Harrison Ford

HARRISON FORD

A Biography

Robert Sellers

ROBERT HALE · LONDON

ISBN 0 7090 4828 9

Robert Hale Limited
Clerkenwell House
Clerkenwell Green
London EC1R 0HT

2 4 6 8 10 9 7 5 3 1

Photoset in North Wales by
Derek Doyle & Associates, Mold, Clwyd.
Printed in Great Britain by
St Edmundsbury Press Ltd, Bury St Edmunds, Suffolk.
Bound by WBC Bookbinders Ltd, Bridgend, Mid-Glamorgan.

Contents

'Harrison, more I think than any other actor
on world screens embodies the Everyman.'
                                    PHILIP NOYCE
                            Director of *Patriot Games*

Illustrations

Foreword

Harrison Ford died in 1957. Medical records clearly show that he had been ill for some time and on 2 December at the motion picture county hospital he silently passed away. Ford was seventy-three.

To many Hollywood Boulevard is the cultural heart of Los Angeles, to others the place is a cesspool of vice and sleaze. Grubby, gaudy and slum-like in places, tourists, nevertheless, flock to the street as they do to the film capital's other golden meccas, Disneyland and the Universal Studio tour. Politely ignoring the pitiful Boulevardiers – the homeless, the teenage dope-heads, the prostitutes – and side-stepping the piles of litter, the happy tourist seeks out his or her favourite name among almost two thousand stars of stage and screen, television and radio. One after the other, on both sides of the street, impressive star symbols honouring current and past greats of showbusiness lie embedded in special paving-stones. A virtual boardwalk of fame. You'll find them all here – Monroe, Bogart, Gable, Chaplin – their individual handprints captured in concrete.

Naturally there's a stone marked 'Harrison Ford'. Hardly surprising – the man is, financially speaking, the most successful film actor in Hollywood history; his movies have taken more dollars at the world's box offices than those of any of his contemporaries or predecessors. But there's a catch: the stone doesn't belong to him. It was put there years ago and belongs to another actor by the name of Harrison Ford, a long-forgotten matinée idol of the silent era, a modest man, born in Kansas in the early 1880s, who made his film debut in 1915. Ford was oblivious of the existence of this man until he was confronted by the Screen Actors Guild (the American equivalent of Britain's Equity) and ordered to choose another screen name, thereby explaining why he is credited as Harrison J. Ford in two of his early pictures. When the belated news of the old man's demise filtered through to Ford he immediately contacted the actor's union, but nobody at their offices could confirm whether or not the old star had indeed died. Ford decided to drop the 'J' regardless.

Stars in their own right and in their own time, separated by almost fifty years, the two men called Harrison Ford share remarkable

11

similarities. Both lived quietly in the hills above Hollywood, kept only a few intimate friends and rejected the razzle-dazzle life of celebrity. In public the old Harrison, like the new, wore dark glasses to avoid being recognized, rarely ate at the smart, showbiz restaurants or attended the latest star-filled movie premiere. The May 1926 edition of *Photoplay* magazine described Ford as a man who 'treasures his privacy' and was 'remote. Aloof. Not only the hermit of Hollywood, but of the entire motion picture industry.' They could almost have been describing the man who would be Indiana Jones.

Throughout the height of Ford's bubblegum fame, practically the whole of the 1980s, the stone on Hollywood Boulevard was left deliberately unchanged. Ford's reason for leaving things the way they stood made sense and was perfectly in keeping with his personality, and suspiciously sentimental. 'If they ever decide to put one there for me, they needn't bother, it's there already,' he professed. 'And I kinda like the idea of using his.'

1

The Grace of Loneliness

Ask Harrison Ford what's the most stupid thing he's ever done and one of those trademark half-smirks will suddenly flash over that perpetually grim face of his. He'll relate the time he drove a Volvo into a telephone pole at thirty-five miles per hour, resulting in a nasty-looking four-inch scar. You know the one: that distinctive horizontal ridge which rests quietly just below his lower lip. A duelling scar we might call it, rather apt for a movie star who specializes in playing a certain breed of action man – the hero so confident of his own masculinity and sexuality that he is unafraid to reveal his sensitive side. The scar betokens authenticity, it signals past mayhem, bygone scraps with hideous villains, near misses and close calls with death, perhaps even a broken heart along the way. Like the famous Kirk Douglas dimple Ford's scar is clearly visible in all of his pictures, but it wasn't until the late eighties that film-makers truly capitalized on this curiously appealing facial disfigurement.

Firstly in Mike Nichols's mocking and wonderfully chic New York comedy *Working Girl*. Ford's character, the world-weary Wall Street broker Jack Trainer, is in bed, post-coital, with Tess McGill (Melanie Griffith). She notices the scar, begins to gently caress it with an inquisitive finger and inquires how it was obtained. At first Trainer lies, making up some cock-and-bull story about a guy pulling a knife on him once in Detroit. The fable so alarms his guest that Trainer opts instead for the truth. He was nineteen and decided to have a pierced ear. His girlfriend agreed to carry out the operation herself but Trainer fainted and knocked his chin on the toilet seat. (This exchange did not feature in the original script, but developed during rehearsals. The toilet gag was Ford's own idea.) In *Indiana Jones and the Last Crusade* a perilous fight aboard a circus train involving the teenage Indy offers us a yet more fanciful explanation for that famous scarred chin. Both examples are neat cinema in-jokes and in true Harrison Ford fashion they leave the real biographical truth unaddressed.

Ironically the authentic story behind Ford's scar is even more

deflating than Jack Trainer's. In his early twenties at the time and living
on dreams of making good as an actor, Ford would drive every morning
through the Laguna Canyon, a treacherously winding road, en route for
Santa Ana where he worked as an assistant buyer in the knick-knacks
and oil paintings section of a large department store. His pride and joy
then was a battered old humpback Volvo. One morning Ford realized
that he had forgotten to put on his seat-belt, and, reaching over to take
the strap off its hook, he momentarily lost concentration. To make
matters worse he was negotiating a blind curve at the time. The car went
out of control, hit a high curb, bounced up and went on two wheels
before greeting a telephone pole head-on. Ford was flung against the
steering wheel but wasn't rendered unconscious and managed to crawl
free of the vehicle. Lucky to be alive ('but I did look a dreadful mess'),
the bloodied figure of Ford stood motionless beside the smoking wreck
of his overturned Volvo and watched as motorist after motorist drove by
offering no assistance. Each carefully and callously manoeuvred their
way around the accident before continuing their journey. 'It pissed me
off so much that no one would stop that I refused to gesture to ask
them,' he told *Vanity Fair* in August 1990. 'So I just stood there until
somebody finally stopped and took me to the hospital.'

Battered and bruised and suffering from minor shock Ford recovered
quickly from his ordeal. But the scar remains, a facial landmark. 'A
terrible job,' the actor says of it now, imagining that instead of stitches
the doctor had used paper-clips. 'I'm sure the guy did the best he could
at the time. It was probably something that should have been done by a
plastic surgeon rather than a resident.' While that scar stands as a
permanent reminder of one rare moment of negligence, it is typical of
the man that the accident happened whilst he was in the act of doing the
safe thing in the safest of cars.

Harrison Ford is not the only movie personality to have stared death
in the face from behind the wheel of a car. Burt Reynolds was the victim
of a near-fatal road smash, the culmination of an over-zealous and
fast-living youth. Strange too that the man predominantly responsible
for Ford's rise to fame, George Lucas, was also involved in a horrific car
accident, just days before his graduation from high school, and had to
spend three months recuperating in hospital. Both he and Ford shared a
fervid and enlightened interest in cars and motor racing as teenagers.
Providence made sure that their first of many celluloid collaborations
was one dominated by the motor car – *American Graffiti*. Lucas was the
more obsessive by a wide margin: he lived and breathed cars, worked for
a time as a mechanic and belonged to a club made up of other auto
freaks. Ford's passion merely ran to leafing through weekly editions of
car manuals and borrowing, as much as he could, his father's car and
those of his friends to perfect his driving skills. At one time he even

considered the possibility of a future as a racing driver, as did Lucas. It was the near death experience that put paid to Lucas's ambition for Grand Prix or Le Mans glory. As for Ford, it was probably apathy.

Very little seemed to occupy the teenage mind of Harrison Ford. By all accounts he was an unambitious youngster, academically lazy, with no desire to rival or emulate his high-achieving father, and something of a loner. At school Ford was often to be found in the lower ranks of achievers, not through any obvious deficiency in the brains department, more due to a blatant stubbornness to concentrate or learn. His disappointing grades were a constant source of bafflement to those infuriated teachers who knew he was capable of better things. Few observers knew in which direction to push him, for the adolescent Ford didn't seem particularly interested in pursuing any kind of respectable career.

A far cry from when as a small boy he was the custodian of earnest ambitions. Most little kids aspire to be engine drivers, astronauts or football players. Ford's first ambition in life was to be a coalman. He wanted to be the man who carried the coal from the front stoop to the coal chute in a wheelbarrow. He was four years old and would watch from his bedroom window as bags of coal were ceremoniously unloaded in front of the house. As the morning progressed he saw the pile diminish until only a black smear on the pavement remained. It was the simple rhythm of the work that so captivated the infant; that and the grating scrape of the shovel on the sidewalk. Here was a job you could see getting done. 'My dad got all dressed up, went to work, came home, sat at the dinner table and bitched like crazy about those bastards at work,' Ford disclosed to *Macleans* in July 1991. 'The coalman, you know, he didn't go home at night and tell his wife how uncooperative the coal was.' Pure Ford logic.

Very little is publicly known about Harrison Ford's background and upbringing. He guards his private life with a passion bordering on the obsessive, resulting in an unwelcome reputation for being a complicated man, an actor whose personality is a veritable maze of which journalists never have and perhaps never will find the true centre. An exasperated media have playfully labelled him as one of Hollywood's toughest interviews: Mr Mum. Occasionally he'll reveal snippets, the odd tantalizing clue to his soul, but as a rule Ford is frustratingly unforthcoming about personal matters. Why? Is it that like some of his celebrated screen roles Ford chooses to shroud himself in an air of mystery? Or maybe he just doesn't have anything to say. Perhaps he's got plenty to talk about but doesn't feel like sharing it with the rest of the world. By Ford's own definition he grew up in normal surroundings and lived an unexceptional youth. And therein lies the real story: how did a lonely, unambitious child from average stock rise to become one of the world's most bankable stars, a leading man whose deceptively limited range has served him through a chain of often brilliant film projects.

Harrison Ford's background offers no indication that he would hack it as a movie star. 'I don't think anyone who had known me as a child would have predicted that I would follow the path I have.' A product of the Midwest and a typically middle-class American family, Ford was born on 13 July 1942 in Chicago, Illinois, the quiet, serious son of an Irish Catholic father and a Russian-Jewish housewife. Ford also had a Jewish grandmother from Flatbush who once frightened him as a small boy by leaving her yellowing false teeth in a glass. Although he quite literally stumbled into acting as a last resort, a substantially large show-business pedigree already existed in the family. In the grand old days of vaudeville Ford's grandfather and namesake, Harrison Needleman, a Brooklyn streetcar worker, was a blacked-up comedian; while his father, Christopher Ford, was an advertising executive and a modest pioneer in the field of television commercials. He conceived the idea of using a see-through washing machine to demonstrate a detergent powder's suds in action and was the first to employ stop-action photography in TV commercials. Years before he had spent time writing and performing for radio in the days when Chicago was seen as the centre of America's wireless industry. When Ford left college his father quit advertising and opened two antique shops in Chicago with his wife, Dorothy. In the late seventies he began a new career as a voice-over artist.

As youths Harrison and his younger brother Terence were often treated to trips to the cinema by their doting father. Ford remembers the first film he ever saw as Walt Disney's *Bambi*. Gawking at the strange flickering images whilst grabbing handfuls of popcorn, the child would be thoroughly entertained but always leave unaffected, no thespian tendencies stirring within. In fact it was his brother's love for acting that was triggered in those halcyon days. Harrison has never been much of a film fan. He has still to see such classics as *Casablanca* or *Gone with the Wind* in their entirety or the works of such great directors as Alfred Hitchcock. Despite this, like most children he fell into the grand ritual of attending Saturday matinee shows, the kind of rip-roaring serials that later inspired the *Indiana Jones* movies. Later in adolescence, going to the picture palaces became an integral part of dating: 'they were a cheap, dark place you could go with a girl.' Ford was never especially bothered what film he saw, although he did go through a spell of frequenting the art-house circuit. This was simply because they were more inclined than the drive-ins and the established theatres to show European movies, which the teenager found more successful as far as dating went.

On the rare occasion you hear Ford reminisce about his upbringing the emphasis is firmly on the sheer normality of it. Unremarkable is a word he likes to use to describe what was an extremely ordinary childhood, full of joy and sadness and the usual hormonal confusions. 'I was never real popular, or real athletic or real anything.' He was neither fish nor fowl. According to Terence both he and Harrison 'came from the most stable, middle-class background you could imagine'. Their parents were not conspicuously wealthy but nor were they on the breadline. Everyone attended church, although neither parent was particularly religious. Ford recalls periods when his family would attend a different place of worship every Sunday 'just to look around'. Window-shopping for God.

The magical allure of belonging to a gang, of harassing the neighbourhood populace and revelling in pranks, appealed to Ford not one jot. He preferred his own company and rarely got into serious trouble or fights with other boys: 'I guess I was what you'd call a loner.' Ford followed this solitary path at a number of schools, beginning with his first grammar school in Chicago: Graham Stuart Elementary (class of '54); then onto East Maine Township Junior High, Des Plaines (class of '56); and finally Maine Township High School, Park Ridge (class of '60).

At his junior-high school Ford was bullied relentlessly, perhaps because he didn't fit in. Shy boys who keep themselves to themselves have always made attractive targets for bullies. Every afternoon during recess the bigger pupils would force Harrison to walk out to the edge of a sharply sloping parking lot and then throw him in. The object was to watch as the victim tried desperately to clamber out. Everytime he succeeded the bullies callously threw him back in. This was the entertainment of the day, and after a time the humiliation of Ford attained a kind of ritual importance. 'The entire school would gather to watch this display,' Ford told *Time* magazine in May 1989. 'I don't know why they did it. Maybe because I wouldn't fight the way they wanted me to. They wanted a fight they could win. And my way of winning was just to hang in there.' Such a character trait, admirable in one so young, is clearly mirrored in Ford's most famous roles – Indiana Jones and Han Solo. Indy's finest quality is that he never gives in, even when all the odds are stacked against him. Ford refused to be a sissy, so he would be Sisyphus. And like Indiana Jones Ford eventually won. Although he was never left badly injured after his ordeals, there were two attractive twin girls whose sympathy for him made it all bearable. Ford's persecution continued into high school. Finally, one day, somebody pushed him too far. Releasing years of pent-up anger Ford whacked the offender, who fell backwards down a flight of stairs. No one picked on him after that.

At home Ford indulged in raising rats out in the garden, starting with a black-and-white pair purely as pets. Inevitably, they started breeding actively, unleashing hordes of young rodents on his unsuspecting household. Pandering to the needs of rats was one of only a few select hobbies in which the young Ford showed any interest; he avoided playing outdoor sports and hated exercise and games. 'I really can't remember what I did instead,' he admitted to the *Daily Mirror* in July 1981. 'I wasn't a sissy or anything like that. I probably just read or cleaned up my room.' A record of his pursuits at Park Ridge, however, tells a different story. They included: the model radio club, class council representative, gymnastics, president of the social science club and disc-jockey for WMTH-FM, the campus radio station, where he was known as Harry Ford. As a teenager Ford certainly started to become a more accessible and active individual. He began going out to parties more and socializing with a growing coterie of friends; at the same time, however, he remained a loner and not particularly popular with the girls.

After high school Ford studied philosophy and English at Ripon, a small liberal arts college in central Wisconsin. Classmates remember 'Harry' as unathletic, unsure of himself and a long way from being a sex symbol. As for Ford he remembers little of his time at Ripon (it's probably best forgotten); he knows only that during his years of academia he possessed no driving ambitions, no thirst to conquer. If truth be told he wasn't really much of an intellectual, barely hanging on by the skin of his teeth, and at the end left without a degree. Ford is honest enough today to confess that whatever he has accomplished in later life was the result of lucky choices and pure happenstance. 'I never had a focused goal or ambition,' he told the *Dallas Morning News* in December 1986. 'I never set out to be held in esteem. I just wanted to be able to hold my head up in private. I couldn't even find a niche in high school. My classmates considered me an oddball, and they were probably right. Not that I cared much for what my classmates thought. I didn't know my classmates then. I don't know them now. I've never been to a reunion.'

Away from college, during the long hot summer breaks, Ford developed an uncanny knack of acquiring jobs for which he was clearly unsuited. He possessed the easy charm and middle-class manners of a well-bred young man and could effortlessly smooth-talk even the most inquisitorial of interviewers. 'I'm real polite. I know how to sit straight and keep my head up. People think I'm not going to steal from them. Getting jobs is like acting.' The best example of this was the time, one summer, Ford managed to talk himself into a position as a chef on a yacht back home on Lake Michigan in Chicago, even though at the time he knew next to nothing about cooking. His mother helped out by lending her son a tatty copy of *The Joy of Cooking*, one of the best manuals for the culinary virgin around. The *Chicago Tribune*'s reader service also came in handy. Ford would call up the newspaper whenever he ran into problems, which was frequently, to ask for their advice. 'This is Harrison again,' he'd bellow down the telephone. 'I know you told me yesterday, but how long do you have to bake a potato? What temperature?' Ford's floating clientele were the idle rich, the pampered heirs to the giant Swift Meat-Packing company. 'All they ever wanted was dead cow anyway. They were very easy to fool,' Ford reminisced to *Playboy* in February 1988. 'Unfortunately, we were out on the water frequently and Lake Michigan can get very choppy. I was deeply seasick most of the time. In retrospect, managing to cook under those circumstances was probably the most heroic thing I've ever done.'

Sadly the success he weaved in the outside job market didn't extend to his class studies. In college he was, by his own admission, downright lazy, an unhappy student bored out of his skull and teetering on the brink of failure. 'I slept pretty well all through my last year, just waking up from time to time to eat a pizza.' That senior year was a disaster, and Ford suffered a 'total academic breakdown.' Failing to complete a thesis on the American playwright Edward Albee (*Who's Afraid of Virginia Woolf?*), he was booted out of college in disgrace just three days before graduation. His parents had made reservations at a local hotel in preparation for attending the ceremony, and his ignominious exit was met with consternation. 'They weren't best pleased I can tell you.'

Having flunked out of Ripon, and thus firmly thrust into the cruel reality of the outside world, with plans to marry his college sweetheart Mary Marquardt in the summer, Ford faced an enormous dilemma. 'I really didn't know what the hell to do with myself.' In those last few bitter months at college Ford refused to attend classes or even sit exams; he apparently felt that the two subjects he was studying were going to get him nowhere in adult life. With no clear job prospects or qualifications to speak of, and no clue as to which career to pursue, Ford was in a mess. 'I couldn't figure out what I wanted to be when I grew up. I think the difficulty was with the idea of growing up. I'm a late bloomer.'

It was during this period of uncertainty that Ford began to seriously consider becoming a professional actor. 'I never came up with a suitable alternative.' Besides, he'd made such a cock-up of his academic career that he was scarcely running the risk of ruining his life by turning to acting. But what did he plan to do if his dramatic pretensions failed? 'Beat the shit out of me!' More than likely he would have become a full-time carpenter, a labourer perhaps, or a farmer, 'although working in a very chic ladies' dress shop wouldn't be entirely without its rewards'. It's ironic that here was a man destined to become one of the most popular of all movie stars, who got into the acting game almost as a last resort, because he was so useless at everything else.

By his third year at college Ford's grade point average had become so low that he decided to try his hand at something else. He knew better than anyone that he was a dead loss as a philosophy major. Weighing out all the options carefully Ford surprisingly picked the drama course. For a shy and introverted young man adopting this most public of crafts was a bold step, one which almost backfired on him. Ford's first stage appearance turned out to be the most frightening ordeal of his young life. The prospect of potentially making a fool out of himself in front of 600 fellow students terrified the 21-year-old. 'I was really, literally pushed up there on the stage. I didn't have the balls to do it without lots of encouragement.' This was the first time he'd ever faced an audience. With knees knocking so loudly you could hear them from the back of the hall, Ford soldiered through his first performance, discovering along the way that the adrenalin it produced was addictive.

Far from being overwhelmed by the experience Ford felt compelled to try again, if only to conquer his dread of performing live. 'It scared me, it scared me something fierce.' Drawn to the challenge of overcoming this fear, Ford felt he would begin to relish the pure process of acting, the pleasure of communicating ideas to an audience and stirring their emotions. 'It's a feeling of power combined with a feeling of community, of having community with all these people.' Ford was subsequently asked to appear in a handful of other college productions, most notably as Mr Antrobus, with a pillow tied around his waist to lend his lanky body a portly exterior, in Thornton Wilder's *The Skin of Our Teeth*. 'I wore a fake moustache and half a pound of talcum powder in my hair. That's when I caught the illness.' Ford's love of the craft had begun, along with the realization that acting was just as valid a career option as teaching, banking or health care.

Theatre also appealed to the young Harrison Ford on account of the lifestyle he believed an actor led. The very idea of being stuck in the same job and the same town all his life filled him with revulsion. From youth, Ford saw his father's job as being a lot more interesting than most of the other kids' dads who lived on the block, and perversely this encouraged him from an early age not to want to pursue a normal, stable career in adult life. Ford left Ripon with no career plan whatsoever, other than a determination not to get sucked into the nine-to-five rat-race like many of his contemporaries. Acting offered the perfect escape route from a hideous life of banality. It also magically fitted his idea of what would be a fun thing to do. There was the attraction of assuming new personalities; acting was a way of living many lives in one short lifetime, of always being exposed to fresh challenges and being part of a team, to experience that wonderful sense of community. It seemed like the best job imaginable.

For years the armed forces has acted as a safety net for the academic drop-out. If you can't find your niche in civvy street, join the marines. In a queer way Ford equated acting with joining the Navy. 'I would travel around the world and meet interesting people. But I wouldn't have to kill them.' He also believed that his wish to become an actor developed from not feeling a part of society. He saw himself as being ostracized from the mainstream. 'My natural state is always to be slightly removed,' Ford related to *Mademoiselle* in February 1988.

The reason I'm not more in the mainstream of life is that from early on I felt myself separate from events that were occurring around me. When I was very young I thought myself a maverick, but by the time I reached twenty-three I realized I was just a stubborn son of a bitch who didn't want to do things the way everyone else wanted me to.

In June 1964 Harrison Ford signed up with the Belfry Players for a season of summer stock (similar to English repertory) in Williams Bay, a quaint resort community on the shores of Lake Geneva in Wisconsin. He was twenty-two, full of enthusiasm and eager to learn all he could about the theatre and the art of acting. Harrison and Mary (who became the company's secretary) soon settled into life at the Belfry and were a popular couple among the troupe's members. They lived together with the other resident actors at Crane Hall, a large mansion house rather like an upmarket dormitory, which stood adjacent to the theatre. Crane Hall still stands today, unlike the theatre which was demolished to make way for a highway. (It's curious that the only two theatres Ford was ever to appear in no longer exist; Ripon's Red Barn Theatre was burnt to the ground the summer he left.) These days Crane Hall is used as an antique shop, and old bedrooms where once Ford might have lived now lie in various states of disuse or are employed as storage space. Visitors browsing in the House of Two Lions Antique Store are blissfully unaware that they may be treading in the thirty-year-old footsteps of Harrison Ford.

On 26 June, at 8.20 pm, the curtain rose at the Belfry Theatre on the company's thirty-first and most ambitious season yet. The cramped but atmospheric auditorium was well attended and there was an air of expectancy as the lights grew dim. The opening night of *Take Her, She's Mine*, a bright comedy which had earlier found some success on Broadway, could hardly have been described as an 'event', if not for the fact that it marked the professional acting debut of Harrison Ford. His portrayal of Alex received much favourable comment; yet no one, least of all Ford, was under the illusion that the Belfry theatre was harbouring a future Hollywood superstar. Ford was seen as nothing more than a pleasant, good-looking young man with none of the qualities of a great actor. He was just one of the guys, part of the team. He didn't stand out; he never would.

Repeatedly cast in roles he believed he was 'totally unsuitable for',

Ford, nevertheless, was far more competent on the stage than he had hitherto suspected. In *Sunday in New York* by Norman Krasna, and Tennessee Williams's powerful *Night of the Iguana* the young actor excelled as a supporting player and won a modicum of respect when he took on the musical role of Preacher Haggler in *Dark of the Moon* by Howard Richardson and William Berney. On the occasions Ford was elevated to the principal part, both were in musicals. *Little Mary Sunshine* was a gently satirical spoof on the MGM Jeanette MacDonald and Nelson Eddy musicals of the forties. Ford flung himself into the 'Nelson Eddy' role of the strait-laced Captain Jim of the forest rangers. According to the programme notes he displayed 'a beautiful singing voice'. Ford took this for the howling joke it was probably meant to be. 'I can sing,' he once admitted, 'very, very badly.' Those dubious vocal cords of his were exercised again for the penultimate show of the season when he played the baseball hero in *Damn Yankees*, a role made famous by Tab Hunter in the 1958 cinema version of the Broadway smash.

By mid September it was all over. Props and costumes were collected and stored, backcloths and sets dismantled, dressing rooms left empty and silent. The Belfry Theatre, which had been so alive with manic activity for the past three months, was now dark. Ford had enjoyed his brief stint with the company and by the end was being hailed as one of its better assets. In one of the theatre programmes he was cited as having been 'outstanding in his varied roles'. But the bright summer evenings were growing increasingly shorter, autumn and winter were close on his heels and the prospect of facing the arctic temperature of another Wisconsin winter haunted Ford. He knew it would soon be time to move on.

About the only thing Ford knew about being an actor was that to succeed he needed to be either in Los Angeles or New York. Such a decision would have to be made quickly, for parts of Wisconsin were already seeing soft snow fall. To help make up his mind he enlisted the services of a coin and left it all to chance – tails he'd go to the West coast, heads the East. He flipped the coin in the air. Heads. Ford didn't fancy New York very much – 'I wasn't going to starve and freeze' – so he kept tossing the coin until it landed on tails. Some might call that cheating, but you can't argue with the fact that he made the right decision. While it's fun to speculate on what might have happened to Harrison Ford if he had acted on the outcome of that first throw and gone on to brave the cold of the Big Apple, Los Angeles was always the better option. For any actor starting out times can be tough, work and a steady income are hard to find, so who wants to be cold and miserable as well. 'Better to be poor in the sunshine than the snow. That was my idea, anyway. So we loaded all our stuff into our Volkswagen, drove off and didn't stop until we saw the Pacific.'

2

You Ain't Got It, Kid

Like the early settlers who came to the West coast around the turn of the century, Harrison Ford and his fledgling bride drove the long distance west from Wisconsin to California full of hopes and dreams of a fresh start. His ignorance of the difficulties of becoming an actor was monumental; the names of most of the major film studios were alien to him; and he had not a single friend or contact in town. Indeed there was very little he did know about his chosen profession, save that Hollywood was probably the place to be. Stardom was the last thing on his mind – to be just a regular, working actor in a television series was about the height of his ambition. What Ford didn't anticipate or prepare for was the bitter disillusionment that followed.

The couple's journey ended once they spied the unmistakable blue of the Pacific. Here was Laguna Beach, a coastal town a good hour's drive south of Los Angeles. After a brief spell working in a paint store the resourceful Ford managed to land a role in a production of *John Brown's Body* at the local playhouse. He also secured an assortment of day jobs to help pay the $75 per month rent. He worked as a yacht broker, a management trainee in a department store and as a late-night pizza chef, an experience which Ford enjoyed. 'I felt I was playing a pizza man,' he recalled to the *Sunday Telegraph* in June 1989. 'Nobody knew who I was or what I was doing and nobody said any more to me than: "A large pie with cheese and pepperoni." And that gave me a lot of time for looking around and thinking.'

While appearing at the Laguna Beach Playhouse Ford's potential was recognized and he was sent over to Columbia studios for an interview. Numerous reports suggest that Ford was spotted by a talent scout working on behalf of Columbia. In fact the man who 'discovered' Ford was a composer by the name of Ian Bernard. He saw the actor performing at the playhouse and sent him to see Billy Gordon, head of casting at Columbia Pictures. To Ford's amusement the whole gruelling experience turned out to be just like the movies. Ushered into a small, walnut-panelled office he found himself face to face with the archetypal Hollywood mogul figure, a Danny de Vito lookalike, a bald, diminutive man smoking a thick cigar and sitting behind a large oak desk on which there stood two telephones. Looming behind him was a second man whom Ford thought resembled one of those unscrupulous touts you find at racecourses. Making himself comfortable in the only seat available, directly facing the desk, Ford waited patiently for a small eternity while the two men made long-distance calls, closed deals and discussed big names and big money. Eventually the bald man looked over at his guest as if he'd just discovered a beetle sunbathing on a crouton in his soup at some fancy eatery. 'Who sent you?' he inquired. Ford answered. The two men looked at one another with blank expressions; the name carried no weight. 'That's all right,' the fat guy said. 'Doesn't matter.' Ford was asked for his name and then other details were tersely requested: how tall was he, how much did he weigh, what were his hobbies, did he possess any special talents, speak any foreign languages. After writing all this information down the bald-headed man said, 'OK, fine, if we find anything for you, we'll let you know.' All very polite but Ford recognized it for what it was, the 'don't call us, we'll call you' routine. Standing up, Ford thanked his hosts and left. Walking down the corridor, on his way back to oblivion, nature called, so when the lift failed to arrive he made a quick dash for the toilets. On his return Gordon's assistant came running down the hall in a panic shouting, 'Come here, come here, he wants you.' Back inside the office, much to Ford's surprise, he was offered a permanent place at Columbia. 'You're not the type we're usually interested in, but how'dya like to be under contract,' beamed the bald-headed man. What else could Ford say but yes. 'Sure I was thrilled. Columbia wanted me. It was my big break.' It would forever remain a mystery why the fat man changed his mind. Doubtless some kind of emergency had arisen and they needed a guy in a hurry. But Ford always knew that if he'd taken the lift straight down it wouldn't have been worth anyone's while chasing after him. As it turned out this was the beginning of a nightmare apprenticeship. He soon discovered that the last thing Hollywood wanted was Harrison Ford, actor. Not yet anyway.

A few months after this extraordinary interview Ford was signed up, for $150 a week ('and all the respect that implies') to a seven-year pact, part of Columbia's short-lived new talent programme. Other signings of the period included Nat King Cole's daughter Carol, Tom Nardini, who became one of the Cat Ballou gang and Todd Armstrong (of Jason and the Argonauts fame), who would share screen time with Ford in his third movie, *The Long Ride Home*. The initial jubilation over being recruited by a big Hollywood studio soon evaporated. His brief tenure there as a novice actor was to prove an unfulfilling affair. Ford had arrived at a turbulent period in Hollywood's history. By the mid sixties all the main studios were concentrating their efforts in overseas production. Columbia, in particular, were investing heavily in the British film industry. It was an odd time: all the major movies were being made over in Europe, while those left behind were dropping acid and smoking dope. 'And I was this baby actor going nowhere.' It was also the fag-end of the contract era, the studio system which had ruled the roost since the twenties. Ford was among the last to experience the sometimes degrading privilege of being under contract to a studio, and soon grew disenchanted with their outdated factory methods of churning out stars who were little more than clones of one another. 'I was sure that the most important thing for an actor was to hold onto what was individual about himself.' This stubborn and rebellious attitude ultimately led to his downfall at Columbia.

For starters everyone was obliged to turn up each morning properly attired in jacket and tie. For a man who enjoys lazing around in jeans this was an acutely humbling ordeal. He was also expected to attend acting class and eat in the executive dining-room. Occasionally Ford would have to act as publicity fodder. Studio executives dreamt up the most brainless promotional ideas for photo layouts. They'd put a Chevrolet Nova on Malibu beach and summon the starlets to play volleyball beside it. Below this fiasco the caption 'Photos courtesy Columbia Pictures' would be printed. Ford, at times, felt like a piece of meat. For the salary of $150 a week the studio thought they owned him body and soul. 'Was I disgruntled? You bet I was. It was horrible. Nobody ever knew your name or cared a damn about you. I went fucking nuts.' Things reached a head when in their collective wisdom, the powers-that-be first tried to make him wear his hair pompadour-style like Elvis Presley. He was later instructed to change his name; Harrison was seen as too pretentious. When Ford, sick and tired of being pestered by the studio big guns, suggested he be rechristened 'Kurt Affair', the most ridiculous name he could think of, the idea was hastily dropped. The acting classes, which lasted for some six months and where Ford was to be groomed and moulded for stardom, were just as unsatisfactory. He found that all they were succeeding in doing was teaching him how to act in acting school, which had nothing to do with the real world. Experience has always been Harrison Ford's best teacher; he knew he'd have to develop a personal process, a way of doing it for himself.

The feature-film debut of Harrison Ford was inauspicious to say the least, a forty-five-second appearance as a bellboy in a hotel lobby. The film in question, *Dead Heat on a Merry Go Round*, a pleasantly diverting crime drama starring James Coburn, has since quietly slipped into obscurity. Just as well, as Ford's brief appearance is one that he would probably like to forget. All he had to say was, 'Paging Mr Jones, paging Mr Jones'. Coburn calls 'Boy!' and motions Ford over. Then one last 'Mr Jones?' from our baby-faced friend before handing over the telegram. And that was it. Little was required by way of real acting and the whole thing took less than a day to shoot. In Ford's own words his indoctrination into the world of cinema 'made absolutely no impression at all. Not a particularly uplifting experience.' For this less-than-inspiring debut performance Ford was severely reprimanded. Soon after the film's completion the vice-president of Columbia requested his presence in the head office. 'Kid,' began the executive ('They always called me kid, probably because they didn't know who the hell I was.') 'Kid, siddown. Lemme tell ya a story,' he continued. 'The first time Tony Curtis ever appeared in a movie he delivered a bag of groceries. A bag of groceries! You took one look at that person and you knew that was a star. You ain't got it, kid. Get back to class because you ain't gonna work again in this studio for six months, maybe a year. Go get your shit together.' Ford was devastated and now totally disillusioned.

As predicted, Ford didn't work for another six months, and when he did the role was so small that his name wasn't even featured on the credits. *Luv*, a comedy based on the Broadway hit about a trio of pseudo-intellectuals, boasted the talents of Jack Lemmon and Peter Falk but was a turkey in all departments. Ford's brief appearance only just qualified as an entertaining moment. He played a hippie (the first of many. Ford was invariably cast in his early years as hippies or cowboys) involved in a car accident with the film's two chief protagonists, Harry (Lemmon) and Ellen (Elaine May). Coming to a screeching halt at a red traffic light Ellen is forced into reverse, only she backs right into a '67 Ford convertible. The hippie Harrison leaps from his vehicle and strides violently up to Harry and Ellen's battered red volkswagen. Peering inside, Ford's anger is temporarily stalled when he sees a woman behind the wheel. Then he spies Harry sitting beside her and punches him full on the nose. Returning to his own car the hippie promptly drives off.

Ford's next two film roles were in period dramas, both of which dwelled, with varying degrees of success, on the American Civil War. *The Long Ride Home* (a.k.a. *A Time for Killing*) chronicles the sometimes violent search by a Union officer (Glenn Ford) for a group of escaped Confederate soldiers led by Captain Bentley (George Hamilton). Ford, as Lieutenant Shaffer, on the side of the Union, and even gets his own death scene. Leading his patrol across a river Shaffer is ambushed by the Confederate renegades. All are slaughtered and Shaffer is dragged from his horse and run through with his own sword. A boring film, *The Long Ride Home* almost led to Ford's banishment from Columbia. It was the last picture he made for them as a contract player.

When his option came up for renewal after eighteen depressing

months Ford was sick and tired of the studio. As it transpired they had
had quite enough of him too and were itching to be rid of him.
Summoned into the lion's den Ford was informed of the studio's
decision in no uncertain manner by the very executive who had earlier
torn a strip off him for his portrayal of a bellboy. As Mike Frankovich,
the head of the studio, was at that time overseeing operations in Europe
it had been left to his lieutenant to decide Ford's fate. 'Kid,' he said,
'when Frankovich gets back I'm gonna tell him we ought to get rid of
you. I don't think you're worth a bunch of shit to us. But I know your
wife is pregnant, you need the money, so I'll give you an extra coupla
weeks. Just go sign the paper my secretary has, OK boy? Now git outta
here.' The thought of being a charity case annoyed Ford deeply, so he
hit out and told the assembled company where they could stick their
charity. The act resulted in him being sacked on the spot. 'I guess I was
never temperamentally suited to being a studio actor.'

Three days after his departure from Columbia, and much to his own
surprise, Ford entered into a similar working relationship with
Universal. Again he was under contract, naked to the strains and
demands of the studio system, but this time it was different. Universal
was immeasurably more satisfying to work for than his old home,
because they operated a policy by which all contract players were greatly
used in the myriad television shows that the company churned out.
Although Ford would later feel betrayed that no one had the guts to use
him outside of the home entertainment medium, between 1967 and
1974 he appeared, in the guise of 'guest star', on numerous American
shows. These included some of the most popular ever made, like *The
Virginian* in which he portrayed a bankrobber who is slain in the gunfight
climax, two episodes of *Gunsmoke*, *Kung Fu*, and *The Partridge Family*,
where he played a teacher on whom one of the Partridge kids had a
crush. The perennially popular detective series *Ironside* presented Ford
with one of his largest television roles. In the episode entitled 'The Past
is Prologue', he received second billing in the guest cast as Tom Stowe,
a Stanford graduate whose father is accused of murder. Some of the
more unfamiliar programmes in which Ford appeared included: *My
Friend Tony*, a formula cops and robbers series, *The FBI* and *Petrocelli*.

An amusing tale is attached to Ford's appearance in an episode of
Love, American Style. One Friday he received a call from the producers
asking if he would play a hippie in the show. 'My character comes to pick
up the daughter of a normal middle-class couple. They were to be
appalled by my appearance, but I was to furnish them with some sort of
helpful hippie philosophy that would mend their troubled marriage,'
Ford related to *Playboy* in March 1988. Arriving promptly on Monday
morning he was immediately escorted over to make-up and ordered to
cut his long hair and shave off the beard he was currently wearing. 'I

tried to explain that I was playing a hippie, but they mumbled something about "America inviting me into its living room" and how we wouldn't want to "offend". And I thought, oh shit, I'm in trouble here.' In wardrobe Harrison was asked to remove his blue chambray work shirt and jeans and replace them with studio-approved clothes, a navy blue shirt with a high collar, a pair of burgundy jeans, made out of some plastic material, and a wide white belt. Just in case he didn't feel embarrassed enough an assistant gave him a scarf with a little ring to put around his neck. 'I thought, somebody has clearly made a mistake here.' Feeling like a complete fool Ford walked on the set, looking to offload his frustrations on the producer ... who turned out to be wearing exactly the same get-up as him. 'He was a hippie producer, I guess. A Hollywood hippie. At least the cheque went through when I got paid.'

It was soon back to western territory for Ford's fourth cinema outing and, as it transpired, his last for a couple of years. *Journey to Shiloh*, a tale set in the Civil War, was nothing more than a programme filler, but at least it gave Ford the opportunity to work with some of his rising contemporaries – James Caan, Michael Sarrazin and Jan-Michael Vincent. The film followed the by now preordained course of a Harrison Ford movie and bombed resoundedly. As Willie Bill Beardon he was required to do little else save look stupid in a buckskin outfit and a floppy hat.

In mid 1969, after two years in TV hell, Ford was loaned out to MGM for what was the most important film of his career thus far, certainly his first brush with a director of prestige, Michelangelo Antonioni. Following on from the success of *Blow Up*, his hypnotic pop-culture parable set in swinging London, Antonioni was invited to America to make *Zabriskie Point*, a fascinating cross-fertilization of 'art' and 'popular' cinema, a study of campus rebellion and the problems of youth. But the film was ignored or misunderstood upon release, and Antonioni would not make another film for five years. There seems to be some confusion regarding Ford's participation in *Zabriskie Point*. Reports claim he can be glimpsed as one of the student revolutionaries in the film's opening sequence; others that he appears in the stunning climactic 'love in' shot in Death Valley; or that his scenes were cut out altogether. I doubt Ford himself can even remember.

The following year was hardly any better. It began with yet another western, this time *The Intruders*, a feeble made-for-television film about the Jesse James gang. And then there was the indignity of being loaned out to his ex-employer, Columbia, for *Getting Straight*. This satirical swipe at campus politics and student unrest was one of many such films released by the major studios during this time to exploit the *Easy Rider* cult. Not for the first time Ford found himself in distinguished company (Elliott Gould, playing a disillusioned Vietnam veteran and Candice

Bergen), but in a role that was about as important as the wallpaper on the set. Yet another hippie – a college art student who wears his hair long with thick sideburns. This really was the last straw. Ford now found himself on the threshold of making one of the most important decisions in his life. He was contemplating quitting acting.

3

Jesus Was a Carpenter Too

Arguably, Harrison Ford was born more suited to the honourable and pure pursuit of carpentry than to the turbulent, rollercoaster world of celebrity. The man has perfect plumb, that is the ability to see at a glance whether a building is perfectly perpendicular or, say, a few degrees out. He knows, too, that the length of a tenpenny nail is three inches and the true dimensions of a two-by-four is one-and-a-half by three-and-a-half inches. He can tell you that the blunt instrument used to bludgeon Carolyn Polhemus to death in Presumed Innocent was not a hammer but a similar-looking tool. Ford's hands are the hands of a workman, large and strong, and his nails are short and to the point, just like their owner.

The famous scar, that hideaway ranch in Wyoming and those carpentry skills are all aspects of the Harrison Ford story that have been mythologized by the media over the years. During interviews at least one, sometimes all three, of these subjects are raised. The actor scarcely tires of answering queries about carpentry, for, as in acting, Ford has a talent and he knows what he's talking about. At the grand age of fifty he has done both for a living and excelled in each. His bookshelves at home still groan under the weight of countless carpentry reference books and the nerve centre of Ford's headquarters in Wyoming is the outbuilding which contains his private office, a garage and an impressive workshop. But he has justly grown tired of relating how his career in carpentry started, of those dark days as a contract player anxious to make a name for himself, shuffling his heels, waiting and suffering in silence.

At least the regular income paid by the studios enabled Mary and him to move out of their shoddy rented apartment and buy a house. The couple's first home was a modest two-bedroom affair high up in the hills above Los Angeles and situated close to the famous Hollywood Bowl. But the cheapness of the asking price was reflected in the state of the building. It needed drastic refurbishment. There was just one problem: the Fords didn't have the money to hire a crew of professionals.

Undeterred, Ford bought some power tools and joined the local library to read up on carpentry and woodwork, subjects about which he knew very little. In what could have proved a foolhardy exercise, not to mention one of considerable expense, Ford proceeded to totally strip and gut his home from top to bottom until all that was left were the bare walls and the ceiling. He then rebuilt the entire house to his own specifications, learning as he went along. For this first attempt at carpentry Ford had used his own home as a guinea pig. 'I taught myself, it's the only way I can do anything.' His fascination for the craft had begun. To his surprise Ford found that he was able to derive a great deal of pleasure and satisfaction from the job. He revelled in the sense of achievement, of putting things together with his hands, of creating beauty out of dead wood. When his acting career reached a stalemate in the late sixties it was to carpentry that he turned for salvation. 'It was the only occupation I had the wardrobe for.'

Hollywood didn't handle the fledgling Ford very kindly. As a contract player he was more or less treated like dirt. Fuelled by anger Harrison revolted against his persecutors at every given opportunity, but today harbours no resentment or an ounce of bitterness towards those who told him he would never make it. If anything, other people's resistance drove him on that little bit more. Later, though he did enjoy informing journalists that the Columbia executive who never rated him was no longer in the film business. 'And I am. I am.' But the way things stood in 1969/70 Ford was beginning to suspect they were right. After five years in Hollywood his career was heading nowhere fast. He was being employed perhaps eight to ten times a year, not nearly enough to assure his family of a comfortable lifestyle. What irritated Ford the most was that neither Columbia nor Universal taught him anything about the industry. During his brief tenure at these two famed studios he learnt little about the rudiments of screen acting, nor was he given the opportunity to appear in productions which would test and broaden his acting horizons. 'I was being given tiny, little spaces to fill, nothing where you could take the space.' In other words, he wasn't getting the parts he thought he deserved, just being endlessly shuttled from one no-hope television guest spot to the next. It would not have been so bad if there had been a little variety among them; but more often than not he was cast in the same kind of role, either as the guy who didn't do it or, 'if there were two bad brothers, I was the sensitive one.'

Condemned, it seemed, to an eternity of playing hippies or idiots, Ford decided to quit this 'Twilight Zone' existence, turn his back on Hollywood and strike out on his own as a full-time carpenter. A brave decision. At Universal Ford was in danger of wearing out his welcome if he continued accepting the same poor-quality material year in year out. He would be a spent force by the time his chance arrived to appear in any decent movies. 'That's when I began to realize that if I didn't take control of my own career and my own life, I'd always be at the mercy of others,' Ford told *You* magazine in January 1987, 'and I'd soon be a worn-out case.' Carpentry provided Harrison with an alternative means of earning a living, of building a financially secure platform from which he could pick and choose from among the acting work on offer, and if necessary hold out until something of quality came along. If that meant not working for six or twelve months, then so be it. To be able to choose – that was the luxury; having the freedom to say 'yes' or the freedom to yell 'go to hell'.

Ford's first professional assignment as a carpenter was the conversion of a three-car garage into an elaborate recording studio for the Brazilian composer/arranger Sergio Mendes (the 'M' in A&M Records). At a cost of $100,000 it was a massive undertaking, a real baptism of fire for the amateur carpenter. Mendes had no idea that Ford was so inexperienced, and if he had known one doubts that the musician would have let him within a mile of his home. 'He didn't ask me if it was my first job and I never told him.' Fortunately the Brazilian lived just three blocks away from the Encino public library and, during breaks in construction, Ford would run over there to browse hurriedly through their DIY section and borrow the odd woodwork textbook. 'I didn't know what the hell I was doing,' Ford confesses today. 'I'd be up there on the roof reading the relevant page, hoping no one would come out and rumble me.' He had to be especially careful in the mornings as Mendes was prone to wander outside soon after rising, wearing a robe and smoking a Havana cigar, to check on how things were progressing. 'I guess he wouldn't have had much faith in me if he'd seen me up there checking out the next step in a book.'

The Mendes job was an unexpected success and news of Ford's achievement spread quickly through the canyons of well-heeled showbusiness folk. But Ford knew nobody else was going to risk hiring him (the Mendes job had been a lucky break), because of his total lack of hands-on experience. The solution was academic: he'd hire a couple of professionals to watch and learn from. He was in business and soon business was booming. Carpenters were a much valued and sought-after commodity in the Los Angeles of the early seventies. Skilled operators were especially thin on the ground, leaving Ford in an enviably strong position to clean up. His little carpentry business went from strength to strength. There was scarcely any shortage of work around, and his hours were always occupied either remodelling homes, building extensions, fitting shelves and cabinets or making furniture. By virtue of his close connections with the entertainment world Ford was fortunate enough to procure work from some of the industry's high flyers. He became, in his own words, 'carpenter to the stars'. His clients included the actress Sally

Kellerman, for whom he built a sun porch; the husband-and-wife screenwriting team of Joan Didion and John Gregory Dunne; Talia Shire (famous for her role as the wife in the *Rocky* movies); and Richard Fleischer, the director of such epic films as *20,000 Leagues Under the Sea* and *Doctor Doolittle*.

At one fell swoop Ford had become something other than a demoralized, unemployed actor, a redundant commodity in Los Angeles. He was now a carpenter, a respected and serviceable member of the community. Attending auditions or meetings with agents and casting directors Ford was no longer the guy who needed the job in order to put food on the table, he now had other responsibilities, places to be. 'I behaved less like a victim,' he told *USA Today* in December 1986. 'I wasn't the bleeding sore that is the out-of-work actor.' He'd also reclaimed some lost pride and confidence within himself, for through carpentry Ford was able to support his family more generously. Soon his new career was paying better than the old one and with this achievement came the kind of self-respect he could never have commanded as a lowly contract player under the dirty thumb of Hollywood. During this self-imposed exile Ford never once contemplated leaving showbusiness altogether; he had invested too much of his life to throw in the towel now. 'I still wanted to be an actor when I grew up.' Let's just say that over the course of the next few years those flames of ambition grew paler. Hardly surprisingly, the stigma of defeat clung to him like a bad suit – half a decade in the world's film capital and Harrison had failed to scrape together even a modest living as an actor.

If truth be told Ford would never have blossomed into victory as a contract artist. He still had a lot of growing up and learning to do. Those early walk-on performances stand today as a testament to how truly awful he was. To begin with those youthful features – the all-American college-boy look, complete with jutting chin, candid stare and greasy side parting – were a great handicap. Even in his mid twenties Ford looked barely out of college. But the man was ageing fast on the inside and going crazy seeing other actors younger than himself making it big. 'I wondered if it would ever be my turn.' Out of pure jealousy Ford never went to see the work of his fellow actors. 'They were getting good stuff. I wasn't.' Later, a positive element crept into this policy· of non-cinema-going, the decisions to resist the temptation of copying the success of other performers rather than developing his own style. 'All I would tell people is to hold on to what is individual about themselves,' he said in conversation with *The Palm Beach Post* in December 1988. 'Not to allow their ambition for success to cause them to try and imitate the success of others. You've got to find it on your own terms.' Sound advice, and Ford eventually did, but it was to be a long, hard slog.

Fortunately he had the inbred common sense never to feel defeated by his own frustration. Rather, in his new guise as 'carpenter to the stars', Ford developed his own exacting criterion, a quality yardstick by which he measured all the job offers that came along. Unless there was a clear career advantage in making a film, and the money was right, he'd shake his head and walk away. In the six years Ford worked as carpenter to the rich and famous in Beverly Hills and beyond he downed his tools for just a handful of television roles and four movies. Not much exposure, but who can argue against the man's wisdom when in those supposedly 'lean' years he worked with directors of the calibre of George Lucas, Francis Ford Coppola and Stanley Kramer. Ford's supreme gamble of holding out for the best job available had paid off handsomely by the middle seventies. The elite of the industry – the decision makers, the agents, the producers – were beginning to associate Ford only with good work. He was getting there.

On screen there is something unsettlingly honest about Harrison Ford. Unlike some major-league stars he is quite happy to share the acting honours or immerse himself in a fine ensemble cast: *Witness* and *Presumed Innocent* immediately spring to mind as examples. Ford is totally dedicated to his movies as a whole and not merely the characters he plays. His acting style has been described as 'nearly Hemingwayesque'. Of course he enjoys the flamboyant roles like Indiana Jones and Allie Fox in which he splendidly, if shamelessly, hogs the limelight. But he prefers it when his characters dominate him, when audiences emotionally connect with the hero's predicament and for two hours can share in the life of a fictional person and forget Harrison Ford even exists. 'I don't want to be a movie star,' he told *TV Times* in June 1986. 'I want to be in movies that are stars.'

In life this tendency towards self-effacement in the service of the greater good reveals itself most dramatically in his woodworking. All those early carpentry jobs betray someone who strained to avoid the audacious, the flashy, someone not consciously drawn to opulence. Stylistically his designs were traditional, rather like the man himself. Technically they all ascribed to the maxim: form follows function. Ford was shrewd or fortunate enough to work only for the wealthiest of people who could afford to let the true craftsman within indulge himself, because when it came to quality no expense was spared. 'Spend the bucks, spend the bucks, that's all he ever said,' one former customer fondly recalled to *Premiere* in March 1988. Ford earnestly subscribes to the old adage that if a job's worth doing it's worth doing well. When people hired Harrison Ford they knew what they were getting: a solid and dedicated professional.

'I believe in the work ethic. That was the middle-class way I was brought up.' Ford's deserved success gave him a whole new perspective on life, one rooted firmly in that central theme of the American dream: money and lots of it. 'I realized the correlation between money and respect,' he told *Films Illustrated* in April 1978. 'Take a lot of money off people and they'll treat you with respect. They'd ask, "How much is all this going to cost me?" And I'd say, "Well, I don't know. All I can tell you is that when it's done, it'll be right." ' As the son of a well-off businessman it is not surprising that Ford is an adherent of the Anglo-Saxon Protestant work ethic that rewards graft rather than flair. Quality above quantity is an ideal that permeates his whole life.

Unquestionably Ford's most valuable customer at this time was a man by the name of Fred Roos, a casting director and one of the actor's few friends from his days at Universal. Roos was working for Francis Ford Coppola when the two of them ran into one another again. 'Harrison was not conventionally good-looking,' Roos told *Premiere* in March 1988. 'He was also tight-lipped, standoffish, and most people thought he had an attitude. He's an incredibly cranky guy. But I thought he was going to be a star. And we got along famously.' Ford had won over his first powerful ally. He also got some decent employment out of the alliance too, building in Roos's house, among other things, a fireplace, a bathroom and a bed. In return Roos began to audition Ford for 'anything he was remotely right for'. The actor would later pay grateful homage to Fred Roos, counting him among those who were instrumental in getting him properly started in the business.

Roos's close association with Coppola led to him being appointed casting director on the second feature of an unknown director called George Lucas: *American Graffiti*. Lucas was against using established stars in his film: he wanted the dozen or so major characters he'd written brought to life with the freshness and vitality that only unknown actors eager for the elusive first break can deliver. Assisted by producer Gary Kurtz, Roos scoured the drama schools and fringe theatres of the San Francisco Bay Area searching for the perfect mix of hot young talent. Several unknowns made it through the final auditions; and some of them were on their way to future fame and fortune: Richard Dreyfuss, who, before Ford, struck it big as Steven Spielberg's one-man repertory company in *Jaws* and *Close Encounters of the Third Kind*; Ron Howard, who went on to star in *Happy Days* and is today a successful director (*Cocoon, Far and Away*); and to a lesser extent, Charles Martin Smith, Candy Clark and Cindy Williams.

Roos had no difficulty including Ford's name among the hundred or so young hopefuls gunning for a place in *American Graffiti*. Whilst fully appreciative of the chance he was being given Ford at first displayed arrogant indifference about becoming involved in the project. Not for artistic reasons, but because of money. The carpentry business had now become so lucrative that if he were to take the *Graffiti* job it would mean a cut in wages. Money at the time was of paramount importance. Mary was expecting the birth of their second son and Ford had fallen behind in his health insurance payments. Originally offered $485 a week to play the part of Bob Falfa Ford turned Lucas and Roos down. 'Come on, guys,' he protested to them over the telephone. 'I've got a wife and two kids to support,' then abruptly hung up. Roos called back informing Ford that they had both gone through the whole budget and were willing to raise his fee to $500 a week. This was a marginal improvement, but still about half of what he could make in the same period as a carpenter. Since Ford now had the luxury of choice he eventually decided to do the film because he believed in the project.

When he first met George Lucas Ford had no sense of destiny, no feeling that this was the turning point. It was an ordinary office interview, fixed by his agent – a matter of routine. Ford doesn't even recall the director very well then, or remember if he spoke. He just sat while other people talked. Ford had no impression of being in the presence of a *Wunderkind*, nor of getting on particularly well with him. But more than any other film-maker George Lucas was responsible for Harrison Ford's meteoric rise to superstardom. Although luck played a significant part in Ford being cast in the three Lucas films which launched his career – *American Graffiti, Star Wars* and *Raiders of the Lost Ark* – it was Lucas nevertheless who exploited Ford's untapped screen potential, as no other director had previously done. In his first scene as Bob Falfa, that mocking face partly hidden beneath a giant white cowboy hat, he exudes star quality. That here was a captivating, new and exciting masculine presence was manifestly clear.

Pictures taken of Ford during his days with Columbia reveal a callow youth with a boyish charm. He looked like an Ivy League postgraduate student, the consummate model of prefecture. This excessively clean-cut image was as much of a hindrance in those early years as his then total lack of experience. Now he was maturing at precisely the right time to take advantage of an emerging new wave of directors: Francis Ford Coppola, Martin Scorsese, Brian de Palma, Steven Spielberg and John Milius. Dubbed the 'movie brats', these men were the first generation to grow up actually wanting to be film-makers. Steeped in movie lore, they set about the task of rejuvenating Hollywood by replacing the old guard they had once revered, driving away the doldrums of the sixties, banishing the uncertainty reigning in the early seventies and reinstating wonder, excitement and the box-office blockbuster. The most significant brat member, in Ford's case, was George Lucas.

Although their influences and approach to cinema differ considerably, remarkable similarities exist between these two artisans. Lucas was born less than two years after Ford in May 1944; their fathers were both self-made businessmen (George Walton Lucas Sr ran a stationery business); and as children both grew up within the comfortable, stable confines of middle-class suburbia. As adolescents Ford and Lucas were slightly introverted, solitary youths who preferred their own company to that of other children. Even today both men are intrinsically shy, hate to socialize, guard their privacy and are wary of the press. They also share a mutual loathing of Los Angeles and Hollywood. At school both led undistinguished academic lives and were later to develop an informed love of the motor car, culminating in serious accidents.

Redirected by his own close brush with death, Lucas moved from cars to cameras. An interest in photography earned him a place at the University of Southern California in the mid sixties where he found himself among a 'miracle' group of other students destined for Hollywood glory: John Carpenter, John Milius, Robert Zemeckis, Dan O'Bannon and others. But Lucas was the star pupil, churning out one innovative short after another. The uncharacteristically bleak futuristic fable *THX 1138* won an award at the National Student film festival and brought him to the attention of the creatively sterile executives of Hollywood. He got a scholarship to observe the making of Francis Ford Coppola's *Finian's Rainbow*, beginning a portentous and sometimes turbulent friendship that still endures. Under the patronage of Coppola Lucas made his first feature-length movie, an expanded version of *THX 1138*. This grim future shocker set in an Orwellian world was misunderstood, mutilated and mispromoted by its distributor Warner Brothers – a barbarism that made Lucas swear he would one day be the master of his own destiny.

Dejected by his first experience of Hollywood Lucas dabbled for a while in various directions, assisting Coppola on *The Godfather* and working as a cameraman on *Gimme Shelter*, David Maysles's documentary of the notorious Rolling Stones gig at Altamont. Working with a legendary sixties band is something else Lucas and Ford share. For a week Ford helped out on a concert-tour film of 'The Doors'. 'I couldn't keep up with those guys.' The actor recalled on MTV's *The Big Picture* in the summer of 1989. 'It was too much. I was part of the camera crew – second camera. I don't think any of it was in focus, not a bit of it.' Boosted by a warm reception at the Cannes Film Festival, THX was acquiring a minor cult following and Lucas was starting to receive offers of work, but nothing to which he wanted to lend his name.

For years Lucas had been peddling the idea of a rock 'n' roll movie about cruising, a sociological study of the American mating ritual. It was to be a simple little tale about a group of teenagers' coming of age in Modesto, a sleepy town in northern California where Lucas himself spent his formative years. Ned Tanen at Universal agreed to finance the modest $750,000 production after everyone else had rejected it, but only if Gary Kurtz was replaced as producer by a more renowned name. So in early 1972 Lucas turned to Coppola, who agreed, if reluctantly, to lend his support. (Universal craftily drafted a clause into the contract stipulating that if Lucas failed, Coppola had to step in as director.) *American Graffiti* was off the grid.

'The boy in the cowboy hat, a sort of shit-kicker-cowboy-truck-driver type,' is Ford's rather apt description of Bob Falfa, the straw-hatted badass he played in *American Graffiti*. Ford wasn't required to do very much in the film, save give mocking speeches out of his car window and partake in a classic bit of teenage ritual jousting – drag racing. Not forgetting a half comic rendition of 'Some Enchanted Evening', delivered in a deep, melodious baritone. Such scenes scarcely ate into the running time and Haskell Wexler's camera was mean on the close-ups, but his sneering performance at least got him noticed.

Released in August 1973 *American Graffiti* was the surprise smash of the year, netting Universal some $55 million, dollar-for-dollar even a greater return on investment than *Star Wars*. The film launched a nostalgia boom for the sights and sounds of the fifties. It also received near unanimous critical acclaim and five Oscar nominations, winning none against a sweep by *The Sting*. For Lucas, *American Graffiti* was an intensely personal work, a compelling portrait of a nation's lost adolescence, pre-Vietnam, pre-Watergate, pre-paranoia. Set in 1962, the year Lucas left high school, the film is an evocative assemblage of the music and attitudes of teenage life and rituals, complete with drive-ins, necking in the back seat and cruising. The period was enchantingly recreated but with hellish sacrifices. The schedule was desperately tight; and involved twenty-eight days of shooting at night. The success of the picture more than compensated for the almost intolerable conditions under which the cast and crew were forced to work, and it enhanced both the director's reputation and bank balance. But it did little for the financial prospects of Ford, who was on a basic salary and didn't reap any of the profits. It felt good, however, to be finally associated with a successful product. So he returned to his carpentry duties at least artistically the richer for having worked with Lucas and for having been given a glimpse of the new American cinema in action. For the first time in his career Ford felt like he had actually made a worthwhile contribution to a movie, not merely been a piece of window-dressing. 'I didn't really feel comfortable acting until *American Graffiti*,' Ford told *Elle* in February 1988. 'That's when I realized I had requirements just as a director has requirements. I'd always been too diffident, too nervous to ask the questions necessary to do my job.'

The aftermath of Ford's convincing portrayal of Bob Falfa was predictable: he was repeatedly offered the same kind of roles, guys in cowboy hats. Hollywood hadn't changed much. The 'movie brats' had not yet taken over the asylum. Luckily Fred Roos, who was now a producer in his own right, remained Ford's guardian angel throughout the mid seventies, winning him first a small role in what turned out to be the most critically revered picture of 1974. Francis Ford Coppola's *The Conversation* is a combination of European 'art' film and Hollywood thriller and centres on a paranoid, alienated surveillance expert (Gene Hackman) who stumbles upon a murder scheme. The appearance of this movie at the time of Watergate served to add credence to Coppola's nightmarish tale of government/corporate eavesdropping. Ford gives a quietly menacing performance as Martin Stett, an evil young henchman, in what was essentially a nothing part. Recognizing the deficiencies in the character Ford tried to make Stett more rounded by turning him into a homosexual. This intelligent input impressed Coppola but failed to bring Ford to the attention of the critics and public alike.

Over the next three years Ford accepted just two acting jobs, both for television. *Dynasty* was a lavish costume drama, an epic saga chronicling an American family's rise to power in the first half of the nineteenth century. Intended as a pilot for a series that was never made, Ford had little to do as usual but managed unselfishly to hold his own against some stiff opposition from the more experienced Sarah Miles and Stacy Keach. Much better was *Judgment: The Court Martial of Lt. William Calley*, directed by Stanley Kramer. This was a stirring dramatization, based on actual trial transcripts, of one of the most controversial court cases in American judicial history. The accused was one William Calley, charged with the murder of seventy Vietnamese – mostly women and children – at My Lai village on 16 March 1968. Ford played Frank Crowder, the main prosecuting witness, who in one emotional scene breaks down under oath. Ford remembers the role as being among the riskiest of his career. He had to develop the part himself, performing without rehearsal or input from Kramer, who was busy riding herd over a large cast. It was a strong indication of how Ford had grown in stature and confidence as an actor.

The year was 1976 and Ford's career again seemed to be going nowhere. His comeback films had been enormously successful, but their renown had not rubbed off on him. When Fred Roos rang Ford up again with a third job it did little to raise the spirits of his friend. The role hardly seemed an auspicious one, an interplanetary knight errant by the name of Solo.

4

A Myth for Our Time

We laugh at them now, those old black-and-white *Flash Gordon* serials of the late thirties with their antiquated special effects. Who can forget the smoke-powered gyroships and hydrocycles which hung precariously from the sky on all too visible strings, the dodgy scenery, farcical dialogue and the worst kind of melodramatic acting? But in those Depression years Buster Crabbe and his fearless cohorts thrilled the world's movie houses, and the legend, 'To be continued next week,' would be greeted with howls of disappointment by fans whose fate it was to wait until the following Saturday morning to discover whether their hero had survived the clutches of the dastardly villain. *Flash Gordon* made cinema history in 1936 by becoming the first space serial ever; nothing quite like it had been seen before. The profound influence the programme wrought over successive generations of film-makers is irrefutable and one that continues to be felt to this day. For without Flash, Ming the Merciless, Dale Arden and the planet Mongo there would assuredly have been no motion picture called *Star Wars*.

Just as *American Graffiti* disclosed aspects of the teenage Lucas, so *Star Wars* captures the mogul as a child. In the process of attending film school George Lucas accumulated a small stockpile of ideas for great movies that he would one day love to make. Among his cherished favourites was the notion of committing to celluloid the ultimate space epic. After *American Graffiti*, associates and friends of the director urged him to make another *THX 1138*, a serious, socially relevant film on the lines of *Taxi Driver*. So disheartened was he with contemporary trends for violence and shock realism in the cinema, Lucas ignored all advice. Consciously or otherwise, he went in completely the opposite direction, declaring an earnest intention to make a children's film, to go, as he put it, 'the Disney route'. Lucas didn't want *Star Wars* to be an intellectual trip like *2001 A Space Odyssey* or *Solaris*, but a rollicking fantasy which recaptured the spirit of those stalwart space heroes of the thirties, Gordon and Buck Rogers. It was to be a modern fairy tale, closer to

Grimm than to Kubrick, and aimed squarely at the youth market, while also shrewdly appealing to the hidden kid in all of us.

Lucas's exploration into the make-believe land of childhood – home of dragons, wizards and damsels in distress, and where good always triumphs over evil – was territory that Hollywood has neglected for some time. Lucas wanted a return to the sense of wonderment and adventure that made the old Saturday matinee cliffhangers so appealing, but to update the genre for contemporary audiences by taking full advantage of the technical wizardry of modern film-making. Lucas thus cleverly conceived *Star Wars* as an expression of his boyhood fantasy life, those lazy hours spent reading comic books or transfixed to the television watching re-runs of *Flash Gordon*. Indeed, Lucas was so strongly influenced by *Flash Gordon*, in particular, that he originally intended his space epic to be a remake of the classic serial. King Features, who owned the rights to the characters created by Alex Raymond, bluntly rebuffed the director's advances. Apparently they wanted too much money and their treasured property in the hands of a more seasoned filmmaker.

Undeterred, Lucas set about fashioning his own story using the space fantasy milieu of the old Buster Crabbe serials as a springboard. Other ideas were thrown in from such diverse fields as pulp literature, war and western movies, Marvel comics and Tolkien. The daunting task of putting down all his ideas for *Star Wars* on paper was a daunting experience for a man who has confessed to loathing the writing process. 'I'm a terrible writer: I hate scripts, I hate plot.' Beginning in January 1973 Lucas set himself a crushing work schedule: eight hours a day, five days a week he sat in his office, pounding draft after draft on his typewriter. It wasn't until March of 1976, shortly before filming began, that the final screenplay emerged and even then Lucas was prone to stay up half the night following a stressful day's shooting attending to rewrites. In all Lucas wrote four entirely different screenplays, searching each time for the right ingredients, characters and plotline. 'It's always been what you might call a good idea in search of a story.'

Star Wars went through various stages of metamorphosis while Lucas was shopping the idea around Hollywood. Originally the hero was to be Luke Starkiller, an elderly general, and later became Luke Skywalker, a wide-eyed eighteen-year-old orphan. Bored and restless for adventure, he is kept on a farm on the remote dustbowl planet of Tatooine by his uncle, who fears the teenager may turn out like his father, a once great Jedi warrior. In one script version Luke was changed into a girl, allegedly because 20th Century Fox wanted some romantic interest; and Han Solo, who evolved from a green-skinned monster to the brash, egotistical interstellar pilot in the version that Harrison Ford accepted, became champion of the universe. Luke eventually regained his rightful gender and Princess Leia was brought in as a third character. For a time Han Solo and Obi Wan Kenobi, a Merlin-type figure, were the same man. Kenobi is one of the last of the Jedi race, a mystic religious order who worship the Force. The universe is in peril from an all-powerful, tyrannical empire, and Luke is out to save a beautiful princess imprisoned by the evil Darth Vader and his cronies, and transport to the rebel forces the secret plans of the Death Star, the imperial spacefort which can destroy planets.

No one in Hollywood was much worked up about *Star Wars*. Most thought the idea an eccentric one, a bit kooky. Universal dismissed Lucas as mad when he handed them a twelve-page outline of the plot in 1973. As part of the *Graffiti* deal the studio had first option on *Star Wars* but declined to put up $25,000 to develop the screenplay further. Alongside Decca's rejection of the Beatles, this surely ranks as the worst decision in entertainment history, one that ultimately cost them a reputed $250 million bonanza. There was one man in Tinseltown, however, who was eager to do business with Lucas – Alan Ladd Jnr of 20th Century Fox, who realized the potential of his ideas and his enthusiasm and agreed to back the film. The budget was tentatively, and somewhat unrealistically, set at three to four million dollars.

The big brass at Fox were totally mystified over Ladd's acquisition of the *Star Wars* property. They were leery of the whole science-fiction genre because of the enormous expense and apparent lack of audience appeal. Lucas worried too that there might not be a big enough demand for this kind of picture. The only really successful major sci-fi film of recent years had been *2001* and that took five years to show a profit. Nevertheless, Fox were eager to work with Lucas who was now a hot director, thanks to the unexpectedly high box-office performance of *American Graffiti*. The deal struck between Lucas and 20th Century Fox was almost without precedent, an extraordinary coup for a man with barely two films to his name. Instead of demanding outrageous sums of money for his services, as the studio had cautiously anticipated, Lucas craved control and set forth his demands with a casual recklessness that stunned many observers. After weeks of heated debate Lucas walked away from the negotiating table with considerable creative freedom over the future of the entire *Star Wars* industry – and forty per cent of the profits.

As work on the script continued apace it became apparent that *Star Wars* was evolving into more than just one story; indeed it was close to becoming a mini-saga. By the time of the second full screenplay there was enough plot material for three films, with ideas sketchily laid out for a further six. From his own hand Lucas had conceived an entire universe, a cosmic Ruritania, and peopled it with weird and wonderful creatures out of the debris of twentieth-century popular mythology. *Star*

Wars is a masterpiece of synthesis. Influences abound from *Lord of the Rings* and *Dune*, to *The Wizard of Oz* (R2D2, C3PO and Chewbacca are the transmogrified trio of the Tin Man, Scarecrow and the cowardly lion) and war movies. In fact, Lucas drew on footage from a number of WWII classics to orchestrate the climactic dogfight in space, and the Samurai tradition of Japan was partly the basis for the Jedi warriors. There is also the obvious influence of comics in the film's balloon dialogue, which Ford had so much trouble with. 'There were times when I issued a threat to tie George up and make him repeat his own dialogue,' Ford joked with *Time* in May 1977. 'I told him: "You can't say this shit, you can only type it." But I was wrong. It worked.' But *Star Wars* borrows most heavily from Flash Gordon: the 'crawl' at the beginning; the paragraphs of plot synopsis trailing off into the stars; the visual punctuation (wipes, fast dissolves and so on); and the film begins smack in the middle of the action, as if you've just walked into chapter four of a long-running weekly serial.

After a tighter third draft was completed Lucas turned his attention to the problem of casting, ignoring pressure from Hollywood to load the film with a cavalcade of famous faces. The *Star Wars* auditions were held over a period of two months at the old Goldwyn Studios in Culver City. The strategy was the one that had worked so well for *Graffiti*, an endless sifting through hundreds of unknown actors for the perfect combination. Lucas joined forces with Brian de Palma, then casting *Carrie*, which also required a group of young performers, to share the burden. Perhaps the most hotly contested role was that of Han Solo. Numerous twists of fate and an incredible run of luck led to Harrison Ford being cast. The actor knew of the auditions – the ever efficient Hollywood grapevine had been alive with the news for weeks now – yet Lucas had let it be known that he wasn't using anybody from *American Graffiti*, which ruled him out. Such a policy made perfect sense. Every film-maker has the right to approach a new project with fresh talent – and anyway, as Ford later earnestly admitted, 'I had no ambitions about being in Star Wars.'

Quite by accident the two men bumped into one another again at the offices of a mutual friend, Francis Ford Coppola. Ford seems to be of the opinion that this so-called 'chance' meeting may have been meticulously preplanned by peripheral forces. In his capacity as carpenter Ford had been 'inveigled' (the actor's own choice of word) by Dean Tavoularis, Coppola's production designer and a friend of Ford's, into installing an elaborate entrance for the director's plush office at Goldwyn. This put Ford in exactly the same location as Lucas, who was holding his interviews on one of the stages. Surely this was more than mere coincidence. Harrison thought so too and felt it would be a little coy of him to be around the place at the same time, so opted instead to carry out his work at night. As luck would have it, something important came up, leaving Ford with no alternative but to work one afternoon at the office; and sure enough that was the day Lucas decided to pay a visit. There was Ford working on his knees by the doorway when a group of men entered. First through the door came Coppola, followed by Lucas, then Fred Roos. Behind them strolled Ford's old *Graffiti* co-star Richard Dreyfuss, who found the sight of a bent-over Ford especially amusing and proceeded to make a joke out of being his assistant. 'That made me feel just great,' Ford said. 'I felt about the size of a pea after they walked through.'

More than any other individual Fred Roos was responsible for Harrison Ford landing the role of Han Solo. He prevailed upon Lucas to consider him after the director had seen just about every other possible candidate. 'He wasn't high on George's list,' Roos remembers. 'He didn't know him like I did.' Three or four weeks before the final casting decision had to be made Ford did a video test, ironically at the same place where he had successfully auditioned for *American Graffiti*. The omens were good. To his surprise the routine was almost identical to his last audition with Lucas. He was requested to read from a couple of loose script pages – there was no scene-setting, no explanations, he just had to get stuck in and do it. A few days later Ford was asked to help out by reading the male parts opposite the contenders for Princess Leia, about fifty people in total. Ford obliged, still believing nothing would come of it, and duly took a week's break from his carpentry. One of the video tests was conducted with a faintly plump little nineteen-year-old American actress who had recently returned from studying drama in London. Her name was Carrie Fisher, the daughter of Debbie Reynolds and Eddie Fisher. 'The first time I saw him I knew he was going to be a star – someone of the order of Bogart and Tracy,' Fisher recalled to *Vanity Fair* in August 1990. 'I mean, you look at Harrison and you listen; he looks like he's carrying a gun, even if he isn't. I think he has qualities that disappeared into the pioneer west. He's this incredibly attractive male animal in every sense of the word. This carpenter stud.'

Around the time of Ford's call-up from Lucas he was busy carrying out domestic chores up at the Beverly Hills home of Sally Kellerman. According to Ms Kellerman, Ford was midway through painting her kitchen and in the process of putting up some bookshelves when the message came through that Lucas wanted to see him. Ford left the Kellerman residence in such a hurry that he forgot his stepladder, a bag of tools, some pots of paint and his overalls. He was never to return for them. Like a museum exhibit these treasured relics of Ford's carpentry days remained for years gathering dust in the Kellerman garage. The actress even painted on one of the walls, above the bag of tools, a simple inscription: 'Harrison Ford left these.'

The audition for *Star Wars* went well and a week or so later, 'after they'd tested everyone else in the world,' Ford won the part, narrowly squeezing out Nick Nolte, Christopher Walken and William Katt. At one stage Lucas seriously considered casting a black actor as Solo, until he envisaged the controversy an interracial romance might cause and chickened out. Likewise, he rejected the idea of having a Eurasian girl for Princess Leia. Initially passed over in an earlier test, Carrie Fisher was recalled and cast as Leia above Amy Irving, Jodie Foster and 400 others. Young Mark Hamill, who had gone through one cattlecall for *Graffiti* when he was nineteen and failed, landed the coveted lead role of Luke Skywalker. As Ford was no great fan of science fiction – unlike Hamill, whose childish enthusiasm for the genre rivals that of Lucas – he approached the whole *Star Wars* project with a certain amount of detachment. To him, Han Solo represented 'just another job'. Those views were to change dramatically once he had read the script.

'The movie sounded a little nuts,' Ford told *Rolling Stone* in June 1981, 'but I didn't give a shit about whether it'd be successful or not. I always thought it was an accessible, human story.' Breaking down Lucas's screenplay until the white of its bare bones were showing, Ford saw that the characters were drawn in a very contemporary light, and the story, in spite of all the fantasy elements, was essentially a simple human drama. 'I mean, I didn't have to act science fiction.' Ford's absolute confidence in *Star Wars* was based on the human side of the story, which revolved around the three principal characters. He earnestly believed that 'that common mythology' was going to work. 'It worked for Grimm in his fairy tales. It worked for Disney, it was going to work for us.'

Although intrinsically a loner, as his name implies, Han Solo was the character to whom most of the audience could relate. He possessed the most contemporary attitudes and was clearly a character rooted in the twentieth century – more like a cowboy from the old West than a space pirate. On release critics and fans compared Ford's performance with that of the young John Wayne. 'If that is so,' he said to *Films Illustrated* in April 1978, 'it was completely unconscious. I didn't know I was doing it, playing it like Wayne at times. I just did what was written down – that's all George's genius. If I'm like Wayne in places, it's my subconscious supplying something that's necessary.' *Star Wars* is indeed very much a western set in space. The celebrated cantina sequence, for example, with its menagerie of exotic monsters, is a reworking of those classic saloon bar showdowns; the scene where Luke returns to a smouldering homestead and finds his surrogate parents slain by imperial forces is a direct reference to John Ford's *The Searchers*; and good and evil are clearly differentiated: heroes dress in white, villains in black. Straight out of the old West rides Han Solo, gun for hire and quick on the draw, with his pistol/blaster slung low in a holster on the hip. Like Luke, Solo is also an orphan, deserted as a baby by space gypsies and reared by wookies, a race of jungle mammals somewhere between a monkey and a grizzly bear. Solo had all the qualities necessary to endear him to the cinema going public. A dashing, reckless adventurer with an infectious, rascally charm, he is tinged by a perceptibly amoral outlook on life. But, through the film, he grows from solitary cynic to fullblown hero.

The statement 'There's none of my personality in Solo. He's no one I know,' was perhaps designed by Ford to avoid being typecast as a hero of comic-strip adventures. It was not entirely true, however. Indeed Lucas said as much when he told reporters that he handpicked the principals for *Star Wars* because 'they're more or less by nature like the characters in the story'. Lucas knew Ford would be ideal to play Solo because of the roguish personality he'd displayed as Bob Falfa. The energy and brooding intensity Ford exudes as Solo is there in *Graffiti*, and in real life, where it is suitably suppressed. Lucas liked Harrison from working with him on *Graffiti*, but when he considered him for *Star Wars* he was afraid of being influenced by the fact that he liked him, that he was familiar with his work, that he was thinking of him for the part because of his previous associations with him. 'So I did tests with a lot of others too. But I just couldn't find anybody who had Ford's qualities as an actor and fitted my concept of the character as well as he did.' Ford himself had no qualms about playing a cartoonish galactic swashbuckler. 'I understood what the part was absolutely. It was the most fully written part, on paper, that I'd had'. And his first starring role. Han Solo was Bob Falfa writ large and he fit Harrison Ford like a glove. It was also the first time in his entire career that Ford had had a character in whom he could actually make his own space ... 'not just fill it anymore. I just went ahead and did it'.

One of the many pleasures of *Star Wars* for Ford was Lucas's ensemble casting. The chemistry between Hamill, Fisher and himself worked so divinely that today it is impossible to imagine anyone else fitting those roles quite so snugly. Lucas took no chances, though, installing a substitute trio of actors who anxiously waited in the wings, ready to step in at a moment's notice if things didn't work out. But at no time would it have been a case of mix and match. The threesome didn't click immediately: it took about a week where they sized each other up, before beginning to grasp exactly what Lucas saw in them as a team. A strong bond of friendship was soon cultivated between them – one which survives to this day.

To support these relatively inexperienced players Lucas signed two of England's finest senior actors: Peter Cushing, veteran of countless Hammer horrors, and Alec Guinness. Ford's one overriding concern during preparatory work for the film, apart from a grave worry that the actors would be overshadowed by all the special effects paraphernalia, was the prospect of acting alongside Guinness, a distinguished thespian and acknowledged master of his craft. It scared him half to death, ('Me in a movie with Alec Guinness!') and resulted in the occasional sleepless night. 'I thought if he laughed at me just the once, I'd pack my bags and go home.' Of course nothing of the sort happened: the two men got on extremely well and Ford left with nothing but admiration for the elder statesman.

Work began officially on *Star Wars* early in 1975, once 20th Century Fox decided to give Lucas's space extravaganza a chance. Top priority was the physical design of the film. To help visualize his ideas and dreams Lucas hired top design consultants and artists, notably Ralph McQuarrie, whose stunning production paintings of the various worlds, characters and costumes heavily influenced the visual style of the entire movie. Deliberately steering clear of the shiny, antiseptic modernism of films like *2001*, Lucas insisted all sets and models be designed to look inhabited and used. Han Solo's ship, the *Millennium Falcon*, for example, really looked as if it had travelled from one end of the galaxy to the other, its durable, grease-smeared bodywork pockmarked by laser blasts and near-misses with meteorites. Only inside the newly constructed Death Star is the futuristic chic one usually associates with the genre on display.

Apart from the media phenomenon that *Star Wars* was to become, the most important and mould-breaking aspect of the production was in the field of special effects. The trilogy sparked a quantum leap in special-effects technology, to the point where today just about anything you can imagine can be actualized on film. In June of 1975 Lucas contracted John Dykstra to supervise the effects for *Star Wars*. In order to produce the quantity and quality of special-effects shots required, Dykstra realized that a complete in-house effects studio would have to be developed. In July an empty warehouse in an unfashionable district of Van Nuys, California, was purchased expressly for this purpose. Within eight months Industrial Light and Magic (ILM), as the place was imaginatively christened, was turned into one of the most advanced facilities of its kind in the world. Dykstra's seventy-five-strong staff were nearly all young technicians, some fresh out of college. Few of the team were older than thirty, some were even under twenty years old. They were children of the sixties, with boundless enthusiasm for their trade and what they were all setting out to achieve. Working under the aegis of Dykstra and other effects luminaries, such as Richard Edlund and Dennis Muren, this motley band of dedicated craftsmen, some versed in traditional movie effects methods like mattes and stop-motion photography, others conversant in state-of-the-art computer technology, were to revolutionize the way effects were created. It took twenty-two months in all to plan, develop and execute the special effects for *Star Wars*, at a cost of $2.5 million.

At first, Lucas though of making Tatooine, where much of the film's opening action takes place, a jungle planet. But the logistical problems and cost of spending months shooting in the Philippines made Lucas edgy; so, with the touch of an eraser, Luke Skywalker's homeworld became a sprawling desert. Southern Tunisia was chosen; the region's unusual terrain and arid landscape seemed an ideal setting. In March 1976, just ahead of the tourist season, the *Star Wars* production crew descended upon Tozeur, a sleepy little oasis town situated close to where North Africa and Arabia meet and the Sahara Desert begins.

On the second day of filming, 26 March, the perennially blue sky temporarily opened up and a torrential downpour reduced the dry yellow lake beds to pools of uninviting mud. George Lucas was not amused to learn that this was the first winter rain in over fifty years. Was this an omen? Was his project fated and doomed to fail? It must have seemed so by the end of the first week, when the location site was ravaged by a sandstorm. Crew-members were forced to wear goggles and the expensive cameras had to be rigorously cleaned out every evening. These were to be just the initial problems in an arduous seventy-day shoot.

In addition to the adverse weather conditions – freezing temperatures in the morning, blazing heat in the afternoon – the biggest location headache was getting the various robots to function properly. When *Star Wars* was released it wasn't Ford or even Alec Guinness who attracted the most attention but a pair of automata: R2D2, a chirpy dustbin-sized droid who communicates via a series of blinking lights and sharp bleeps; and C3PO (played by Anthony Daniels), a golden anthropoid with all the insufferable qualities of an English butler on the slide. The metal duo's love/hate relationship was likened by many critics to Laurel and Hardy, and the *New York Times* called them, 'the year's best new comedy team'. On day one in Tunisia they worked like a dream, but the remainder of the shoot was a nightmare. For the most part R2D2 was operated in extreme discomfort by Kenny Baker, at three feet eight inches the smallest man in England. At other times a remote-controlled replica was used, which due to strange radio signals emanating from the sand frequently went haywire, wandering off on its own accord and crashing. So much for the modern technology which the movie celebrated.

After a fortnight of stressful location filming in Tunisia operations relocated to London, in the grip of a heatwave. Elstree studios, a dingy, depressing dinosaur of an edifice and long past its prime, was home for the next two months. Lucas had chosen Elstree because it was the only studio in America or Europe which provided him with nine large sound stages simultaneously. With a predominantly British cast and crew Lucas and his three leading actors felt themselves to be strangers in a strange land. Lucas, in particular, never really adjusted to making the movie in Britain. He was unhappy with the working conditions and incensed at always being at the mercy of the all-powerful union, who insisted their members clock off promptly at 5.30 pm, no matter how near a scene was to completion. In this atmosphere of mutual distrust and dislike there emerged two definite camps, the British contingent and the American one. Ford, revelling in the opportunity to shine at last in a role of substance, was determined to have fun amidst the monotony and grinding routine that was demoralizing everyone. Although his madcap practical jokes never reached the inspired lunacy practised on the *Graffiti* set when he, Paul le Mat and Bo Hopkins urinated in the ice-making machine, they did end up alienating the two camps still further. 'The only damper on the pure fun,' he said, 'was the almost unanimous attitude of the English crew that we were totally out of our minds.' Such larking about runs counter to the popular conception of Ford as a quiet, solitary animal on a film set. On the whole, though, this is a fair portrait. While he interacted socially with Lucas, Hamill and Fisher, Ford was very reserved around everyone else. 'We had a good working relationship more than a friendship,' Peter Mayhew, the actor who portrayed Han Solo's co-pilot Chewbacca, recalled to *Cinefantastique* in the spring of 1978. 'I don't think anyone got on that well with him as he really isn't that sort of person.'

Filming continued at a snail's pace in a climate of workmanlike intensity. The near insurmountable technical problems, inherent in a film of such scale, served to compound existing problems and add to the general feeling of misery. It was not a happy ship. Lucas, under enormous pressure, feuded with his cinematographer Gil Taylor, and even fired an editor with whom he didn't get along. Then he fell victim to violent psychosomatic headaches and stomach pains, followed by bouts of exhaustion and depression. Lucas's first experience of working on a major Hollywood production – *Graffiti* had a team of about eighteen people, while *Star Wars* employed around 900 – proved so gruelling that he has never personally directed a film since. '*Star Wars* was one of the worst periods in my life.'

More calamities were to follow. The picture was running dangerously behind schedule and over budget, the special effects weren't very special and nowhere near ready, and Fox were sorely tempted to pull the plug on Lucas's dream. Only Ladd's faith in the project dissuaded them. The post-production period saw Lucas at his most desperate. Ford and the rest of the cast had gone home, leaving their director to slog away eighteen hours a day trying to get the film finished in time for its Memorial Day première (he was still solidly working on it until a week before the opening). Meanwhile, over at ILM teams were put on an around-the-clock work schedule. Editing with his wife Marcia (who cut *Graffiti*), Lucas finally had a roughcut, minus key SFX shots, ready to show expectant studio executives, keen to see how their money had been spent. Their silent, sullen reaction spoke volumes. They were baffled to say the least. What is a wookie? they asked, and emerged from the screening with grim expectations for its commercial viability in the marketplace.

The first finished version, previewed on 1 May 1977 at a packed North Point Theatre in San Francisco, played to rousing cheers and applause. Yet there was no hint of the miracle to come. Satisfied, Lucas left the cinema that mild Sunday morning confident that *Star Wars* would at the very least earn back its investment, but not sure of much beyond that. Nobody was, least of all Ford, who got his chance to see the film at a cast and crew screening at the headquarters of the Academy of Motion Picture Arts and Science in Beverly Hills on 21 May. 'I didn't realize we were onto a winner. I thought either it would reach a wide audience who would recognize it as a fun, space-age western, or it would be so silly that my two kids would be embarrassed for me to even leave the house. I didn't even know that there were so many out there interested in this kind of material.'

Neither did Fox, then in financial dire straits, whose hopes for summer glory and survival were pinned on *Lucky Lady*, a light period comedy featuring the expensive talents of Burt Reynolds, Gene Hackman and Liza Minnelli (which bombed). In their opinion George Lucas and his silly little space film with its cast of nobodies stood no chance. They couldn't even figure out how to sell it properly: was it a comedy, an adventure, or a *2001* clone? Thirteen different publicity campaigns were scrapped. This rejected PR line perhaps summed up *Star Wars* better than any: 'Never before in cinema history has so much time, money and technology been spent ... just for fun.'

The moment of truth came on Wednesday 25 May when *Star Wars* opened, without great fanfare, in cinemas across America. Immediately, the film attracted an astonishing outpouring of critical praise and generated an almost unprecedented audience response. Within a few weeks box-office records were tumbling; Fox executives accepted congratulations on their foresight as the value of the company's shares doubled on Wall Street; and theatres, paying the price for not recognizing a hit, were fighting in the courts to show the film. By August *Star Wars* had taken $100 million, until then the fastest-grossing motion picture in history. (The final cost of *Star Wars* was $10.5 million, remarkably cheap considering its stunning production values. Lucas later called *Star Wars*, 'the most expensive low-budget movie ever made'.) No one was more surprised than Lucas, whose reaction upon fathering a worldwide phenomenon was one of bafflement. He had even resigned himself to the fact that the press were going to rubbish his work because of its lighthearted entertainment value, but was surprised when the majority of newspapers accepted the film for what it was and enjoyed it on that level. 'An escapist masterpiece, one of the greatest adventure movies ever made' – Newsday; 'A grand and glorious film, the best movie of the year' – Time; 'The most elaborate, most beautiful movie serial ever made' – New York Times. Of course there were some detractors, who, while praising the technical proficiency on show, dismissed the film as corny. 'Star Wars is childish, even for a cartoon' – Village Voice. They got no argument from Harrison Ford. 'Sure, Star Wars is preposterous. But it's so wonderfully made.' Lucas, for that matter, later described his masterpiece as 'a rather simplistic movie', and derived some puckish pleasure from those 'serious' critics who searched for hidden meanings or philosophical enlightenment amidst the whirring spaceships and flashing ray guns. The whole point was that there was no message; this was pure unashamed escapism breathtakingly staged. The film's simple good-over-evil moralism, combined with its romantic streak, did not find favour, perhaps, with sci-fi purists. But the reason for the film's fundamental appeal to both young and old lay precisely in its deliberately old-fashioned plot, which had its roots deep in American popular culture. This was a myth for our times, a Wizard of Oz for the seventies.

'I didn't take the success of Star Wars personally,' Ford said as he, Hamill and Fisher became the subjects of a steady barrage of media coverage. Sadly, nothing much in the way of individual recognition for his performance was forthcoming. Ford had been a positive force that refused to be upstaged by the film's brazen technology, but he avoided any egotistical scene stealing. Second in the cast list, the three young leads were generally lumped together, often disparagingly, with any acting plaudits going to Alec Guinness. Though Variety acknowledged: 'Harrison Ford is outstanding.' By Christmas Ford's face was known across the globe when the toys and games market was flooded with Star Wars souvenirs. The film's enormous success heralded a new age in movie 'tie-in' merchandising – everything from comics, sleeping bags, models, wallpaper and ice cream – which by the tenth anniversary of Star Wars had amassed over $2.6 billion in retail sales. They used to send Ford boxes of these goods as they were manufactured, little bendy action figures of himself, the lot, but he usually just gave them away, unopened. Inevitably there were frictions, Ford could sometimes get quite childishly upset. 'Mark gets to be a puzzle, why don't I?' he'd blast. Those sorts of arguments went on. 'Wait a minute,' the others would harp. 'Why don't I get to be on the pencil box for chrissakes! I mean, if I'm gonna be in this and I'm gonna end up being two sizes of dolls, a belt and a cookie, then why don't I get to be on an eraser too?'

In 1978 Star Wars reaped six Academy Awards, all for technical merit; the actors and Lucas went unrewarded. Nominated for best film, best direction and best screenplay, on the night these accolades deservedly passed to Woody Allen's *Annie Hall*. In July Fox reissued the film, bringing in another $46 million in only five weeks. After worldwide ticket sales of $600 million, Lucas and *Star Wars* became the undisputed box-office champion of all time, having rudely usurped fellow movie brat Spielberg's *Jaws*. (Revenge was sweet though when *ET* smashed *Star Wars'* seemingly invincible $193 million record for rental profits.) These astonishing profits helped Lucas fulfil his goal to become an independent film-maker. Feeling generous, he rewarded his main actors with a percentage of the profits. Ford's own 0.66 per cent netted him a cool million dollars. His financial independence was assured. The money was well spent: a new home in a canyon above Beverly Hills and a large, fully equipped workshop where he would spend much of his spare time.

Star Wars is undoubtedly one of the most important films ever made, less for its dramatic content than for the way it revolutionized hi-tech filmmaking. Just as significantly, it made Hollywood stand up and take notice of the massive international thirst for epic fantasy movies. Whereas *American Graffiti* took a worn-out genre (the teenage drive-in/beach-party movies) and reanimated it, *Star Wars* breathed new life into the space fantasy. Lucas began a trend that turned the commercial cinema into a vast extension of the children's Saturday matinee, virtually killing off the adult film as a money-making proposition for ten years, and opened the floodgates for a boom in science fiction that still reverberates today.

Dramatically *Star Wars* leaves a lot to be desired. Though lovingly crafted, full of verve and visual ingenuity and acted with real charm and gusto, it is a hollow spectacle, where special effects preside over derivative ideas and unoriginal plotlines. 'I don't think it's altogether that well made a movie either,' Lucas later said, 'because I was working under extremely difficult conditions.' But its effect on so many areas of the entertainment industry cannot be denied. For that fact alone, *Star Wars* stands as a landmark of the cinema.

5

Going Solo

Star Wars catapulted Ford into the mainstream movie world, and critics hailed him as an overnight success. Ford laughed at the irony, the night in question had lasted fifteen years! Fifteen tough years of bit parts, of lean periods full of anger and frustration, of walking out on the Hollywood system. In the end he won through by sheer determination and staying power. From the beginning Ford knew that it would take at least a decade to make his name and that staying the course was what counted. The sheer process of attrition would wear the others down. So he just never gave up, nor did it ever occur to him that he might have made the wrong choice; instead he became more stubborn and tenacious in his quest. It's a personal characteristic: this is a man who never quits. No drugs, no alcohol; Ford was just addicted to his job. Whether building houses or acting, his ambition was always the same – to do good work. Until eventually, as he liked to joke, 'there were only six 35-year-old actors left'.

Ford believes in accident as an instrument of fate, not in determinism, that hard work and a proper frame of mind prepared him for the lucky breaks that finally came along. His career was absurdly slow in taking off but at least this allowed him to gain some maturity before being confronted with fame. He had spent years laboriously climbing to the top of his profession, getting wiser and tougher at every rung. Unknown and twenty-five, a role like Han Solo might have destroyed Ford. Without the benefit of a long apprenticeship, battle-hardened and thick-skinned, he might never have handled the sudden pressures of stardom resulting from *Star Wars*. It was great to be a late bloomer Ford testified: it goes against everything society tells you, which is to claw and grasp and get there quick.

Ford was now a household item, his face adorning a variety of products from posters to badges, wallpaper to lunchboxes. Yet after the success of *Star Wars* more people recognized Han Solo than knew or understood Harrison Ford, the actor who gave him life, a state of affairs lasting years. *Star Wars* was by no means a personal triumph, but Ford was being handed a golden opportunity which he could either nurture into a career or fritter away. It was unquestionably the turning point in his life, or at least, as the actor liked to jibe, 'that was the point my accountant chose'. He would be forever grateful to George Lucas for the recognition and professional acclaim it generated. 'I guess I owe a lot to George for bringing me back from the wilderness in terms of my career', Ford told *Film Review* in June 1978. 'He's been responsible for a lot of good things happening to me.' Still he didn't want to build his career solely on the back of Han Solo.

Importantly *Star Wars* gave Ford financial security and the creative freedom which accompanies it. He received numerous job offers which were respectable in terms of salary but which weren't intrinsically worthwhile. He didn't want to abuse what *Star Wars* had given him, so he refused the carbon-copy sci-fi films, rejected the crude Han Solo replicas. Already Hollywood sought to typecast him. The last thing Ford wanted at the dawn of his career was to become too closely associated by producers and audiences with any single role or genre. Recurring parts are a blessing and a curse for a film actor. On the one hand, they can lead to a freeing-up of choices and a king's ransom for sequel work. On the other, they can lead to a well-upholstered captivity. Another obstacle encountered by any star associated with a single character type is a prejudice among directors when they cast their films. Why choose someone with all that baggage, when another actor can come to a role unburdened by public preconceptions? (Ford would soon make things twice as difficult by amassing a worldwide following for two heroes – Han Solo and Indiana Jones.) Thus began a personal crusade to work against the powerful and all-consuming *Star Wars* image by deliberately inhabiting a variety of film roles so as constantly to alter the public's perception of him. In some ways Ford was able to escape the perils of typecasting quite early on through some carefully considered career decisions, beginning with *Heroes*. The anonymity of his roles in films like *Heroes* and later in *Apocalypse Now* suggested then a certain reticence about being typecast as a high-action player. But this obsession to work against type led Ford into a series of misfires and puddings which almost wrecked his career.

On paper *Heroes* was a shrewd and calculated move. In execution it turned out an honourable failure. Strongly advised against playing a character who only occupied fifteen minutes of screen time, Ford saw it as vital to get something on film quickly that was the complete antithesis of *Star Wars*. In this respect *Heroes* was an important step. 'After that, I felt secure that I was not going to be typecast.' Kenny Boyd, a tragic Vietnam veteran unable to cope with civilian life, seemed to fit Ford's new game-plan perfectly. Boyd was a Missouri farmhand, living rough in a tumbledown motor home and occasionally indulging in drag racing; he was light years away from the buccaneering Han Solo. Ford signed the contract in the full knowledge that the role was underdeveloped, the pay cheque minimal and that the spotlight belonged to Henry Winkler – himself, ironically, trying to escape from the graven image of The Fonz in television's *Happy Days*.

Like so many other post-Vietnam films of the late seventies, *Heroes* cashed in on the neurosis of a nation putting itself on the couch. Winkler plays Jack Dunne, a veteran of the war who clings to a dream of starting a worm farm with some former army colleagues. On his travels he meets another lost soul Carol (Sally Field) and discovers his old buddies are either dead or, like himself, deeply and incurably scarred. Released in November 1977 *Heroes* caused hardly a ripple, meeting with mediocre reviews on both sides of the Atlantic. Ford's persuasive, touching performance as the outwardly cheerful, but inwardly pathetic Boyd, passed largely unnoticed.

Although a flop *Heroes* served the purpose for which Ford had agreed to become involved. He never expected the film to pull in big dollars at the nation's box office, nor did he particularly care if the public decided to stay away. Far more important was that those in the business caught the show. He also happens to like the film a great deal and enjoyed working with its young director, Jeremy Paul Kagan, who allowed a certain amount of freedom when it came to rephrasing dialogue. Ten days before shooting Kagan changed Boyd from a Mid-western to a Missouri farmer. Because the new accent affected the flow of speech, Ford got the chance to work on changing the screenplay with him. The sudden alteration also presented Ford with the opportunity of fully researching a character for the first time. Hopping on to a plane bound for Missouri, tape recorder in hand, he travelled around for three days taping conversations with local townsfolk, perfecting the new accent, and by coincidence meeting up with a young man similar in spirit to Boyd, a car fanatic who worked at an auto-part shop. Ford introduced himself as a writer in the throes of researching a novel to avoid an afternoon of fending off inevitable questions about Hollywood. 'It puts a certain distance between them and you.'

The subject of the Vietnam War was to be shockingly and more triumphantly exploited in Ford's next project. *Heroes* might have been the first post-Vietnam comedy, but *Apocalypse Now* still ranks as the masterpiece of that terrible conflict. The war in Vietnam, the horrors of which were brought home vividly every night on television, caused massive domestic unrest in the United States. Ford's own view of the Vietnam War says much about the man. Like many of his generation he was disillusioned with his country's involvement in South-east Asia and increasingly sickened at the seemingly senseless slaughter of many of his

contemporaries. Protest rallies and peace marches were common –
some people even burnt their draft cards in open defiance of
government policy. Ford's resentment against being drafted was
straightforward enough and based purely on ethical, rather than political
grounds. He simply did not want to get involved in the taking of human
life. 'I'm not a spiritual person,' Ford told the magazine *Options* in April
1987. 'I am a practical, logical, pragmatic kind of person. I do have
ethical values though.' When his call-up came, Ford went along and
presented himself as a conscientious objector. 'I had to do that without
any history of religious training, so what I talked about was ethics and
fairness, and the final fairness is not killing someone else.' Willing to do
alternative service, Ford was not prepared to kill for his country, a moral
conviction which is still rigorously upheld. When the moment came to
write a thesis on why he wouldn't fight, Ford unearthed his scrappy
notes from the failed philosophy course at Ripon to support his tenuous
argument. Happily the ploy worked, confusing the authorities to such a
degree they put his name way down the list rather than try to counteract
it. That Ford was a married man and a father to boot also played to his
advantage. With single men readily available to act as cannon fodder,
those with wives and families to support were allowed to stay at home.

The tangled origins of *Apocalypse Now* stretch back to the late sixties
when fellow USC (University of Southern California) students George
Lucas and John Milius dreamt up the idea of adapting Joseph Conrad's
novel *Heart of Darkness*. They won the support of Francis Ford Coppola
to develop the project, which foundered at the first hurdle.
Unperturbed, Lucas concentrated all his efforts on *American Graffiti*,
content to leave *Apocalypse Now* on the back-burner. The subject
surfaced again in 1973 when Lucas's mind was scheming the exploits of
Luke Skywalker and Han Solo. Still, the desire to make his Vietnam
picture had not dwindled over the years and he enlisted Milius to write
the screenplay while Gary Kurtz scouted for locations in the Far East.
But after several contractual and personal differences of opinion with
Coppola Lucas withdrew in protest. Where he had originally envisaged
making a 16mm documentary-style film, Coppola chose to make a
spectacular star-studded anti-war psychedelic trip.

Ford's involvement in *Apocalypse Now* was engineered once again by
Fred Roos, co-producer of the film with Coppola. Ford saw in the
character being offered, a US Army intelligence colonel, a chance to
present the public with yet another image change. Ford immersed
himself into what was nothing more than a cameo role. He cut his hair
dangerously short and hid behind a pair of steel-rimmed glasses, the
kind Indiana Jones wears when he's not out bullwhipping the hide off
foreign types. The ruse worked perfectly; in his ten-minute appearance
Ford is barely recognizable. At his own request the character was named

after his *Star Wars* director; the name tag on his army shirt reads 'Colonel G. Lucas'. When Lucas first viewed the footage the scene was already halfway over before he recognized Ford, which pleased the actor no end. 'That's exactly the way I want it and I hope I can maintain that anonymity because I think it's important, considering the incredible occurrence of the image of *Star Wars*.'

Ford shares his one sequence with Martin Sheen, who plays the lead character Willard, an army captain and sometime assassin. Ford refers to it as 'the laundry list scene – it tells the audience all they need to know for the rest of the movie'. With an air of detachment and coldness Ford briefs Willard on his mission. He is to sail up the Nung River into Cambodia where he is to seek out and 'terminate with extreme prejudice' a renegade American colonel. The latter, played with mumbling majesty by Marlon Brando, is waging his own private war against the Vietcong with an army of natives, who worship him as a living god. Coppola's production began shooting the same month as *Star Wars*, and Ford was left with the daunting task of having to choose between the two. He concluded that Han Solo would be the more career enhancing. How right he was. 'And am I glad, because some guys went to the Philippines to make *Apocalypse Now* for three months and stayed a year.' His *Star Wars* duties at an end and with Coppola's movie only a third of the way completed, over schedule and over budget, the saintly Fred Roos conjured up a role for Ford, one which would only require his services for three weeks. But he turned it down. Finally Roos came up with the part of Colonel Lucas, nine days' work maximum. Ford packed his bags and headed for the Philippines. It was to be a fateful journey.

What he witnessed when he arrived was nothing short of a madhouse. Ford had walked into a maelstrom. In one corner poor Martin Sheen, selected only after Robert Redford, Al Pacino and Jack Nicholson had said no to Willard, was recuperating from a near-fatal heart attack brought on by the demands of filming; in the other the alchemist Coppola had mortgaged his home and put his own marriage at risk to complete the movie. A spiralling budget didn't help – $31 million at the final count – much of which was spent in creating stunning set pieces. Most notable of these, perhaps, was the helicopter attack on a coastal village to the strains of Wagner's 'The Ride of the Valkyries'. Even the gods were against them, sending Typhoon Olga to wreck the shoot. All of this led Coppola to announce memorably, '*Apocalypse Now* is not a movie. It is not about Vietnam. It is Vietnam.'

Possibly the only person on location having a good time, Ford thoroughly enjoyed his brief stint on the picture and the experience of working with Coppola again. 'Francis really is delightful. He allows you enormous freedom. He lets you make a choice and then moves everything to support you, to make it work for you.'

Another source of pleasure was his burgeoning friendship with Coppola's assistant, a bright, long-limbed Californian called Melissa Mathison. The two of them had hit it off from the moment they met, partly because she too was as un-Hollywood as it was possible to be. This despite the fact that she grew up there, the daughter of author and journalist Richard Mathison, ex-bureau chief of *Newsweek*. Like all future lovers meeting for the first time, Harrison and Melissa found they shared many common beliefs and were remarkably well suited as a pair. Soon both felt as if they had known one another for years. Melissa was an extremely intelligent woman and fully aware of the fraught situation in which she now found herself. But so close had they become in such a relatively short space of time, that when Ford left the Philippines for America they agreed to keep in touch. This new and unexpected relationship was to place an even greater strain on Ford's already crumbling marriage.

For some time he and Mary had been steadily growing apart. In every marriage break-up various contributory factors are to blame. Ford, in his guilt-ridden defence, simply chose the most logical. He blamed the eventual split partly on the cynicism and bitterness which stemmed from his early disillusionment with Hollywood. Certainly, to begin with, there were the normal pressures associated with being poor and unfulfilled, but countless times Mary proved her love, and when his career took off with *Star Wars* she would try and bring the children over for odd visits wherever he was filming. Never once did she reproach her husband. But as Ford's film commitments escalated, so their relationship suffered as a consequence. The length of time he was spending away from home grew longer and more painful. It was a truly terrible time, with Ford's driving ambition getting in the way of his being an attentive father and husband. In those hectic years after *Star Wars* Ford was selfish and self-centred, and before he knew it there was no more marriage to come home to. Quite simply their love was torn apart little by little. 'The cinema separated us and I will never forgive it for that.'

Friends and colleagues, however, speculated that Ford's new-found stardom was not necessarily the sole cause of the split; rather, they had both married too young. When Carrie Fisher met the couple in London during the filming of *Star Wars* she noted that 'the bloom was sort of off the rose. Mary was Harrison's wife – that was what she did,' the actress disclosed to *Vanity Fair* in August 1990. 'She was a phenomenal cook and the mother of his kids. I don't think they split up because he got famous. They'd been married for fifteen years, since they were kids, and it had just gone its course.'

The rain hammers down with unrelenting force against the bulky picture windows of the five-star Ambassador Hotel. Outside bleak patches of fog methodically roll up from the slate-grey Adriatic to shroud the neighbouring hills in its misty embrace. If the fog were to lift, even slightly, the view would be of a spa resort out of season: large, imposing buildings boarded up for the winter, empty streets and leaf-strewn swimming pools, unattended, forgotten. For a tourist retreat devoid of tourists there is an inordinate amount of activity going on. World War II has returned to soil the majestic Yugoslavian landscape. Ammo dumps are being blown up, German infantry slaughtered and assorted army vehicles wasted. Overseeing the mayhem is one Guy Hamilton, who presides over cast and crew as a general would his troops prior to battle. That was before the rains came. Now the new heroes of Navarone sit redundantly in their respective hotel suites, slowly cracking under the strain of doing nothing.

Seventeen years earlier Gregory Peck, David Niven and other assorted heroes scaled an impenetrable cliff face to silence the monolithic guns of Navarone. They made cinema history and $56 million into the bargain. Master storyteller Alistair MacLean repeated his success with a best-selling follow-up, the film rights of which were inevitably seized. *Force Ten from Navarone* takes place just two years after the original mission. This time Major Mallory and Sergeant Miller (Peck and Niven now replaced by Robert Shaw and Edward Fox) are sent to Yugoslavia, along with young and brash American Lieutenant-Colonel Barnsby (Ford), to assassinate the Nazi spy who betrayed them at Navarone and to help blow up a strategically important bridge.

On their arrival in Yugoslavia Hamilton's 140-strong unit were welcomed with open arms. By a stroke of luck Marshal Tito, the Yugoslav president, was a movie buff and his administration ably supported the production, with the local militia only too willing to turn their tanks into Churchills or Panzers at a cost. But three months of hard location work in barren countryside eventually took its toll, and the miserable weather only served to compound the agony. 'OK, I'll try and think of something positive to say about this location,' Ford muttered to a journalist from *Photoplay* magazine. Pondering the matter in silence the star lit a small cigar. It didn't help. 'No,' he replied shaking his head. 'No ... but give me time.' Suddenly, Ford is inspired. 'I tell you, the hardest thing we have to do on this film is get up in the morning.'

To bolster everyone's dampened spirits and, perhaps, to prevent a full-scale mutiny, the cast devised their own mini-Olympics. Activities ranged from archery, *boules*, arm wrestling and darts, all undertaken for money, of course, with Guy Hamilton happy to perpetuate a sense of rivalry between the Limeys and the Yanks.

The fog which had disrupted shooting for days turned out to be merely the prelude to even darker calamities ahead. Soon the location was under attack from severe gale storms and heavy snow. As the weather grew steadily worse, the crew were forced to abandon Yugoslavia and continue filming in Jersey. The storm followed them, sweeping across Europe and the English Channel. It was soon blowing down trees on the island and halting further progress on *Force Ten from Navarone*. While in Jersey, the actors all kept pretty much to themselves. Robert Shaw, the life and soul of the party in Yugoslavia, made himself invisible, and holed up in a house way up in the hills with his wife and eight of his ten children (tragically, Shaw would die before the film's release). As for Ford, looking offscreen, as the *Observer* put it 'like a bespectacled, very tweed-and-corduroy American assistant professor,' he booked himself into a picturesque manor house hotel along with co-star Edward Fox. At the time, Fox was busily preparing for his role in television's *Edward and Mrs Simpson*, and the two men spent one quiet Sunday lunchtime discussing the project and idly speculating on the true nature of Mrs Simpson.

Like most Alistair MacLean thrillers *Force Ten* displays all the cliché'd arrogance of the 'Boy's Own' paper, with enough red herrings to fill Billingsgate market, a plentiful stock of stereotypes and an unhealthy disregard for life and limb. Its old-fashioned 'war-is-fun' attitude caused consternation among some critics, while others revelled in the absurdity of its stiff-upper-lip heroics. 'Hugely enjoyable and outrageously impossible' – *London Evening News*; 'It is appalling' – *Financial Times*. 'The bridge blowing climax would shame Thunderbirds'; 'The action adventure movie of the year' – *Hollywood Reporter*. Brought out in the same year as *The Deer Hunter*, *Force Ten* was refreshingly empty of any sanctimonious speeches about the horrors of conflict. One could expect no sincere statements about the futility of war here: this is a schoolboy romp which, if caught in the right mood, is unashamedly enjoyable nonsense.

Sitting alone in his dressing room at Shepperton Studios, London, adorned in the khaki-green uniform of an American Ranger and sporting a short-back-and-sides haircut Ford tried vainly to legitimize his involvement in *Force Ten*. Such earnest sentiment as, 'Barnsby's a man of real capacity. He flies, he fights, he's got brains,' impressed no one. 'An interesting character. I think it'll work.' ... Later, in an interview for *Films and Filming* in September 1981, Ford conceded that the role had been rubbish. 'I was lost, because I didn't know what the story was about. I didn't have anything to act. There was no reason for my character being there. I had no part of the story that was important to tell. I had a hard time taking stage with the bullshit that I was supposed to be doing.' His reasons for accepting in the first place were valid enough, if a little mercenary. Hollywood only really takes notice when actors are commanding vast fortunes and receiving top billing *Force Ten* was important in that the cast was a package of big star names which included Ford. 'That was a job I did for money.' Ford sees nothing dishonourable in making movies purely for financial benefit, but it isn't his style – the potential for embarrassment and humiliation is too great. 'I won't ever do that again. It wasn't a bad film; there were honest people involved making an honest effort. But it wasn't the right thing for me to do.'

Hanging up his army regalia, Ford was eager to get back home to carry out building alterations and some much needed repair work on a collapsing marriage. At the same time, Kris Kristofferson walked out on the British production *Hanover Street*, leaving it without a leading man at the last minute. Geneviève Bujold, his co-star, soon followed suit. Obligingly Ford agreed to take over, a decision which kept him away from home again at a crucial period. Since *Star Wars* Ford's punishing work schedule meant that most of the time he was filming, sometimes on the other side of the world from Mary and the children. The pressure on their relationship was intense. Fortunately he'd been able to take them all with him to Yugoslavia, where for a few months at least they were together as a family. Ford expressed publicly the hope that in the near future his family would always be able to accompany him on location, even though by now he had resigned himself to the fact that his marriage was probably over.

In *Hanover Street* Ford once again found himself playing an American serviceman stationed in war-torn England – this time as Lieutenant David Halloran, a B-52 pilot who falls in love with a married woman (Lesley-Anne Down). Also, to his dismay, he faced another long stretch of work in wet and windy Elstree. 'I'm getting kinda used to the weather,' he told a journalist, resignedly. In the space of only a few years Ford had made three out of five films in London and still to come was the *Star Wars* sequel, slated for a March '79 kick-off. London was fast becoming his second home. Curiously, Ford had always been director Peter Hyams's first choice to play Halloran, but the backers had refused to put up the money on account of not knowing who Harrison Ford was. *Star Wars* changed all that. Currently on a roll after the impressive *Capricorn One*, Hyams had been impressed by Ford's performance as Han Solo – 'he jumped off the screen for me'. In his opinion the actor possessed 'a fierce, burning sexual energy', which would lend the love affair story some much needed credibility.

Ford's prime motivation for doing *Hanover Street*, stupid as it may sound, was that he had yet to kiss a girl on screen, 'and I thought I'd better do that pretty soon or they'd cut me out of that category altogether'. Previously his characters had all been macho types – 'totally sexless' – and it was about time he played a more down-to-earth romantic role if he was going to succeed as an 'all-purpose movie actor'.

These factors, above the prospect of securing top billing for the first time, were enough to lure him into a project in which from the outset he had little faith. Hyams's ragbag of a script unnerved him greatly and early hopes that it would be altered as filming progressed were dashed. As a consequence, the making of *Hanover Street* is one of Ford's least favourite topics of conversation. Afterwards he didn't want anything to do with the wretched mess.

Critics happily agreed with Ford's sentiments, ruthlessly mauling the movie upon release. 'This cretinous film should be firmly boycotted by the entire nation' – *New Statesman*; 'It plumbs new depths of banality' – *Sunday Express*; 'If your taste inclines towards a weepie of no socially redeeming merit whatsoever, take a six-pack of tissues over to Hanover Street, where Peter Hyams has left a parcel of grandiose absurdity' – *Sunday Telegraph*; 'This is the most unbelievable claptrap, featuring stupendously abysmal and embarrassing dialogue. Somebody called Harrison Ford delivers his lines like it was all a terrible mistake' – *Daily Mirror*.

In an earlier age Harrison Ford might well have carved out a career for himself playing western heroes, as his old namesake had done in the silent days. Gerald Nachman of the *San Francisco Chronicle* wrote in March 1988, 'The last principled movie cowboy was Steve McQueen, who had a cool gimlet-eyed look, but even he grew too citified, too complex. There are no more guys with that jut-jawed Cooper-Wayne-McQueen don't-mess-with-me squint except Harrison Ford, who has a two-fisted swagger and an air of menace tempered with justice, the William S. Hart look.' Instead Ford established his reputation playing heroes who were distillations of the classical western adventurer – the stranger, the drifter, the outcast. Both Han Solo and Indiana Jones were based, in part, on the mythical lonesome cowboy. Indeed many viewed *Star Wars* as a western set in space. Sadly the western's epitaph had long since been written by the time of Ford's rise to prominence and to date has enjoyed only sporadic resurrections (*Young Guns* and *The Unforgiven*). The soaring heights of the forties and fifties have never since been reached, however – which possibly explains why *The Frisco Kid*, a comedy-western reminiscent of both Mel Brooks and Preston Sturges, is Harrison Ford's least-known major work.

While terrible uneven, *The Frisco Kid* is nevertheless worth a curious peek, if only to watch Ford playing a genuine cowboy hero, a real gun-toting, quick-on-the-draw outlaw. It is an offbeat story of a Polish rabbi, amusingly played by Gene Wilder, crossing America during the 1850s gold rush and developing a friendship with a young bank robber,

Tommy Lillard (Ford). Having recently returned from Europe after the sad debacle of *Hanover Street*, Ford abandoned plans for a six-month sabbatical to star in *The Frisco Kid*. 'It's such a wonderful script,' he said, and he was looking forward to the chance of working with veteran director Robert Aldrich. Made during the breezy, bitter winter of 1978, Ford basked in the tranquillity of filming back home among the familiar wilderness plains of Colorado and Arizona – quite a change from the draughty, outdated confines of a London studio. And he knew *The Frisco Kid* represented the best chance yet of success in the wake of *Star Wars*. He was wrong. 'A rambling, overlong, sentimental, sometimes endearing comedy. Undoubtedly the silliest film ever made by its esteemed director' – *Financial Times*; 'It is a fairly profound disaster area' – *Guardian*. Reviews such as these condemned *The Frisco Kid* to an early grave.

Classically Ford was to pay the price for his fame in the most severe terms. The failure of his first marriage plagued him for years. As a man who believes so devotedly in the concept of wedlock the guilt must have been enormous, sometimes too much to bear. Although Mary secured custody of the children both parties remained as amicable as possible under the circumstances, with Ford granted unrestricted and regular access to his sons. 'I'm proud of them. And I enjoy their company. We spend as much time as we can together.' In public Harrison never spoke ill of his first wife nor failed to acknowledge her generous support during the lean years. She played an instrumental part in urging her husband to do *Star Wars*, ironically unaware that his resulting fame would tear them apart. 'I owe everything to Mary,' Ford told *Cine-Review*. 'Without her, I wouldn't be in the cinema today, because I wouldn't have accepted the role of Han Solo. When Lucas made me the offer I hadn't been in front of a movie camera for three years. Mary wasn't only beautiful and kind, she gave me the confidence to accept. She pushed me back into the cinema.'

Ford was also gracious enough to lay a large portion of the blame for his marriage break-up upon himself. He was correct to do so, for the struggling actor was not always easy to live with. The stresses of his occupation often manifested themselves in deep mood swings. When the dark side of his personality took over Ford could get aggressively foul-tempered and grumpy. 'I was definitely not Mr sweetness and light,' he informed *Parade* magazine in December 1988. 'And, frankly, I was an inadequate husband and father in my first marriage.' This is a remarkable confession, especially from the lips of a man renowned for keeping his mouth firmly shut on such intimate matters.

Ford and Melissa Mathison had by this time become more than just lovers, and this was a relationship which Ford would find, so soon after splitting up with Mary, literally revivifying. Soon the couple were scouting the greater Los Angeles area for a suitable first home, bypassing the palm-lined avenues of Beverly Hills and Bel Air. They finally settled on an Alpine chalet-style affair up in the hills of Benedict Canyon, just five miles away from Mary and the kids. Erected in 1941, the house was chosen because of its secluded position at the end of one of many identical cul-de-sacs as well as for its less than ostentatious air. The two-bedroom house was simple and modest, far removed from the decadent movie star mansions that surrounded it, and far away from the tourist coach routes. As unobtrusive as the owner, it was fashioned out of dark cedar and blood-coloured brick and dominated by two huge chimneys that pointed like blunt fingers towards the heavens. There was no swimming pool or tennis court, only a garden patio so small that Ben and Willard were forced to play basketball out in the street when they came to visit their father.

The task of remodelling the house, an estimated two-month job, fell on the shoulders of local craftsmen, as Ford had a previous engagement with George Lucas. Returning after four months working on *The Empire Strikes Back* the house still wasn't finished. All the hardwood floors had just had their first coat of varnish the day before and the surfaces were soaking wet when he walked through the door. So the couple lived in the basement while Ford toiled on the house to get it ready. A month went by before he and Melissa could move back in. Neither complained. 'That was a good re-entry into reality', Ford said. 'I didn't mind at all', No longer a living, carpentry became a form of private therapy after the strains of film-making. He still enjoyed the craft immensely and jokingly planned that if ever his career should fall apart, he would open a furniture factory.

The kids visited Benedict Canyon most weekends. 'We're best friends. I like to think I'm a fun dad.' Ford told *Photoplay* in May 1982. 'My boys come first for me. I try and include them in every part of my life.' As a family they particularly enjoyed sitting around the television watching videos. 'We saw Star Wars repeatedly, until even I could speak the other characters' lines.' Melissa certainly benefited from Ben and Willard's weekly trips. She crafted the dialogue for the child characters in *ET* by listening to them chatter and argue. She even pointed to the mother in *ET* as being the fictional extension of her relationship with Ford at the time. 'She's sort of the ideal mother, which is what being a girlfriend is like,' Mathison told the *Mail on Sunday* in November 1982. 'I get all the pleasure of Harrison's kids without having to discipline them or lay down the law.' Both Ben and Willard were delighted when they saw *ET* for the first time. Ford, by contrast, wasn't very impressed. 'That creature,' he said in conversation with *Time Out* in September 1982. 'Two weekends ago I called him an ugly little fuck. And Steven went apeshit.' This in spite of a cameo appearance in the film as Elliott's headmaster, which Spielberg ended up chopping out of the finished print. This marked the first time Ford had ended up on the cutting-room floor since his fledgling days at Columbia.

The movies Ford made in the wake of *Star Wars*, in an effort to consolidate his position, are mostly forgotten now. All were major flops, which tarnished his newfound leading-man lustre. However, he did take the opportunity to deepen the ironic-romantic, self-effacing streak that informs all of his best portrayals. Only his return to a character from whom he'd tried so desperately to escape – Han Solo – brought him back into the focus of an adoring mass audience. *The Empire Strikes Back* was to resurrect Harrison Ford's career, and set off an avalanche of fantasy blockbusters which would make him the most popular actor in the Western world. But there were valuable lessons to be learned from those first ill-judged solo outings. Perhaps the most significant was an understanding of the totalitarian role of the director. Film is a director's medium and all actors are servants to him. From 1980 onwards Ford endeavoured to work only with the very best, people like Steven Spielberg and Roman Polanski. 'It also took me a while to learn to relax enough to enjoy it,' he told *Movies USA* in May 1989. 'Realizing that you couldn't get it absolutely right every time was a big thing for me – the willingness to go on and not worry about the one that got away.' Ford refuses to dwell on the past; he knows from bitter experience that unlike some actors (notably Michael Caine), he cannot be good in a bad picture. 'Failures are inevitable. Unfortunately, in film, they live forever and they're forty feet wide and twenty feet high.' I guess that's the price you pay.

6

Ford Strikes Back

The temperature is thirty degrees below zero, a forty-knot gale is whipping up a blizzard. Snow covers a group of outlying mountains, which jut out of the landscape like sleeping gods in a blanket of magnificent white. This is Finse in Norway, a village 5,000 feet above sea level on the rail link between Oslo and the port of Bergen. Boasting a population of less than a hundred, the place is so inaccessible that during the winter months it can only be reached by helicopter, train or foolhardy climb. A remote wilderness, both hauntingly beautiful and alien, it could be an uncharted continent on some far-distant planet. Hoth, perhaps, an ice world that lies somewhere in the universe of George Lucas, and to which Han and his rebel confederates have fled from a revenge-seeking empire. High above the village, desolate and precipitous, stands a glacier sheathed in a veil of blue ice. On this foreboding icescape take place the opening sequences of *The Empire Strikes Back*, Darth Vader's merciless attack on the rebel's stronghold.

The expected bright Norwegian spring weather failed to emerge when on 5 March 1979 the *Star Wars* bandwagon hit town for a scheduled two-week stop. Base camp was the Finse ski lodge – once used as the training site for Robert (Falcon) Scott's ill-fated Antarctic expedition – but the extreme conditions, the worst in living memory, severely hampered production. For two days the first unit were cut off by avalanches. Gary Kurtz, director Irvin Kershner and Mark Hamill were all stranded in the snowy terrain until railroad rescue parties could dig them out. Arctic blizzards reigned for the remainder of the first week, confining everyone to barracks. Though a few daring sorties were made, little by way of action was captured on camera. Already the film was beginning to drift behind schedule.

Han Solo makes his first appearance in *Empire* astride a stop-action animated beast called a tauntaun. Later, in an act of unselfish bravery, he rescues Luke, stranded in the cold, from certain death. Originally slated for filming on the Elstree lot, it was decided instead to shoot these scenes on location, and a notice requesting the immediate presence of Harrison Ford in Finse was summarily dispatched. Ford responded promptly and jumped on the first available flight out of London. The trip over turned out to be an ordeal of nightmarish proportions, which almost resulted in him missing his first camera call. Landing in Oslo Ford boarded a train which took him as far as the ski resort of Geilo, thirty miles east of Finse. Instead of there being a car or helicopter on standby to take Ford directly to the location site, the actor was told to proceed single-handedly as best he could. By now the Scandinavian winter had closed in around him, evening had fallen, as had the temperature to well below zero. Two unpleasant taxi rides later and Ford arrived in Ultaoset, twenty-three miles short of his final destination, where he hitched a lift on a snow plough for the remainder of the journey. He finally arrived at midnight, cold and exhausted.

A little shaken by the experience, Ford was nevertheless up and about early the following morning ready to start work. This professionalism endeared him to the frostbitten crew and moved the unit publicist Alan Arnold to write: 'He looked a bit dazed and bleary eyed. He had gotten very little sleep, but he could not have been more courteous. His manner reminded me of something I had not encountered since dealing with actors from the past, romantic stars like Cary Grant. I have seldom seen it in the younger generation of actors who tend to be self-conscious. Yet here was Harrison – urbane, self-assured and charming after having been up half the night. What a pleasant change.' Had Arnold known of Ford's private sentiments he might have been less charitable in his praise. Ford may have been physically freezing cold, but his temper was rising to boiling point. 'I kept asking myself how I got into this whole mess.' Ever the professional, Ford persevered; he had little choice, because all the trains were buried in snow.

In the beginning Ford declined to sign anything that would contractually oblige him to return a second time as Han Solo. Years of bitter experience with Columbia had taught him to be forever wary of studio contracts. 'I wasn't going to make that mistake again.' When *Star Wars* was released to overwhelming public acceptance it was inevitable that a sequel would follow. An announcement was made by George Lucas to the effect that the second instalment of the middle trilogy in his nine-part space saga was entering pre-production and that all the principals, save Ford, had already signed. The very idea of Han Solo being absent from the *Millennium Falcon*'s cockpit was enough to send alarm bells ringing in *Star Wars* fan circles. As it transpired Ford was only too glad to return. The actor's fiercely independent stance, refusing to enter into early discussions with Lucas, led to rumours that his head had inflated in size and he was difficult to work with. In fact he had merely felt it premature to be discussing sequels before *Star Wars* had been released. When Ford finally sat down to negotiate with Lucas, he swiftly decided to reprise the role of Solo. In fact he was raring to give it another go – having already played the man once Ford saw a chance to improve on his original performance. The real icing on the cake was the dominant part Han Solo was to play in the new film. Gone was the youthful gung-ho spirit of *Star Wars*, which was replaced by a more sardonic adult tone. 'It's part of the natural progression really,' Ford told *Starlog* in August 1980. 'You'd expect development of the characters in a second act. I was expecting it and wasn't surprised when I saw a different version of Han Solo in the script. We get to know him better.'

The man responsible for much of the maturing of Han Solo was Lawrence Kasdan, who also put the first fumbling sentences into the mouth of Indiana Jones. A stocky, advertising copywriter, with only two screenplays to his credit, Kasdan was plucked from relative obscurity by Steven Spielberg to write *Raiders of the Lost Ark*. It took him six months to produce the shooting script for Indy's inaugural adventure, which he presented to his employer George Lucas one Saturday afternoon. Lucas gratefully received the bulky package but seemed in no great hurry to read it. Instead he took the young writer out to a restaurant. Over lunch, Lucas informed him of the tragic and sudden death of Leigh Brackett. The prolific author, a collaborator on Howard Hawks's *The Big Sleep*, had been hired to write *The Empire Strikes Back*. Already in her sixties and riddled with cancer, she gamely tackled Lucas's mammoth enterprise after a single meeting in which he outlined the basic story. By March 1978 Brackett had completed a rough first draft. When Lucas called her up two weeks later to discuss it he discovered she had died in hospital. Already nearing pre-production time, Lucas attended to the urgent rewrites himself. Now he was asking Kasdan to continue his work. A big *Star Wars* fan, Kasdan was naturally thrilled, but thought Lucas really ought to read his script for *Raiders* first. 'Well, I just get a feeling about people,' Lucas replied. 'Of course, if I hate *Raiders*, I'll take back this offer.' He didn't and twenty-four hours later Kasdan got the job.

While Ford and Hamill frolicked in the snow in Norway, sets were under construction in London. *The Empire Strikes Back* was to be on a far grander scale than its illustrious predecessor, with a longer, more punishing shooting schedule and twice as many sets, sixty-four in total. To accommodate the film at Elstree Studios an additional facility had to be built. On completion, the *Star Wars* stage, as it came to be known, was one of the largest in the world, big enough to host an FA cup final. On 12 March Kershner assembled his crew in London and work on the interiors began. For four months filming occupied every available foot of stage space at Elstree. After an initial visit, Lucas kept in contact with Kershner and Kurtz by telephone from the States, virtually supervising the entire production from his studio office in San Rafael. Nothing got by without his approval. Save for the odd foray across the Atlantic, Lucas stayed firmly rooted in the bay area, home of the new ILM workshop, where he was personally supervising the stunning new special effects.

The first scenes shot at Elstree all involved Harrison Ford and took place in the hold of the *Millennium Falcon*. Within the rusty innards of this steel beast, the pervading atmosphere was of some curious homecoming. The warm familiarity of Han Solo acted as both a comfort and a protection for a man whose own fragile reality was crashing around his ears. *Empire* arrived at a particularly trying period for Ford. On a personal level his life was a mess; he was divorcing his wife and on the verge of reinventing himself, reshaping his life. In an effort to escape the inner turmoil, he flung himself into the film, working as hard as he dared. In the process, he succeeded in striking up a good rapport with Irvin Kershner. The 57-year-old director had a conspicuously uncommercial record behind him and no experience of complex special effects. He was therefore a surprise choice to helm the sequel of cinema's biggest-ever blockbuster. In his favour was an unbroken reputation as a brisk, precise worker, a knowledge of film technique lacking in the current crop of young hotshots and a healthy suspicion of Hollywood, something he shared with Lucas.

Aware that *Empire* would have to develop the main characters established only superficially in *Star Wars*, Lucas also appreciated Kershner's ability to capture on film human dramas and relationships. Working with actors was Kershner's forte, more so than that of Lucas, whose interests lay more in the technical aspects of film-making. Kershner was the complete opposite: for him actors came first and, as a result, he wrought greater performances out of his cast. Notably Ford, who gives his best portrayal of Han Solo. 'Harrison I adored,' Kershner said after filming. 'He was so creative and so much fun.' Delighted with the freedom to contribute his own ideas, Ford's natural flair for improvisation and phrase-making came into its own. According to Mark Hamill, Ford plays his changes as if they were in the script and often without anyone noticing the difference. Ford improvised a line during the *Millennium Falcon*'s escape from the Death Star in *Star Wars*. Luke's gleeful whoop upon shooting down a pursuing Tie fighter is wonderfully put down by Solo's quick-witted jibe: 'Great kid! Don't get cocky.' In another scene Solo and Luke break into the cell block to release the princess, and a bemused Han speaks uneasily into a communicator before blasting it to smithereens. To appear convincingly flustered and desperate Ford deliberately never learnt his lines and was eager to improvise the whole thing in one take. 'Stop me if I'm really bad,' he told Lucas. The scene played perfectly as an expression of frustration pushed to the extreme and is indicative of the minor felicities which

Ford managed to milk from a role that could have been swamped by the special effects. 'Harrison's ideas are usually superb,' Hamill told *Prevue* in October 1983. 'He has more freedom to bring bits to Solo; there's no question that he's added much to his role. When the story gets a little too arch, too corny or old-fashioned, Harrison will express exasperation or scepticism. He represents a portion of the audience that's too sophisticated to see the story from a young person's viewpoint'.

In *Empire* Ford's creative input was on overdrive. His most valuable and certainly most contentious idea occurred in one of the film's most emotionally charged moments. It was Ford's major scene. Solo is about to be frozen in carbon, and veiled hints have been dropped throughout the movie concerning Leia's true feelings for the space buccaneer. At last she says those magic words: 'I love you.' In the original script Ford was to have lamely replied, 'I love you, too.' Yuk, he thought; where was the power and drama in that? A stronger exit line was required. Ford approached Kershner. 'I think she ought to say, "I love you", and I'll say, "I know".' The director thought the idea was inspired; it was exactly the kind of crowd-pleasing arrogance Solo would come out with, his way of saying all is not lost. But Lucas didn't like it, nor did Kasdan, who complained bitterly – nor for that matter Carrie Fisher, who normally found Ford's suggestions useful and well-considered. But not this time and the pair had a blazing row off-set. When Lucas viewed the sequence it gave him pause, because he didn't feel a laugh line was appropriate at so serious a juncture. Ford convinced him otherwise – that it served to relieve the tension of a grim situation, and the exchange remained to become one of the most hotly discussed features of the entire film.

From Lucas's point of view the making of *Empire* was a disaster from start to finish. Kershner's sensitive handling of the actors may have paid dividends on the screen, but it did little for the blood pressure of his employer. Lucas was becoming more and more exasperated with Kershner over the delays he was incurring, and he felt far from satisfied with the footage he was seeing. 'I felt it wasn't working at all,' the harassed tycoon commented at the time. 'I was running out of money and I had a movie I thought was no good.' His patience and temper were at near breaking-point. *Empire* was turning into a terrifyingly expensive white elephant. Provisionally set at $15 million, the budget was to balloon to more than $33 million. Kerschner was ordered to speed things up, scenes were cut and the actors forced to rehearse on their one rest day a week. Even so, *Empire* still went six weeks over schedule and was further marred by the unexpected loss of John Barry, the Academy-Award-winning production designer of *Star Wars*, who fell ill and died a fortnight after starting work.

The Empire Strikes Back was the cinematic event of 1980. This time fans were not queuing up two hours in advance of the morning show; the lines of sleeping bags began to mass on the pavement outside the Egyptian Theatre in Hollywood three days before the grand 21 May unveiling. No one was particularly surprised when *Empire* broke theatre records everywhere or that Lucas was in the black within three months, or that *Empire* proved to be the second most popular film ever. 'Every bit as visually astounding, fast moving, noisy, swashbuckling and unbelievable as its parent' – *Sunday Telegraph*. 'This epic is a Wagnerian pop movie – grandiose, thrilling, imperially generous in scale and a bit ponderous' – *New York*. In general the critics were enthusiastic, although there were those cynical few who found it difficult to see the film as anything more than an extended commercial specifically designed to sell more model kits and comic books. 'The quality is already beginning to diminish. The film fails to involve and seldom charms' – *The Times*. 'Hamill, Fisher and Ford flounder in roles that are certain to doom their careers regardless of the series' success' – *Cinefantastique*.

Comparisons with *Star Wars* were inevitable – and unfair. Act II of Lucas's middle trilogy, *Empire* contained the heaviest material, the most crucial events and the most harrowing cliffhangers. The central story of any trilogy or drama is always the most formidable to realize. Kershner had no grand finale to lead up to; he had to make the best out of a decidedly unexciting denouement. And though it was emotionally powerful, it lacked the slam-bang action thrills that distinguished the rebel attack on the Death Star in the first instalment. One of the criticisms lodged against *Empire* was that the construction of the film was unbalanced, with the most spectacular stuff occurring in the opening reel and the rest of the tale being a dark and sombre mish-mash of seemingly disconnected scenes. Complaints that nothing of any real substance actually happened – no deaths, no victory and no defeat, only temporary crisis – were justified. *Empire* does end unresolved, leaving the audience dangling on a contrivance of the plot. But then that is the devilish purpose of a second act: to whet the appetite for the eventual raising of the curtain on the third and final act.

In its defence *Empire* is a vastly richer piece of work than *Star Wars*. The complex story, with its fertile embellishment of the central characters, lends the enterprise a greater depth than its simple-minded predecessor. *Empire* is really about the coming of age of Luke Skywalker. His cosmic education at the hands of Yoda, the grand custodian of Jedi science, is, however, one of the film's imaginative shortcomings. Yoda is certainly not the awe-inspiring wizard figure we had imagined, but, rather, a cuddly soft toy afflicted with the voice of Fozzie bear. The naïve romantic sparring between Han and Leia is *Empire*'s real human highlight, though as in *Star Wars*, the eye-popping special effects tend to dwarf the actors. One man who disagreed was

Lawrence Kasdan. 'Han and Leia's relationship is not at all what I envisioned. I thought that their romance had a touch of falseness about it'. Kasdan was aggrieved that his dialogue for those all-important love scenes was radically altered by the actors during filming. 'I'm thrilled with Harrison Ford in Raiders, he's shockingly good as Indiana Jones, because I was one of the people who wasn't crazy about him in Empire'.

The toughest and most traumatic of the *Star Wars* trilogy to capture on celluloid, *The Empire Strikes Back* is also Harrison Ford's favourite. 'It's the first time I've ever seen anything I've done that I'm happy with. I don't think I ever walked away from a scene thinking that I hadn't given it my best shot'. Surprisingly, Ford never bothered to read the script pages for the scenes in which he did not appear. 'I asked Irvin if I had to read this section or that. He said there was no need to. So, when I finally saw the finished movie, I learned for the first time all the things that happened to Luke. It was great.' The secrecy surrounding the making of this sequel was even more strict than that which hid *Star Wars* from view until première night. Most of the key plot developments were kept confidential. To keep everyone guessing, including the cast and crew, false lines of dialogue were sprinkled throughout the script. The same practice was exercised on *Return of the Jedi*. The pervading air of mystery led to feverish rumour-mongering among fans. The gossip chiefly revolved around the fate of Han Solo. Many believed the romantic triangle of Luke, Leia and Solo would ripen in the new movie and that Solo would be killed in combat to leave the field clear for Luke, or that both would die and the saga would continue with the princess as the new lead. Other assorted rumours included: Solo being captured by the empire and crossing light sabres with Darth Vader, the *Millennium Falcon* falling into a black hole and going back in time; and Han and Chewbacca encountering time travellers from thirteenth-century earth defending themselves with flimsy bows and arrows against hordes of Imperial stormtroopers. Even the press got in on the act. One Hollywood trade paper reported that Mick Jagger was going to provide the soundtrack and that Spielberg would direct the third follow-up.

The most fascinating and prophetic rumour concerned a scene in which Luke persuades Darth Vader to turn his back on the *Empire* and join the rebels. But the revelation that Vader is Luke's father took everyone by surprise. This shattering admission was so top-secret it wasn't even in the script. No one in the entire cast, except Hamill, was told. When the sequence was shot, David Prowse, the bodybuilder who played Vader, was speaking entirely different dialogue; the confession was dubbed in later during post-production by James Earl Jones. At the London première Prowse was sitting directly behind Kershner. When the scene revealed itself the strongman leaned over and thumped the director on the back. 'Why didn't you tell me!' he implored.

7

A Tale of Flying Wings,
Nazis and Snakes

Raiders of the Lost Ark is the result of one of the most significant film-making collaborations in motion-picture history. Directed by Steven Spielberg, conceived and produced by George Lucas, *Raiders* marked the first time during their eleven-year friendship that these two important film-makers had worked together. Their decision to join forces was reached in late May 1977, while both were vacationing in Hawaii. Lucas had flown there to avoid the opening of *Star Wars*, which he fervently believed would be a monumental disaster, while Spielberg was on the island relaxing from the headaches caused by *Close Encounters of the Third Kind*. For the first few days Lucas was a bag of nerves, taut and uncomfortable, until one evening over dinner he received a phone call which changed the complexion of the entire holiday. It was from Ashley Boone, Twentieth Century Fox's marketing chief – *Star Wars* was breaking box-office records in its first week. Lucas was reborn, the child-man again, laughing and instigating new plans, new ideas. The following morning, as the men built sandcastles on the golden beach in front of their hotel and watched them resist the surf for thirty suspenseful minutes, both fondly fell into their accustomed fantasy routine of which films they wanted to make next.

Spielberg's wish had always been to direct a James Bond epic with Sean Connery. *Dr No* and those other classic sixties 007 thrillers made such a lasting impression on the teenager that when United Artists (the distributors of the Bond series) offered him a choice of projects after *Sugarland Express* it seemed a propitious moment to declare his candidacy for the Bond director's chair. But the Bond hierarchy chose to rebuff his advances. It seemed their blind allegiance to the motto 'Bond is British' apparently applied to those behind the camera too. (If United Artists had agreed, Spielberg would most likely have ended up directing *The Man with the Golden Gun*. Instead he went on to make

Jaws.) But the desire to direct a Bond-type action yarn remained. 'I've got something better than Bond,' Lucas told his colleague and began spinning a tale about an archaeologist whose search for ancient artefacts leads him into many perilous adventures.

The concept of a film trilogy featuring the daredevil Indiana Jones began as a daydream way before Lucas had even created *Star Wars*. Indeed it had been a toss-up as to which hero he would commit to celluloid immortality first: Luke Skywalker or Indiana Jones. The inspiration behind *Raiders of the Lost Ark* was very personal indeed. Like *Star Wars*, Lucas was once again harking back to pleasures past – this time paying grateful homage to the rip-roaring Republic serials and backlot cheapies of the thirties and forties, most notably *Don Winslow of the Navy*, a cliffhanger about a two-fisted serviceman who politely ridded the world of Nazis. This was a whole genre that had lain dormant in American funhouses for decades. Lucas's champion was to be a throwback to all the square-jawed heroes of Hollywood's B-picture heyday. Moreover in the grand tradition of Clark Kent he was to be two separate people: a mild-mannered college professor one minute, and explorer extraordinaire, dashing off to foreign climes, the next.

Enlisting the aid of Philip Kaufman, the film's basic premise soon took shape. Set in 1936, Indiana Jones is recruited by the US government to foil a dastardly German plot to uncover the Ark of the Covenant, within which are stowed the broken tablets of the Ten Commandments. Beyond its obvious value as the ultimate object of religious veneration, the ark supposedly bestows mystical destructive powers on its worldly possessor. (Hitler himself was an occultist and an avid student of religious doctrine and artefacts.) An army who marched with the Ark before it would be truly invincible.

Spielberg was entranced. Sure enough, all the 'Bondian' elements were present, despite the lack of hardware and gimmickry. Indeed, *Raiders* was little more than a James Bond movie set in the 1930s, but exhibited more wit and panache than any of the spy's recent adventures, including *For Your Eyes Only*, which Indy took to the cleaners at the box office of summer 1981. *Raiders* also had a sense of narrative pace and sheer exuberance that had been sadly missing from the 007 series since the sixties and showed up just how lifeless and mechanical the Bond movies had become. Like Lucas, Spielberg had grown up on a staple diet of the same old serials, and the chance of 'reinventing' them for a new generation of cinemagoers was tempting beyond expression. Alas, Kaufman was slated to direct. Spielberg would just have to sit tight and wait (and pray). Six months after their holiday in Hawaii, Lucas rang Spielberg. 'You still interested in the movie I told you about in Hawaii? Well Phil's not doing it. I'm not doing it. I've retired! I'm not directing anymore. So, it's yours if you want it' Spielberg accepted on the spot and although both had films to complete first (*Empire* and *1941* respectively), tentative plans to begin production in 1980 were drawn up.

Everyone's unlikely first choice to play Indiana Jones was a then unknown TV actor called Tom Selleck. Recently returned from Hawaii, where he'd made his debut as Magnum in the pilot episode of a proposed series, Selleck was offered the *Raiders* job out of the blue. Despite a lack of film experience his audition had impressed all at Lucasfilm. However, and in defiance of Lucas's appeals. CBS refused to release Selleck from the Magnum contract. Nor were they prepared to hold off production until the following season in order that he could make the Spielberg movie. The decision proved ironic, for the moment cameras rolled on *Magnum* a Hollywood actors' strike halted filming, while *Raiders*, based in London, was free to continue. Selleck was left twiddling his thumbs in the Pacific, reflecting on the painful fact that in the end he could have handled both assignments. Resigned now to his bad fortune, and a star in his own right, Selleck begrudges Ford nothing. 'It's hard to imagine anyone being better than Harrison. He was quite wonderful.'

The sudden unavailability of Selleck left the makers with just a few weeks to find a new leading male before shooting commenced. Numerous actors passed before Lucas's video cameras before Harrison Ford became Selleck's plainly obvious substitute. It was during an afternoon screening of *The Empire Strikes Back* that Spielberg realized Ford was the perfect man for the job and immediately called Lucas. 'He's been right under our noses.' After a deliberate silence Lucas spoke. 'I know who you're going to say.' 'Who?' asked Spielberg. 'Harrison Ford,' replied Lucas. Lucas had his own special reason for choosing Ford: the actor's unique charisma was ideal for the type of characters the producer developed. He would also be especially skilled at portraying Indy's occasional vulnerability, the trait which made him far more attractive to audiences than if he had been some invincible superman. Lucas approached him the very next day.

Although he often confessed that the part of Indiana Jones only became his 'by default', Ford's laconic charisma better suited the character than what would probably have been a more comedy-orientated approach by Selleck. Ford also fitted Spielberg's own vision of what Indy looked like, an odd amalgam of Errol Flynn from *The Adventures of Don Juan* and Humphrey Bogart as Fred C. Dobbs in *The Treasure of the Sierra Madre*. 'Harrison can be villainous and romantic all at once,' Spielberg said. The character's name derived from Lucas's pet dog, Indiana, a malemute who used to sit with his master during writing sessions. Spielberg disapproved of the original name of Indiana Smith on the grounds that it sounded too much like Nevada Smith, a character played by Steve McQueen in a 1966 movie. Lucas then suggested Indiana Jones; and the name stuck.

Neither was Spielberg enamoured of some of the human qualities bestowed upon Indy either. Created to satisfy a nostalgic affection for bygone cliffhangers, *Raiders* partly evolved from a fervent early academic interest Lucas had in archaeology and social science. Indiana is part college professor, part soldier of fortune and it is this nefarious side of his nature which leads him in search of treasure and personal gain, dabbling in the occult, and destroying the past more often than preserving it. He is an overtly dark hero, saturnine and lecherous, an outright looter of native cultural and religious artefacts and valuables. 'Indiana Jones is an archaeologist. In his spare time he's a grave robber,' as Ford aptly put it.

But as originally envisaged by Lucas, Indy was also a 1930s playboy spending nights out on the town and indulging in the high life, a habit financed by the museums who buy his stolen antiquities. At the request of Lucas Kasdan wrote, under duress, an alternative version of the scene where Brody (Denholm Elliot) visits Indy's home. Brody is welcomed indoors by a tuxedo-wearing Indiana, and a beautiful Jean Harlow-type blonde sipping champagne is glimpsed in the living-room. It was this character trait that did not find favour with Spielberg. The director felt that Indiana's two sides (teacher and adventurer) made him complicated enough without adding the playboy element. He also wanted to make Jones a more sleazy, slovenly kind of man, with a grumpy and grizzled view of everything – more Fred C. Dobbs than Clark Gable. For a time he was anxious to make Indy an alcoholic, but Lucas wanted none of that. In the end, they compromised: the playboy image was dropped (although vestiges of this other life were paraded in the opening sequence of *Indiana Jones and the Temple of Doom*), and Indy became the loner that all heroes must be.

While surprised at Lucas's telephone call asking if he'd play Indiana Jones, Ford was not offended by being second choice. Indeed, he never expected to be chosen at all due to being so clearly identified as Han Solo: 'It must have seemed kinda silly to them both to put me into *Raiders*.' Still, Lucas was keen for Ford to meet formally with Spielberg, whom the actor had previously met once only casually. After reading the script Ford took Melissa and his son Willard over to the director's home. The two men hit it off immediately. 'Steven was bubbly and enthusiastic,' Ford told journalist Derek Taylor. 'He seemed he might be fun to work with. So I agreed and took the part.' Ford's interest in *Raiders* was surprising, since accepting meant playing the lead in yet another fantasy blockbuster, something he had deliberately avoided in the wake of *Star Wars*. The fact that in the preceding three months Ford had been unable to find any decent projects might have played a significant part in his decision. Most likely it was the realization that this was the best character he had ever been offered, in a film that promised to be a terrific piece of entertainment.

Ford's only immediate reservation, because both *The Empire Strikes Back* and *Raiders* were written by the same hand, was the similarity between the characters of Solo and Indy. Both were fast-talking, smooth, devil-may-care adventurers, adroit at battling their way out of tricky situations. Spielberg, though, drew clear distinctions between the two men; Indiana was by far the more complex. 'I think that Han Solo in Star Wars is a boyish hero,' he said. 'But in Raiders Ford plays a grown-up.' Still the nagging worries remained. 'So Steven and I talked about it and he offered me the chance to be very involved in making the film,' Ford told *The Times* in July 1981. 'Steven and I sat on the plane from LA and went through the script line by line for ten hours. By the time we got to Heathrow, we'd worked out the whole film.'

Signed for *Raiders*, Ford immediately found himself at a striking disadvantage, being unfamiliar with the classic serial heroes on which Lucas had based Indiana Jones. Sure he had read his fair share of comics as a youngster, but not of the pulp variety (Mickey Mouse and Donald Duck had been his favourites), and all he remembered from adolescent visits to the Saturday morning cinema club were the Hopalong Cassidys and Sky Kings. 'George and Steven may be living out their childhood fantasies on film,' he told *Time* in May 1989. 'But I didn't come from the same crate of oranges.' Instead Ford created Indy in his own image. Part of his acting technique is always to try and invest as much of himself into the character he plays. Indiana Jones was a man roughly Ford's own age, and physically they shared corresponding abilities and capacities. At the same time they were a million miles apart. 'He is braver, stronger, smarter and more willing to suffer than I am,' Ford jokingly explained to *Movieline* in December 1988. 'Other than that, we're the same guy. I have never, in life, been an extremely heroic person.'

The now famous external appearance of Indiana Jones is credited to Lucas. 'He was quite explicit in his vision of Indiana,' Ford said, 'in terms of personality and attitude.' He insisted on the leather jacket and the wide-brimmed felt hat, which made things unpleasant for Ford on location in Tunisia. 'I kept saying: Jesus, is there any reason for this ... suffering!' And, of course, there's that ever-present bullwhip. In order for audiences to believe that Indy was a true expert with the bullwhip, Ford was required to learn how to use the unwieldy weapon as if it were second nature. The problem remained of how he was going to learn, as experts who could teach him were few and far between. Luckily Glen Randall, the stunt coordinator, had used the whip before and offered to coach the actor. Randall visited Ford's home three or four times to give lessons, and then it was up to Ford to practise on his own until he got the technique right. 'I lashed myself about the head and shoulders for at least a couple of weeks before I really figured the thing out.' Such dedication won the admiration not only of Randall, but many of the other stuntmen too, because the ten-foot bullwhip he was using could prove quite lethal in the hands of the uninitiated. Ford stuck to his task and by the start of filming was so proficient with the whip that it was incorporated into several of the fight scenes.

Sharing the limelight with Indy was the delightful Karen Allen, a New York stage actress whose only previous screen credit of any note was as Al Pacino's girlfriend in the objectionable *Cruising*. As Marion Ravenwood, a bitter and spurned plaything of Indy's from years past, she turns in a memorable performance. So too do the entire supporting cast who, as in *Star Wars*, are comprised mostly of British character actors. Paul Freeman was notable as Belloq, Jones's debonair adversary; Ronald Lacey hammed it up gloriously as an odious Gestapo officer; John Rhys-Davies won the role of Sallah, Indiana's Arabian sidekick, over Spielberg's first choice Danny de Vito, who lost out when his agent wanted too much money; and, lastly, the late Denholm Elliott, in splendid form as Brody.

Principal photography on *Raiders of the Lost Ark* began on 23 June 1980 in the historic French coastal resort of La Rochelle, located 100 miles north of Bordeaux. Its primary attraction were the antiquated World War II submarine pens that lay close by – huge gloomy caverns built deep into the rock, with fading Hitlerian graffiti carved on the damp, eerie walls. When cast and crew arrived it was raining and the Atlantic looked choppy and uninviting. Each morning for the next five days everyone was ferried out to a 1930s-era tramp steamer, anchored in open water three miles from the coast, which doubled for the *Bantu Wind*, the pirate ship carrying Indy, Marion and the ark to safety when it is ambushed by a German U-boat. All manner of equipment had to be transferred between vessels across a four-foot gap swelling with waves. In defiance of the conditions filming progressed well and the production moved to London ahead of schedule to Elstree Studios. There, five of the main sound stages had been reserved for two mammoth sets, the Well of Souls and the Peruvian temple. Constructed over three months, under the supervision of Norman Reynolds, fresh from designing *Empire*, they were deemed the most costly interiors built in a decade.

The first major sequence shot at Elstree featured the Peruvian temple. Here Indy encounters an ingenious system of booby traps devised by some ancient architect to protect the golden idol of the Chachapoyon warriors: poison darts fly from the mouths of grotesque stone faces, spears shoot out from nowhere to impale their prey and tarantulas await in the cobweb-strewn darkness. Fifty live specimens were recruited by Spielberg and draped on to the clothes of Ford, much to the actor's discomfort. Tarantulas are fragile creatures, and not as dangerous as myth presumes. But even so ...

Spiders don't bother Indiana Jones. His creators, though, recognizing that audiences relate more readily to heroes with some weakness, decided to bestow upon him that other great common phobia: fear of snakes. Ironically, as a teenager Ford loved snakes and for a time collected them. When he was sixteen he went away to a boy scout camp and became a junior counsellor in the nature department there. He used to run around the camp grounds trying to catch as many different types of snakes as he could, later putting what he found on display. On release, one of the most talked-about scenes in *Raiders* was the descent into the Well of Souls. Indy discovers as he lowers himself into the tomb that the floor is a slithering mass of poisonous snakes. Six thousand of them, ranging from grass snakes and other innocuous breeds, specially reared in the Netherlands, to a smattering of deadlies (cobras, pythons and boa constrictors), were deposited on the set despite the obvious dangers. Elstree was crawling with reptiles and the presence of a number of professional handlers hardly allayed the fears of the crew. Caution was the order of the day; cobras can paralyse a person in thirty seconds and can kill inside three minutes, while boa constrictors can crush a man in three seconds if they feel so inclined. The pythons, although not poisonous, can bite and tend not to let go when they do. Of course, precautions were taken – no cobra scene could be filmed without a qualified doctor standing by to administer serum. Unfortunately the day before work was due to begin the anti-toxin serum, which, like the cobras, came from India, was found to be a year out of date. A second shipment which arrived from Paris had also gone bad. Just as the schedule on the Well of Souls set was looking in jeopardy fresh serum arrived. Although fond of snakes, Ford was always careful around them and wore special protective clothing, high rubber boots, gloves and strengthened bite-proof canvas trousers and jacket. Poor Karen Allen was less lucky, having to play the scene in a white evening gown with nothing on her feet and bare arms. Ironically, on returning home after making *Raiders*, Ford was bitten by a snake in his own garden.

In a film of non-stop action like *Raiders*, the physical demands on the principal actor are enormous. Martin Grace, one of Ford's main stuntmen, handled some of the snake shots that were considered too risky for Harrison to try himself. But for the most part, Ford insisted on carrying out his own stunt work. He believes, and rightly so, that the more death-defying feats he performs on camera the more convincing his character becomes. Audiences have grown so sophisticated over the years that today they can tell when they're being cheated, when the stuntmen take over from the star. And anyway, the physical stuff is Ford's forte and a major part of his acting style and he enjoys getting stuck in, there's a certain foolish pleasure in having bogus near-death experiences, life becomes interesting during a duel to the death on a rocky outcropping in the middle of a storm in *Patriot Games* or hanging precariously from the turret of a moving tank as Indiana Jones. Martin Grace was certainly impressed, calling Ford a very athletic actor and capable, with guidance, of accomplishing a great deal. 'A little instruction and he's there.' Spielberg handed out his own tribute when he told *Starlog* in September 1981. 'Harrison Ford is physical to a fault. It's really him doing some of the most incredible things; Harrison was always in there prepared to do a stunt. Glen Randall was our stunt gaffer and he wouldn't let Harrison do any stunts that were potentially fatal. But Harrison did most everything else. Anything that simply promised serious injury or total disability, Harrison did; anything that promised death through fatal miscalculation the other guys did.'

One stunt that could so easily have proved to be the gruesome exception involved the huge boulder which terrorizes Indy in that crackling opening sequence. The twelve-foot rock would have killed whoever it ran over. Still bravely clinging to his theory that the more action scenes he personally got involved in the easier it would be for the audience to identify with his character, Ford was convinced he could outrun the boulder and wanted to give it a try. Spielberg was not convinced and disagreed with the idea vehemently. It was still only the second week of shooting, absolutely the worst time to have your leading man pulverized beneath an eighty-ton rock (well, 800 pounds of fibreglass, wood and plaster, but still heavy enough to do some damage). Glen Randall, however, felt Ford could manage all right. Besides, a double would seem phoney. 'I looked a little scared in the rock scene, didn't I,' Ford recalls. 'I'd have been crazy not to be. Had I tripped, I could have been in big trouble'. The stunt went ahead and worked wonderfully, but it was close, Ford had to race the rock ten times. 'He won ten times and beat the odds,' Spielberg says. 'He was lucky and I was an idiot for letting him try'.

Ford's luck nearly ran out in Tunisia. All stuntmen, sooner or later, acquire injuries of some sort – it's an occupational hazard. Ford is a very physical actor, but he's no stuntman, and severe demands were imposed on his body throughout the filming of *Raiders*. Because Indy is rarely off screen there was little respite. At one point Ford was required to be dragged behind a five ton truck. 'Just one more useless experience,' he muttered dolefully. In fact he rather enjoyed the ride. 'It actually felt just as I imagined it would, only to do it for money rather than have that happen by accident makes a big difference.'

Ford always ran the risk of getting hurt, which he frequently did. At times he felt more like 'a battered football player' than a film star. He was very fortunate to walk away unscathed from one incident, a fight involving Indy and a Nazi heavy under the whirring propellers of an archaic flying wing. Indy is knocked down into the path of the aeroplane's wheels and does a backward somersault to avoid being crushed. The scene was successfully rehearsed a number of times, but when the moment came to commit it to celluloid Ford's right foot slipped in the sand and shot sideways. He caught his toe under the tyre of the advancing flying wing, which proceeded to crawl up his tibia. 'Luckily the brakes worked – inches before my knee was crushed, but I was pinned to the sand.' Around forty members of the crew proceeded to rock the aeroplane off Ford's leg. 'I was a lot more careful about stunt work after that.' What had saved him? The blistering heat had made the rubber wheels soft and pliable. 'That was our closest call,' Spielberg commented. Ford merely took the whole thing in his stride: he got up and walked away laughing, shrugging it off as another near miss. 'It was real exciting,' he told *Starlog* in July 1981. 'The crew's reaction was the normal one associated with having a film's star run over by an aeroplane when the movie is only half completed.'

It was another aeroplane accident on the last day of filming that almost robbed Ford of his life. The picture's action-packed opening, where Indy is chased by natives, was filmed in Kauai, Hawaii. The idea was for Ford to swing gallantly on a vine, jump into the water, swim towards the aeroplane, wobbling uneasily on pontoons, get in and fly off, all in one master shot. (If you look closely here you can spot a Lucas in-joke. The plane's registration reads: OB 3PO.) To emphasize Indy's panic Ford came up with the idea of leaving the door open and dangling his legs outside. This proved to be a grave miscalculation, as the aerodynamics were affected. When the plane reached an altitude of twenty feet, it disappeared behind an outcrop of trees and crashed. The unit, including Melissa Mathison, were all watching from the dock when they heard the awful smash. There was dead silence. Miraculously, Ford and the pilot escaped unscathed. 'But we had to do it again, of course.'

With interior work in London completed, the unit caught a charter flight from Luton airport to Tunisia, touching down on a primitive sandstrip near the town of Tozeur, the same canyon area used for the Tatooine sequences in *Star Wars*. Once settled into the air-conditioned luxury of the Sahara Palace hotel, work began at Sedala, site of Belloq's Nazi-backed excavation of the lost city of Tanis, which had been dug out of the desert by an army of extras in 130-degree heat. Conditions were horrendous and there was no respite from the scorching sun even under the shade of a parasol or palm tree. The only relief came when the wind picked up slightly around 4 pm, cooling the breeze to a bearable 110 degrees. The logistics of filming in so desolate a patch of desert, sixty kilometres from the nearest permanent settlement, were awesome. Water consumption was prodigious in order to avoid dehydration. Unfortunately, dysentery became rife among people working flat out for twelve hours a day in intense and unaccustomed heat. Spielberg, by cleverly sticking to a regime of British tinned foods, avoided any illness. Ford was less lucky: he succumbed early on and never fully recovered. Somehow he managed to soldier on in the face of gastric pains and diarrhoea – 'Tunisian revenge' as crew members playfully called it. This sorry experience somewhat sullied his impression of the country. 'Dysentery, that'll do it every time! That does spoil a nation for you. To see it from a toilet seat. It was a very tough location.' Add to that the physical and mental demands of the Indiana Jones character – Ford had only five days off during the entire shoot – and he was glad when it was all finally over. 'Hardest job I'll ever have.'

One morning Ford, now entering his fifth week of dysentery, felt particularly rough. 'He was all stooped over,' Spielberg remembers. 'Couldn't stand up straight and kept having to run to the bathroom.' He was, therefore, scarcely looking forward to a bruising encounter with a blood-curdling Arab swordsman. During the hour-and-a-half morning drive to the location he dreamt up the inspired notion of having Indy, with an exasperated look, calmly and nonchalantly shoot the man dead. Who needed another protracted fight scene anyway and three more days in this ghastly hell hole. Storming over to Spielberg with the idea, the director, snapping his fingers, exclaimed, 'I was just thinking the same thing.' It turned out to be the funniest sight gag in the film and chimed well with the kind of lackadaisical resignation which lies behind so much of Ford's heroics. The moment was also indicative of the relationship between Spielberg and his star. For Ford, who always craves a stimulating atmosphere of collaboration, working with Spielberg was a pure joy. The sparkling exchange of ideas, the great sense of fun generated on set and Spielberg's willingness to involve him as much as possible in the creative process made the film one of the most enjoyable of Ford's career. For the first time on a film Ford watched the rushes every day. It was on *Raiders* that both artists developed the brilliant working relationship and mutual professional respect that would carry them through two further tough Indy projects. 'Harrison contributes so much to the writing of the scripts, to just the general feeling of the films,' Spielberg once explained. 'He's one of the most inventive actors I've ever worked with. He deals on a level that is so human, so identifiable. His ideas are all of our ideas. In one pure flash, Harrison will come up with something and it's absolutely right.'

Artistically, *Raiders of the Lost Ark* represented a real coming of age for Spielberg. In recent years the *Wunderkind* had lost his way. So what if *1941* was a dazzling technical triumph, it was juvenile in the extreme; whilst the special edition (with only a few new scenes) of *Close Encounters of the Third Kind* was little more than a rip-off. Still reeling from the box office débâcle of *1941* and accusations of profligacy, Spielberg was determined to prove that he could work just as fast and cheaply as anyone else, make a blockbuster for $20 million and make it look like it cost $40 million. Raiders is a masterpiece of economic moviemaking, an object lesson in how to blend the art of storytelling with the highest levels of technical know-how, planning, cost control and commercial acumen. Taking his cue from Lucas, who wanted the film to move like an express train from the first frame, Spielberg set himself the seemingly impossible task of completing the job in a breakneck seventy-three days. If those classic action films of the thirties and forties, like *Robin Hood* and *The Sea Hawk*, could be shot inside two months, what made *Raiders* so different? Working almost exclusively from pre-drawn storyboards, Spielberg filmed Kasdan's script pretty much as written, and for the first time called on the services of a second unit director. Spielberg at last had learned the subtle art of delegation.

Nothing was wasted and every conceivable corner was cut. Everyone worked at a maddening pace, averaging a record-breaking thirty-five set-ups a day on location and half that number in the studio. Spielberg found that by allowing a bare minimum of just three or four takes on each shot instead of his customary twenty to twenty-five, he was able to get a lot more spontaneity into the film without the self-indulgence and pretentiousness that nearly crippled *Close Encounters*. That *Raiders* with all its production values, spectacle, worldwide locations was in the can within two and half months (barring the obligatory ILM magic), represented something of a personal triumph for Spielberg. And it was just that he and Ford were to reap considerable rewards.

As strange as it may seem today, Spielberg and his cohorts had no idea Indiana would prove such a massive hit. The first time Ford watched *Raiders* with an audience he was bowled over by the enthusiasm of the reaction. But competition for the 1981 box-office sweepstakes was fierce – *Superman 2, Cannonball Run* and Bond no 12 among other heavyweight offerings. *Starlog* in July of that year caught Ford in a silly mood and pressed him to give his reasons why audiences should flock to *Raiders*. 'Besides the full frontal nudity, the sex with a camel, the free place setting we're giving away in theatres, and the opportunity to win the presidential yacht? Folks will see it I guess because it's going to be a hell of a lot of fun. If not, I'd ask for my money back.'

The arrival of *Raiders* was a godsend for an industry hit by acute economic downturns because of an increasingly fragmented and more competitive entertainment market, from cable to video. After a year of big-budget flops, which had seen reputations ruined and studios sold, Hollywood seemed to have returned to the formula on which its name was built – old-fashioned high adventure. Costing half the money Michael Cimino was permitted to squander on his white elephant *Heaven's Gate* (*Raiders* took more dollars on opening day than *Heaven's Gate* managed in its entire run), Spielberg's unashamed revival of the old episodic cliffhangers of Hollywood's golden age was an instant smash. As with *Star Wars* Lucas had again taken an old discarded genre and successfully revamped it for the eighties. Once more the movie houses of the nation gasped at scenes of hair's-breadth escapes, cursed tombs, hidden treasure and Nazi villains. Critics and public alike lapped it up. 'One of the best adventure yarns in years' – *Daily Express*; 'Fantastic entertainment' – *Daily Mirror*.

Some of the more intellectual critics, the 'cinema-as-art' brigade, were predictably depressed by it all, seeing so much talent and expense lavished on an essentially mindless piece of pap. They labelled it as further proof of the artistic bankruptcy of the movie brat generation, who were capable only of making movies by plagiarizing the past, instead of producing genuinely original works. Valid opinions in their way, but this film simply rode roughshod over the humourless criticism. 'Raiders is a cynical, exploitative, ultimately boring exercise,' carped *Village Voice*, 'which isn't even a competent action film.' This is mighty hard to agree with. From the opening shot of the famous Paramount logo dissolving into a real mountain to the climax of godly wrath, *Raiders* is a pure cinematic joy, with an infectious, roistering spirit of fun and boundless energy. So fast is the action that there is no time to work out the improbability of it all. Ford's understated sneer beautifully counter-points the most outlandish mayhem; while that sly smirk of his which sneaks out when he's having a good time swatting Nazis, allows audiences in on the absurdity of the gag. It's a real rollercoaster ride of a movie. Lucas sees his films as being closer to amusement park rides than to plays or novels. 'You get in line for a second ride.' *Raiders* brought back the excitement of the Saturday matinee, gave us a hero to cheer for and provided two hours of unadulterated enjoyment. One left the cinema with the feeling that, like the best films of childhood, it will take up permanent residence in the memory.

Scarcely noticed above all the special effects and techno-wizardry of *Star Wars*, Ford as Indiana Jones suddenly found himself the centre of attention. For the first time he was being called upon to use his charisma and ability to carry a movie single handed. At the time it terrified him. Thankfully the nerves Ford experienced on the set never transferred to the screen, and his remarkable and memorable portrayal won him the best notices of his career thus far. 'Harrison Ford's gorgeous performance calls up memories of Bogart, Gable and Wayne among others' – *Films Illustrated*; 'Ford emerges as a matinee movie idol of old, with a touch of the Errol Flynns,' a critic from *Photoplay* commented. 'Ford, with his strong offbeat features and light cynicism has the potential to become a grand romantic hero in the line of Clark Gable,' wrote another. Even Lawrence Kasdan made the old Hollywood star comparison for *Starlog* in September 1981. 'One of my great delights with Indiana Jones is the way in which Harrison Ford brought him to life. Harrison has great charisma without being cocky and shows that he's a real movie star. His performance is actually very close to what Clark Gable used to do. Gable was an odd mixture, because he wasn't an athlete or a muscular guy, but he always had an enormous masculinity that never left him.' But the vintage star to whom Ford was being repeatedly and inappropriately compared was Humphrey Bogart. This was preposterous, and Ford knew it. 'Always somebody else,' he complained. 'Tracy, Bogart or Gable. It doesn't mean a thing. It means absolutely nothing.'

However, critics were right in paralleling Ford with the stars of Hollywood's yesteryear. Many contemporary actor/stars, notably Robert de Niro, pour themselves into a character and are all but unrecognizable from one movie to the next. Stars of the past like Cary Grant, John Wayne and Gary Cooper poured the role into themselves. The actor in whose footsteps Ford was treading, more so than Bogart, was probably Gary Cooper. His plainly chiselled good looks are often troubled by interior ruminations, just as Cooper's were when struggling with his pacifism in *Sergeant York*. Ford also has the very American virtues of straightforwardness and courage in the face of corruption which Cooper epitomized in *High Noon*. Whoever Gary Cooper played he was always unmistakably 'Coop', and the same is largely true of Harrison Ford. His most famous characters – Han Solo, Indiana Jones and John Book – are all believably different but at the same time identical; all are clearly Harrison Ford. 'The roles get lost in Harrison,' Carrie Fisher told *Time* in February 1985. 'I don't think that there's a lot that is dissimilar between the character and the person. It's no accident that he plays a lot of heroes. He plays somebody you can rely on, who will take care of whatever it is, from a kid's hurt finger, to a murder, to saving the galaxy. He has that quality.' It was hard then to imagine Ford ever being convincing as a creep or a villain (that is, until *The Mosquito Coast*). Like Cooper, he lacks malice and the disposition to appear dishonest. Endlessly typed as the good guy, perhaps in perpetuity, Allie Fox (of *The Mosquito Coast*) is the closest Ford will ever come to playing a villain.

The international appeal of *Raiders of the Lost Ark* (in Paris the film stayed in one Champs-Elysées cinema for eighty-nine weeks) prompted Ford to undertake an extensive European promotional tour. He attended the London opening in July and several festivals, including the highbrow Venice film festival, where *Raiders* went through the roof, and Deauville. Ford, almost unrecognizable in a full beard, the trademark of his Hollywood 'movie brat' pals, drove himself down from Paris with his two sons to attend the Deauville festival, a ten-day feast of American movies on French soil, stopping off *en route* to visit the occasional obscure art museum.

The success of *Raiders*, and most importantly the phenomenal public reaction to Ford's latest screen persona created innumerable problems for the actor, despite its rewards. With Burt Reynolds destined to appear in one meaningless car chase picture after another and Eastwood's career hitting a low point, Ford, the rank outsider, had emerged as *the* action hero for the eighties, the world's number one box-office draw. More importantly Ford had become a pulp star to a whole new generation of moviegoers, the ideal comic book hero for the Lucas/Spielberg blockbuster productions, which were proving the most consistently popular entertainments of the day. People kept referring to him as Lucas's one-man repertory company. Ford came to view the hero worship engendered by the *Star Wars* and Indiana Jones films as a burden. As far as he's concerned there are no such things as heroes – 'a hero's a guy in a cape' – only ordinary people moved by extraordinary circumstances to behave in a heroic manner, exactly the kind of roles Ford likes to play. 'I don't look for heroes, I would never play a character if he was labelled a hero in advance.' Indiana Jones, for instance, is a character who stumbles into life-threatening situations and is compelled only by his own instinct for self-preservation to act heroically. Although the world begged to differ, Ford was never to think of Indiana Jones or himself as being particularly heroic.

What Ford found even more unnerving, and still does, was the whole idea of public hero-worship itself. 'One of my discomforts with this culture is this obsession with success and celebrity, this endless search for heroes. I don't believe that adopting heroes from movies and making them the focus of our lives does any of us any good,' he preaches. This is one of Ford's stock hang-ups and stems, perhaps, from the fact that he never had any real childhood heroes himself. Why? 'I've always seen clay feet on people,' he told *American Way* in February 1987. 'I think I have a tendency to see dilemmas in everything, to see contradiction and irony. It's easy to develop attachments, to see in somebody else's example a path, a route, a way to get through life. But it's never happened to me. Maybe that's why you see the loner in me.'

The young Ford, it appears, was a lot like the Ford of today: serious, thoughtful and almost painfully practical. In a way he's disappointingly square; as a teenager he was a counsellor at a scout camp and the decency is still there. Sure, he spent the usual quota of time at the Saturday matinees watching the likes of Gene Autry, but saw them only as pleasing diversions. He was not like the other kids who turned such men into personal heroes. In a decade saturated with cultural icons – Elvis, James Dean, Marlon Brando, Monroe and the stars of rock 'n' roll – Ford had no media idols whatsoever. There was a period of about six months when he considered Hank Sauer, an outfield player for the Chicago Cubs baseball team, as something rather special, but chiefly

Ford picked out his champions from the many biographies he enjoyed reading. His two main heroes Abraham Lincoln and George Washington Carver, were unusual choices to say the least. 'One of them invented a 101 uses for the peanut,' he explained. 'I thought that was neat, and the other freed the slaves and I thought that was pretty good too.' Lincoln especially was a major idol of Ford's, but also his last. 'I have not had a hero since.' Ford was twelve years old.

If Ford has no idols of his own he is fully aware of the heroic role he plays for millions of youngsters. Helen Mirren, who portrayed his wife in *The Mosquito Coast*, cites the 'great sense of responsibility' he showed towards young fans who visited the set. 'He was always very caring and very conscious of them and very much aware of the responsibility he had inherited by becoming their hero. He was always direct, but he seemed to know that he shouldn't destroy the image for them. I found something very tender about that.' The consideration and sense of obligation Ford displays when confronted by young fans perhaps derives from a childhood encounter with the actor who played Sky King, the aerial ace – a meeting which left him utterly disillusioned. 'He turned out to be short, heavyset and unconventional looking. It intrigued me, how different showbusiness was from what people thought,' Ford told *Time* in May 1989. 'And maybe that disposition gave me a reality register that has been a fixture in my life.'

On occasion Ford has exploited his 'hero' image for beneficial effect. In 1986 he appeared in a series of radio and TV advertisements condemning the looting and vandalism of archaeological sites. The pitch was part of an unprecedented campaign by scientists to counteract the alarming increase in the desecration of historical sites in the US. Ford, though, claims to be against making other kinds of commercials, and he doesn't do product endorsements on principle. 'I could have made a lot of money doing adverts,' he told the *New York Times* in May 1989. 'And I've chosen not to do that. Keeping an image that's free of that kind of thing is important to me.' But like many of his fellow American stars this hasn't stopped him from making lucrative commercials in Japan where no one can see them, promoting the Honda motor company for one. But on the whole it's a rare event when Ford lends his name to a product, charity or political cause. He does feel passionate about numerous issues – homelessness and Aids, for example. But despite being a member of several organizations, he is no kind of Hollywood spokesman, preferring to work quietly behind the scenes, and funding causes which range from child care to conservation. There have been exceptions. He agreed to make a public service announcement for aphasia in the mid eighties for the Will Rogers Institute. More recently, like the rest of Hollywood in the wake of eighties over consumption, he has caught the 'green' bug, lending his support to Friends of the Earth and other environmental causes. 'I'm an actor, I don't tell people who to vote for. I don't tell them how to conduct their lives.' Ford remains staunchly critical of other stars who use their fame as a platform to impose their political views on the nation. 'I really can't stomach celebrity spokespeople. There are people with much greater understanding than actors or sports heroes. And I'm real impatient with our society's need to listen to celebrities' opinions on issues. I support a lot of things, but I don't want to talk about it. I'm more likely to put my money where my mouth is.'

The year was 1981 when Ford finally became a genuine superstar. He had appeared in leading roles for years without being able to establish a leading-man identity with audiences. *The Empire Strikes Back* brought Ford back into the public eye after a disastrous run of flops, but it was *Raiders of the Lost Ark* which truly propelled him to stardom. Even if he was second choice for Indiana Jones, the public responded to this brash all-American adventurer. Harrison Ford's name alone guaranteed an audience. 'That was the one that proved I didn't have to play Han Solo to be a hit.' Spielberg, speaking to *Vanity Fair* in August 1990, agreed. 'I don't think Star Wars really made Harrison a movie star. If anybody got real famous there, it was probably C3PO and Chewbacca. I think he became a star somewhere in between Raiders and Witness.' He also became a very rich man all over again. Ford neither confirmed nor denied reports that he received seven per cent of the gross of *Raiders* Assuming this figure to be roughly correct, the role earned him something in the region of $10 million.

There was naturally a down side. Ford had never previously thought of himself as being much of a movie star and still cringes at the mere thought of it. The degree of anonymity he preserved after the phenomenal cult of *Star Wars* was truly remarkable. By 1981 he could still walk down any street in the world virtually unrecognized. And that was just the way he liked it. It helped that Ford was born with a 'very plastic', almost forgettable face, certainly not as distinctive as, say, Robert Redford's. In his opinion Carrie Fisher and Mark Hamill had much more memorable physiognomies and were therefore spotted by autograph hunters more frequently. However, Ford is the only *Star Wars* regular to have achieved star status outside of the series.

Much was made in those early days of Ford's ability to blend like a chameleon into his surroundings; of having the kind of face that only excited recognition on the screen. During the making of *Empire* and *Raiders* his rich Midwestern accent usually meant he was mistaken for an American tourist more often than cinema's rising new star. Seven years later, at midday on a roadside in California, two middle-aged men chat easily as they wait for filming to resume on *Indiana Jones and the Last Crusade*. A woman in a car pulls up. 'Hey look, there's Sean Connery,' she tells her children, who crane forward, pointing excitedly. 'So what am I, chopped liver?' asks Harrison Ford. The anecdote is a perfect illustration of Ford, the man. While Connery never fails to radiate star power or trigger instant recognition, Ford has managed to remain as understated as the man next door. Or so he would like. Ford used to thrive on being able to walk into a local pub (he loves English beer) without being hassled or asked to pose for photographs. Despite having already appeared in three of the highest-earning films in history, his face could still melt inconspicuously into the crowd. Spielberg told *Mail on Sunday* in November 1982, 'What's so attractive about Harrison is that you wouldn't notice him on the street, you might not even know him at a small cocktail party of a dozen people. He really is a chameleon. When he's acting, he becomes the character he's playing and afterwards he reverts to being Harrison Ford, woodcutter and furniture-maker. His magic is that he's a very accessible, common guy.'

Ford learned early on how best to camouflage himself in public. It's how you hold yourself that counts, the way you walk and talk. Behave like a star and you'll be noticed. 'It's the look at me attitude that gets you into trouble. The secret is not to catch anyone's eyes,' he told the *Daily Express* in December 1984. 'Keep your head down and count the cracks in the sidewalk.' Ford has a forceful, contained way of walking, mixed with a large dose of stealth, so that strangers have difficulty recognizing him. When they succeed, his momentum makes it tough for them to approach. When the unthinkable does happen, he isn't stupid enough to resent it; Ford knows on which side his bread is buttered. Generally people are very courteous and Ford always tries to be polite in return. He will happily sign autographs, 'if I'm not having sex at the time or doing something important.' He just finds it very difficult coping with crowds and all that sychophantic attention. Ford never believed he'd be successful at acting to the point where it would impinge on his personal life, or anyone else's for that matter. 'I have this funny thing that happens to me,' he explained to *You* magazine in August 1988. 'When I see famous people on the street, I turn away so as not to embarrass them by staring. But sometimes it's someone I know, only I've forgotten I know them – I think I'm only imagining I know them, because they're famous. Jack Nicholson has been a friend for fifteen years but every time I see him, my instinct is to turn away, to preserve his privacy. I have to remind myself that I can't do that, I do know Jack and I've got to say hi.'

The popularity of *Raiders* meant that it was now impossible to maintain any level of anonymity. That loss of privacy turned out to be a very frightening and traumatic process. Gradually fame changed Ford from the unseen observer, an actor's natural state, to the observed. Nineteen eighty-one was the last year in which his face would truly remain his own. It now belonged to the world. And Ford was not amused.

8

Do Androids Dream?

The vast industrial wasteland stretches for miles, and lofty smokestacks belch out their orange and yellow sulphurous breath into the air. Beyond this infernal landscape lies a metropolis in ruin, a retrofitted cityscape of gargantuan new architecture grafted on to decayed pre-existing buildings, some of which are 500 storeys high. They are home to the elite. Street level is a netherworld labyrinth of punks, villains, survivors and no-hopers, a garbage-strewn society of multicultural chaos. In the skies a hovering blimp bombards the populace with all manner of commercials and propaganda, while flying patrol cars soar through concrete canyons, past massive advertising video screens on the sides of hyper-industrialized skyscrapers. This is Los Angeles *circa* 2019.

Director Ridley Scott and his staff of designers gave birth to their own vision of the near future; dark, garish, congested and chaotic, it is arguably the most dense, detailed and fully realized future society ever put on screen. Certainly it is the best thing that's happened in megalopolis movies since Fritz Lang. Christened 'Ridleyville' by the crew in honour of its British-born creator, this bleak view conforms to Philip K. Dick's literary prophecy of a future where the cities of the world are falling apart, decaying hulks all but abandoned by those who have survived the apocalypse in favour of colonies off the planet. Only the dregs of humanity remain behind.

Released on an unsuspecting public in June 1982, *Blade Runner* was rejected out of hand by the masses, earning a lowly $14 million in America. In a summer blighted by sci-fi films, the smart money was riding on *Blade Runner* to be the season's surefire hit. Ford himself saw his performance as a tough cop as an important step towards more serious roles. The writing was on the wall, though, at sell-out test screenings in Denver and Dallas earlier in the year. Diehard Ford fans, anticipating the next *Raiders of the Lost Ark*, found Scott's slow, downbeat, noirish film confusing and sharply at odds with their *Star Wars*/Spielberg vision of the future. Some even stomped out of the theatre in puzzled disgust. Audiences expecting Indiana Jones or Han Solo were destined to end up disappointed with both the movie and Ford's believably dour characterization. Deckard is no knight in shining armour, he's a humourless, melancholic, dogged individual who, on encountering a foe, usually gets beaten to the ground.

Press reaction was divided between those who appreciated the visual exotica and those who found the impressive technical virtuosity no compensation for a lame and muddled narrative. (Scott has been criticized as a film-maker who creates static tableaux rather than moving pictures. *Raiders* and *Star Wars* moved like greased lightning, whereas *Blade Runner* simply camouflages its stagnation under a wealth of decorative detail.) Most critics were grouped in the former category. 'One of the most compelling and fascinating films since A Clockwork Orange' – *Daily Express*; 'A case could be made for Blade Runner as the best sci-fi film of the past decade' – *Starlog*; 'A masterpiece. It will come to be regarded as one of the all-time sci-fi classics' – *Starburst*; 'The most inventive and satisfying sci-fi film of the eighties' – *American Film*.

As a result of the poor preview response Scott lost control over the final cut and the moneymen took charge. Frantic last-minute 'improvements' – an explanatory narration and a ludicrously contrived happy ending – both failed to make a difficult film more palatable. This crude surgery has been the target for criticism ever since. Today *Blade Runner* has earned its place as probably *the* cult classic of the eighties, a firm favourite among the sci-fi and art student set and one of the most accomplished films of its genre. Scott's revolutionary design and stunning visual style influenced an entire decade. It gave rise to the cyberpunk literary explosion of the mid-eighties, and has been replicated in countless other movies, pop videos and television commercials. The film's idolization continued unabated into the nineties when the director's cut of the film was issued to cinemas in both America and Britain, to great critical acclaim and box-office success. The legend that is *Blade Runner* lives on.

But how did it all start? Cranked out with the aid of amphetamines during the height of the Vietnam War, Philip K. Dick's *Do Androids Dream of Electric Sheep?* is regarded very much as a product of its time. The novel chronicles the exploits of Rick Deckard, a lone-wolf cop tracking down murderous androids in a post-nuclear San Francisco. The near-eradication of earth's animal life has resulted in the measurement of wealth by ownership of livestock. If people can't afford genuine animals they settle for working models. Deckard himself keeps a robot sheep on his apartment roof, but hopes the bounty on the replicants will be enough to buy a real one. The electric sheep idea was an early casualty in the translation of *Do Androids Dream?* into *Blade Runner*. Martin Scorsese was the first film-maker to express interest in the work back in 1969, a year after publication, but the option finally went to Herb Jaffe. He completed a script in 1973 which horrified the father. Dick's highly intelligent novel had been reduced to pulp level. In 1977 Jaffe withdrew, leaving the path free for former actor Hampton Fancher and his partner Brian Kelly to run with the property for a while. They first approached British producer Michael Deeley, who twice refused them on the grounds that Dick's weighty ponderings would not easily translate from page to film. He was proved wrong when Fancher later returned with a self-penned scenario bristling with commercial possibilities. Deeley was hooked and *The Android*, as it was then known, was tentatively given the green light. (The film went through several title changes, including *Mechanismo* and *Dangerous Days*, before Ridley Scott settled on *Blade Runner*. At one point Scott was keen on the title *Gotham City* but Batman creator Bob Kane refused permission for him to use it).

While Deeley shopped around for possible backers Fancher worked on several screenplays, each successive draft leaving Dick's original concept further behind until there was very little of his book left. Fancher's work was anathema to Dick. In his eyes, Hollywood had raped his story, turning it into a simple-minded private-eye fantasy with an over-reliance on cliché-ridden Chandlerisms. 'When I read it,' the author said, 'I thought that I will move to the Soviet Union where I am completely unknown and work making light bulbs in a factory and never even look at a book again and pretend that I can't read.' Most significantly, Fancher had ignored the book's primary philosophical issue: if you fight evil, you will end up becoming evil. The terrible acts perpetrated by Deckard in the name of the law have the curious effect of making the androids seem more human and vice versa. Fortunately, this oversight was rectified in subsequent drafts. *Blade Runner* is far from being completely faithful to the book but at least it is intellectually and spiritually true to its thematic core.

Ridley Scott was in London working on *Alien* when he first came into contact with *Blade Runner*. He agreed to get involved only after his own attempts to bring Frank Herbert's epic *Dune* saga to the screen had failed. Heavily influenced by the hallucinatory quality of the comic *Heavy Metal* and the work of *Moebius* (Jean Girard), Scott, the grand architect, first recruited some top graphic designers to assist in the visual realization of Los Angeles forty years from now. The conceptualization of *Blade Runner*'s exotic vehicles and sets were assigned to renowned futurologist and industrial designer Syd Mead; while one of the business's true masters, Douglas Trumbull (*2001, Close Encounters*) was hired to create the elaborate special effects.

Scott's second and perhaps more daunting challenge was finding the right actor to play Rick Deckard. After wistfully toying with the impossibility of procuring a thirty-year-old version of Robert Mitchum,

Scott became interested in Harrison Ford. Ford, however, was not interested in him. The script was OK, the premise ambitious and the part interesting; what turned his stomach was the choice of London as the base of operations. He was making *The Empire Strikes Back* at Elstree when first approached to star in *Blade Runner*, and the thought of working yet again in the English capital was deeply unappealing. 'I'd been too long in one place. You've got to travel on ... travel on.' Besides he missed home and his children, and felt he could stand London no longer. He was fed up with being treated like a gullible Yank tourist, continually being overcharged and exploited. 'England's a tourist economy now,' he argued in *The Times* in July 1981. 'And that's no state for a developed nation to be in.' Ford is enamoured of the British film community, he just thinks the place itself stinks. 'I'm allergic to this fucking country,' he once protested.

What initially drew Scott to Ford was an 'unusual quality' which shines through in two pictures, *The Conversation* and *Apocalypse Now*. It's a strange, slightly sinister side, very low-key and sombre, as if he were almost a different person. It fit the nature of both Deckard and the film very well. The only other actor considered for the part was Dustin Hoffman, then seeking more stimulating material to accommodate his prodigious talent. He reacted with astonishment to the offer. 'Why the hell do you want me to play this macho character?' he asked Ridley. In the end Hoffman proved unsuitable. Certainly *Blade Runner* would have turned out quite a different type of film had he accepted. Instead the scales tipped back in favour of Ford, who more than any other actor fitted Deckard's requirements perfectly.

As production had since relocated to Los Angeles, Ford agreed to the part when approached a second time. Deckard is the standard seedy private eye haunted by doubts, drink and defeatism and Ford saw in him the chance to play an anti-hero. His character is as far removed from Han Solo and Indiana Jones as one could possibly imagine. Unfortunately, Ridley Scott didn't quite see it like that. Ford's Indy image was exactly the look he was after for Deckard – the felt hat, the bedraggled, unshaven appearance, the slightly long and unkempt hair. Ford rebelled against Scott on all counts when they first met on the set of *Raiders*. 'I've got this great idea,' Scott informed Ford. 'We're going to do this Philip Marlowe-ish character. Bogart and that sort of thing.' Ford's reply was undiplomatic and to the point. 'Just done it. Can't do it.' Ridley continued: 'What I want is this sort of unshaved individual——' Ford butted in again. 'Can't do that. I've just done it.'

If there ever has been a driving force guiding Ford's career it has been the keen determination to seek out projects that contrast with the last thing he's done. 'If I've just made a comedy, I won't read comedies.' It is no accident, for example, that *Frantic* followed *The Mosquito Coast* or

Presumed Innocent succeeded *Indiana Jones and the Last Crusade*. By alternating very different roles in this manner Ford has largely managed to avoid typecasting while simultaneously increasing his range as an actor. Convinced that you have to demonstrate an enduring versatility to maintain a long career in the business, he looks for something different at every opportunity. 'Nobody wants to repeat themselves endlessly.' With *Blade Runner* Ford felt obliged to work against his *Raiders* image. Tuned into his star's entreaties Scott changed gears completely and began altering his original perception of Deckard, beginning with the hair. The severe crew-cut was actually Ford's own personal touch. With the hat gone Scott still wanted something to distinguish his police hero. 'So I got that haircut,' said Ford, 'figuring it would give the character definition, a certain look.' Ford's intention had always been to have the hair very short to give the impression of a man who had long ago given up on himself and was unconscious of his own personal appearance. Ford employed the same technique eight years later when he played Rusty Sabich in *Presumed Innocent*. But it took some negotiating to get Ridley's approval. 'He was afraid it would make me less gorgeous,' Ford quipped. The condition was that Ford's hair could only be touched in the presence of the director. The actual haircut was a four-hour ordeal, with long pauses along the way for stern consideration by Scott. In the end he applauded Ford's resolve. 'It was a frightening process cutting his hair off,' he told *Film Comment* in July 1982. 'It was a brave thing for him to do.'

Next came the clothes, which were 'new wave' in design – patterned shirt and narrow tie with a pair of trousers, made from light wool, and a dirty trenchcoat, the prerequisite for any *film noir* hero. Ford joked that Deckard now looked like 'a middle-aged Elvis Costello'. Deckard cuts a pathetic figure: he's tough, sardonic and sticks to his task with a dogged stoicism that wins our admiration, but like many of us he's prone to fallibility and has allowed his once well-honed skills as an investigator to become blunted. He wanders the choked and threatening streets of Los Angeles in 2019, where genetically engineered humans or replicants are employed as slave labour for high-risk jobs on planetary colonies or as futuristic soldiers. Periodically they attempt to escape their servitude and return to earth. These are 'retired' (or killed) by specially trained detectives called 'blade runners'. Deckard is the best. The Nexus-6 is the ultimate replicant, in almost every respect superhuman and one of the finest products of science. It is comprised as much from flesh and blood as from plastic and electronics. So sophisticated has genetic engineering become that you can't tell who are replicants and who are not. And since the replicants have memory implants, a human cannot even be sure that he isn't one himself. A group of Nexus-6s have escaped from Mars and fled to Los Angeles in search of their creator. They need to discover how to override their built-in obsolescence, which condemns them to a mere four-year lifespan. Back on the streets, having been ordered out of early retirement, Deckard realizes he is no match against the Nexus-6. His mission is further complicated by burgeoning romantic feelings for Rachel (Sean Young), herself an android and a potentially fatal respect for his dynamic Nordic antagonist Roy Batty (Rutger Hauer), the renegade leader.

In early drafts of the script *Blade Runner* included a prologue sequence which explained why Deckard came to be a retired 'rep-detect'. The view is of a wide expanse of farmland, and a tractor tills the soil. At the controls sits a colossal farmer. Enter Deckard walking towards an old-fashioned farmhouse. Once inside, he confronts the farmer, who moves aggressively towards Deckard. The detective pulls out his gun and fires. Surveying his handiwork Deckard takes hold of the farmer's lower jaw and with an almighty heave wrenches out the jawbone. A serial number is clearly emblazoned inside. The farmer was a replicant, an old model, a Nexus-2 or 3. The purpose of this scene was to demonstrate how the Blade Runner's job had changed over the years. When the replicants were grossly artificial it was easy, morally speaking, to destroy them. However, as technology advanced and they became more lifelike, developing real feelings and human empathy, Deckard began to view his job as a abhorrent obscenity. He could no longer condone the extermination of these beings, human or not. The deletion of the prologue diluted this theme. It was one of the reasons why Ford originally wanted to play the part – the ambivalence of the character intrigued him. There was an element of psychological depth at work that he had never before had to convey on film. Echoes of Deckard's moral dilemma remain, though, in the voiceover when he describes his disgust at killing Zhora, the snake dancer (Joanna Cassidy).

Another early idea, and one of Scott's favourites, was to show the extraterrestrial origins of Batty. Within a huge crater stands a vast furnace into which a conveyor belt is feeding legions of dead replicants. From out of this mass of bodies rise the figure of Batty and his five fugitive cohorts. They easily overpower the guards and take control. This brilliantly imaginative concept, sadly never filmed because of cost, was devised by writer David Peoples, who was brought in to polish up the final shooting script, and whose contributions met with Philip K. Dick's grudging approval.

After a year of exhausting pre-production work *Blade Runner* got underway on 9 March 1981 at Burbank Studios. Warner Brothers' legendary New York street set, where Cagney and Bogart cast their shadows throughout the forties, was transformed into Scott's nightmarish vision of our near future. The task was to show a metropolis gone sour, with its garish neon displays, dirty sidewalks and crumbling technological infrastructure. Scott wanted a dense, crowded feel futuristic, yet darkly reminiscent of seedy *film noir* and the major cities of today – a heady mixture of Hong Kong, New York, Piccadilly Circus and Tokyo's Ginza district. Background detail was all-important, from the shabbily dressed milling crowd, the newsstand with its depressingly violent magazines to parking meters that can kill if tampered with.

The momentous teaming of Ford and Scott, of which great things were expected, failed to gel from day one. Here was a director whose visual sensibilities took precedent over narrative structure, a legacy from his days as an artist and long apprenticeship making television advertisements. Determined to get involved in every aspect of the film, his eye for detail was meticulous and bordered on obsession. He would spend hours behind the camera lining up shots. Props, lights, vehicles, extras – all had to be exactly on their marks. Shooting was sometimes disrupted while Scott called for certain objects within the frame to be shifted a fraction of an inch for the sake of aesthetic balance. All of this infuriated Ford, who dislikes loafing about idly on set. Perhaps more than anyone, however, Ford recognizes that such films are technically very complex and long delays between takes are commonplace. 'I sit and stare at the walls or walk around in my trailer,' he told *The Times* in July 1981. 'Either I'm thinking about the next scene or I'm in a state of mental suspension. I can't read or concentrate on anything else. It's the worst thing about being an actor for me.' But at times Scott's perfectionism went too far. As did his natural inclination to operate the camera himself. Ford, while appreciative of the results, was happy when the Hollywood film union put a halt to it. 'Scott likes to watch the performance through the lens. As an actor I'm glad he wasn't able to do that. I think that when a director is looking through the camera he's watching the edges to be sure where everything is. I want a director to be helping me with the whole scene, the performance.'

Problems were compounded by the fact that the story was played out under the veil of darkness. 'Night filming does tend to drive everybody a little wacko after a while,' Ford observed. Lunch was usually held after midnight and shooting would wrap up at four or five in the morning. Ford had been here before on *American Graffiti*, but he'd been young and hungry then. Accustomed to the pampered cocoon of Lucasworld, he was unprepared for the perils of Ridleyville. Scott and his designers had perhaps made the movie's *mise-en-scène* too persuasively real. After four months of high-pressure twelve-hour days, the dark, surreal atmosphere with its steam, noise and smoke began to affect the crew. They were visibly demoralized and depressed. The set even smelled like a sleazy metropolis, with the ever-present stench of burnt coffee and boiling noodles. Scott's vision of a Los Angeles plagued with acid rain, caused by out-of-control industrialization, added further to everyone's discomfort. Seven sprinklers were used, and the continual starting and stopping of this rain system resulted in a perpetual damp chill on the set. By the close of filming a set dresser, a prop man, one camera crew and a special effects team had walked out in protest. Veterans of previous Hollywood campaigns spoke of this as being the toughest of their careers. Tempers flared and most aimed their resentment squarely at the director, calling him 'dominating' and 'a megalomaniac'. Others admired his integrity and regarded him as one of cinema's visionary masters, whose attention to pictorial composition is unrivalled. Others testify that it was Ford and not Scott who behaved like a prima donna on the set.

The friction between Ford and Scott escalated to the point where they almost exchanged blows. 'It was a gruelling movie and Ridley demanded so many takes that it finally wore Harrison out,' a colleague told *Premiere* in March 1988. 'I know he was ready to kill Ridley. One night on the set he really would have taken him on if he hadn't been talked out of it.' In the grand finale, a suspenseful cat-and-mouse chase between Deckard and Batty in a derelict building, Ford was required to run through a flooded room while crew hands threw wild pigeons at him. Being defecated on by sixty frantically flapping birds was really the last straw. Not surprisingly *Blade Runner* is not among Ford's favourite films. 'There was nothing for me to do but stand around and give some vain attempt to give some focus to Ridley's sets,' he told *The Boston Sunday Globe* in July 1991. 'I think a lot of people enjoy it, and that's their prerogative.'

Ford also tangled with Ridley on the film's ending. The director wanted to leave audiences pondering on whether or not Deckard is a replicant himself. Ford loathed the idea. In a movie as bleak as *Blade Runner*, he argued, audiences needed some kind of hero, someone to cheer for. The studio agreed, inserting a new upbeat ending which has remained a bone of contention among fans ever since. (In the director's cut the suggestion that Deckard is indeed a replicant is more pronounced.) Perhaps Ford's sorest point concerns his now infamous and much maligned voiceover. Comparisons with the *film noir* classics of the forties were inevitable and it was Scott's intention from the beginning to exploit the Bogart/Marlowe image. On this point, as with so many others, Ford did not see eye to eye with his director. The narration, one of the staple ingredients of any detective yarn, was written into Ford's contract. But it was always his ambition to wriggle out of the obligation, as he felt the film just didn't need one. In the end Ford walked into the studio and recorded the voiceover without argument, 'on the theory it was such drivel they'd never use it'. But they did.

For others, though, *Blade Runner* was an enjoyable moviemaking experience, and both Rutger Hauer and Sean Young had nothing but praise for their director. The fledgling Ms Young was constantly frustrated at the way she was treated by Ford. 'He was very tough to work with.' Young found him too distant, and he never wanted to rehearse with her or discuss their scenes together. In fact, he seemed more pally and open with the technical crew than any of the performers. 'It's where he can feel earthy,' said Young. 'That's where he feels safest.' Kelly McGillis also found Ford to be aloof on the set of *Witness*. He kept himself very separate from her during filming and they never interacted socially. 'He's a very private person,' McGillis said. 'He doesn't open up easily to people. What I liked best about him was his professionalism.' Young was, however, taken with Ford's sense of fun: 'I don't think people know that he's really a very good comedian.' She was also impressed by his technical mastery of screen acting. 'Harrison was the one who taught me how to kiss,' she revealed to *Premiere* in September 1988. 'We did the first take and I was really going at it, when he said to me, "No, no, no, you don't want to do it too much, because on film it won't look right. The lighter you do it, the better it looks." What a beard that guy had. He completely tore up my face.'

One actress who did enjoy working with Ford was Alison Doody. Her experiences with him on the set of *Indiana Jones and the Last Crusade*, in which she played an Arian ice maiden, indicated the extent to which the actor had mellowed since the early eighties. Ford often joked around to relieve the tension. Before their big love scene he noticed that Doody was embarrassed and very nervous so he kept trying to make her laugh. Standing behind Spielberg, puckering up his lips and making silly kissing noises, he simpered, 'Alison, I'm ready.' They would also talk scenes through together, and Ford was always willing to sort out any problems the actress had. When Doody was hounded by the British tabloids for quotations about what it was like to kiss Ford, she turned to her co-star for guidance. 'Tell them,' he advised, 'that Harrison Ford is so famous he doesn't even use his own tongue.' Melanie Griffith also enjoyed her time with Ford. 'He was so easy to act with,' she told *TV Guide* in October 1990, 'because you look in his eyes and there's a real person there. He listens, he reacts, he gives a lot. He helped me enormously.'

Pretty much left to his own devices during filming, Ford's discussions with Scott tended to revolve around practical matters rather than character motivation. But despite the lack of guidance, Ford still managed a skilfully dark and tenacious performance – a little monotonous, perhaps, but it acted as a compelling contrast to Rutger Hauer's archangel-like villain. 'Harrison is an absolutely magnificent actor,' David Peoples told *Starlog* in May 1982. 'He becomes Deckard. I mean, you don't see him act like Deckard, he is Deckard. Harrison is fantastic in the picture and he just has this enormous broad range.

Harrison can become a different person without adopting a strange accent or a different costume or strange mannerisms or anything like that. He doesn't need that crutch.' Even Ridley Scott was full of praise. 'Harrison has an immense understanding of the entire moviemaking process. You can't fool him at all – he always knows exactly what's happening. His contributions were tremendous, on a story level as well as to his own character. He brought many ideas to me – in fact it got bloody embarrassing. They were so good, there was no way I could wriggle out of using them. For example, Harrison figured he should go for utter reality, almost like de Niro's Travis Bickle in Taxi Driver – the substance of the central character was essential. Harrison developed and kept it that way – he takes full credit for that, not me.'

Just after the beginning of the new year, Philip K. Dick was invited to Warner Brothers' Burbank Studios by Ridley Scott to view some of Douglas Trumbull's dazzling special effects footage. Both men were wary of meeting for the first time. In the press Dick had trashed the film and Scott had admitted never having finished reading the book, branding it as 'too difficult'. Their meeting resulted in a congenial truce. Dick was visibly moved by what he saw. 'If I died and went to heaven tomorrow, I'd be a happy man. Seeing this is like experiencing a vision of the world through my own mind.' Sadly Dick never did live to see the final print. Several weeks later, on 2 March, the author died of a heart attack at his home. He was fifty-four.

After a long, tiresome obsession with sequels a nineties Hollywood, following in the footsteps of the record industry, moved into a 'remix' phase. Colourized and widescreen films, films with restored footage and re-issues of classics were in vogue. Perhaps mindful of this new trend, Warner Brothers recently permitted Ridley Scott to restore *Blade Runner* to its original format. Out went Ford's emotionless voiceover and the tacked-on 'happy ending' of Deckard and Rachel speeding off towards the unpolluted North-west. The aerial shots of beautiful countryside were actually out-takes from the opening of *The Shining*.

The structural alterations made by Scott were minimal, but the improvement is vast. The 1992 director's cut is far more a film of dread, tension and grief, and pulses with a hypnotic darkness that in 1982 – the *ET* era – must have seemed jarring and excessive. The restored original ending – an elevator door closing on Rachel's face – makes all the difference. Instead of the falsely upbeat finale which Warners sanctioned, we are left with the sense that her and Deckard's plight is unresolved. Perhaps most significant of all is the inclusion of the now legendary unicorn sequence, which has languished in a storage facility in London since 1982. Deckard's dream of seeing a magnificent unicorn in a forest entirely alters the movie's atmosphere, and leads to the conclusion that Deckard himself is a replicant, though unaware of it. The final scene, in which Deckard finds an origami unicorn left by fellow Blade Runner Gaff (Edward James Olmos), had little meaning in the '82 version. In the new cut the significance is obvious. Much is made of the importance of false memories implanted into replicants, and the only way Gaff could have known about Deckard's unicorn dream is that he has access to the detective's memory-implant. Not surprisingly, Ford has no intention of seeing the director's cut; nor, for that matter, has he any interest in the rumours of a possible sequel. 'It seems to me that there's no potential in the character,' Ford said in 1982. 'No reason to develop it further.' One of the reasons why Ford believes the film failed in the first place was that audiences had no emotional empathy with his character.

But the baroque and squalid environment created by Ridley Scott does indeed have enormous scope for new characters and situations. The thought of a *Blade Runner 2* is a tempting prospect, and the first film's cult following would almost certainly ensure box-office success. One thing's for sure, though: Harrison Ford won't be in it.

9

A Superstar for the Eighties

Harrison Ford is considered a perfectionist in the industry, a stickler for detail. His clash of egos with Ridley Scott is therefore all the more puzzling. Both artists are cut from the same cloth and approach their work with the same diligence and technical precision. Scott acknowledged as much in the February 1985 issue of *Time*: 'After going over the storyline, he'll turn to the details. He wants to know not only what the character looks like but what he'd wear, right down to the kind of shoes and the type of gun he would carry, where he would live and how.' Ford once described himself as a 'perfectionist and a realist', which is a combination fraught with potential conflict. He is never completely satisfied with any of his films or his own contributions in them. 'I don't think I will ever get to the point where I think I'll be as good as I want to be. That's just an aspect of my character that I don't think I will ever change.' This continual search for perfection can be very wearing, for both him and his colleagues. Those closest to him perceive a residual gloominess, perhaps an after-effect from his lean years – this despite millions in the bank.

Certainly he can be moody and grumpy at times. Above all Ford is an intensely serious man, sometimes unremittingly so, and he plans each move in a practical and logical way. But when he does get overcome with emotion, it's his nature that he will cry alone. 'I am independent. But not solitary. I don't go to anyone for advice or for a shoulder to lean on. My questions are for me to answer. That is my nature. I turn inward and even my wife cannot reach me then.' This is a staunch individualist who knows what he wants, a man who is shaped by his own ambitions, requirements and love for family. And true to his middle-class roots Ford is well mannered. During a night shoot for *Working Girl* Ford and Melanie Griffith were huddled together in a taxi. The scene should only have taken an hour, but had dragged on for two. Harrison, temporarily losing his temper, shouted, 'What the hell is going on here?' Douglas Wick, the film's executive producer later said, 'By the standards of a normal leading man, it was well within the well-behaved category. But he came to me afterwards and apologized.'

Ford's manners are perfect and he expects nothing less than the same in return. Yet regardless of his undeniable charm and screen magnetism, Ford remains curiously aloof in person. He's so laconic that Bonnie Bedelia, during the making of *Presumed Innocent*, called him, 'the Perry Como of actors'. Distant and prone to reticence, Ford is often mistaken for being surly. He has a reputation for being difficult and testy which he feels is undeserved, although he does go to greater lengths than most to control what is known about him. Courteous in public, yes, but also grim-faced. There are times when he entertains with sardonic humour, others when he chills with a stony glare. And he can sulk if he chooses to. Ford is not easy to get along with, and, indeed, few claim to know him intimately. Some believe him to be much more of a man's man, one who finds it difficult to relate or even talk to women.

Perhaps Ford's worst characteristics emerge during interviews. A myth has grown over the years that Ford is Hollywood's toughest press subject, a movie star who approaches an interview with the grim stoicism of a patient undergoing electrolysis. He's annoyingly dull and reserved, and lacks the ingratiating charm of many celebrities. For most actors the press spotlight is the perfect occasion to show off and regurgitate the same old stories that have been boring reporters for years. By contrast, Ford looks upon the journalist with the same scrupulous caution as a chess grand master might survey his opponent. He knows they are all waiting for that one unguarded moment, that fatal slip of the tongue where he reveals more about his past or personal life than intended. Ford faces every interview as an unpleasant if necessary chore. They are a good opportunity to promote a new film, and the only reason he submits to them is as an obligation to the producers.

The fact that Ford, *à la* Garbo, returns between films to the complete seclusion of his home in Wyoming has earned him the reputation of being uncooperative. It is a charge that he resents. 'I think I cooperate as much as possible with the press,' he told the *Radio Times* in September 1990. 'I've always made myself available when I have a film to publicize.' When he does make himself available he hardly ever discusses his family, his politics or any other private matter, so there would be little point unless he had a product to sell. It is a natural reserve that Ford inherited from his parents. He abhors self-promotion and avoids the intrusive tabloid scandal sheets. The fact that his wife once worked for *People* magazine still slightly embarrasses him. Ford's wariness towards the press is well documented and founded on the belief that actors who pursue too much publicity are in danger of becoming mere 'personalities' with short shelf lives. The press get tired of them, then find someone else to exploit. Ford attributes much of his longevity in the industry to never having been fashionable or 'flavour of the month'. Often criticized for shrouding himself in a cloak of mystery, his behaviour actually serves a practical purpose. The more the public knows about him, he feels, the harder it will be to be accepted in a role. 'People have a pretty good idea of some of the characters I've played,' Ford told *For Him* in September 1990. 'They don't have any idea who I am. That's a situation I encourage. That's the correct way for an actor to conduct himself. My position has always been that the movie itself says a lot more than I can. And I don't want to sound more interesting in the newspapers than I look on the screen.'

Even Melissa Mathison cheerfully calls her husband 'a terrible interview'. Before surrendering to the perils of the tape recorder or note-pad Ford braces himself and brings his well-honed inner censors to rigid attention. He speaks quietly in measured tones with a low monotone voice and little expression. The San Diego Union newspaper wrote that Ford sounded like a 'mellow, slightly stoned FM disc jockey'. Ford is notorious for becoming terse and monosyllabic when he detects the conversation drifting towards the personal and assumes that no-nonsense look of his, which is cultivated to keep intruders at bay.

Over the years his attitude has irritated a large portion of the press. The *Bergen County Record* complained that Ford 'turns prissy and pettifogging in answering even the softest questions'. Hilary Bonner of the *Mail on Sunday* watched as Ford fidgeted uncomfortably throughout their meeting. 'I think he may be the only actor I have ever met who genuinely does not like talking about himself,' she wrote. And the *Dayton Daily News* found Ford to be a dour man, 'answering some questions with curt yeses and nos, others with barely repressed disdain.' Jeffrey Abrams (the screenwriter of *Regarding Henry*) was asked to interview Ford during the run-up to the film's release. His first attempt occurred on an aeroplane bound for New York. After ten minutes, tired of hearing the same old questions raised, Ford took the cassette from the recorder and broke it in half. 'Let's start again. Put another tape in.' 'I don't have another tape.' End of interview. Ford can also turn hostile, especially when questions get too close to home. One scene in *Frantic* shows Ford snorting cocaine under duress. This was something of great concern to the actor so he convinced Polanski to include a shot showing him washing the foul powder out of his nose. When a reporter from *You* magazine inquired whether this reflected his own attitude towards drugs Ford pounced. Crashing one hand on the table and jutting his head forward, he yelled, 'That's none of your fucking business.' The poor newshound recoiled in shock. 'I thought Ford was going to nut me, but he immediately regained his composure.'

Publicity tours and press junkets are the worst, particularly when they cut into Ford's hard-earned free time. Few actors enjoy this type of ordeal. One day you might be in London, next Paris, then Tokyo, Sydney or New York. You never get to see much of the city because you're stuck in a hotel room all day long talking to an endless stream of reporters. Ford refers to them as 'cattle calls' and often finds it difficult to talk seriously about his work in such false surroundings or to avoid running through the sessions on automatic pilot. The publicity circus surrounding the *Star Wars* series was by far the actor's most uncomfortable experience. Shortly after the opening of *Star Wars*, Ford, Hamill and Fisher were invited on to a live talk show in Ford's home town of Chicago. It turned out to be a nightmare. The host had begun the evening all smiles, but when the show went on air his whole attitude changed and he turned on his guests. 'Let me begin', he started with, 'by saying that it's certainly *not* a great picture. In fact there's nothing great about it. The script isn't great and these actors are certainly not great.' Ford and co. sat there dumbstruck. 'We're listening to this,' Hamill recalled to *Starlog* in February 1979, 'and the three of us are just dying.' The host closed his speech by declaring that *Star Wars* was hardly in the same league as the work of Ingmar Bergman. 'I looked over at Harrison,' Hamill continued, 'and I could see the veins on his neck popping out.' Not finished yet, the host then had the audacity to produce his daughter and demand they give her their autographs. All on live TV. The subsequent promotional tour was just as horrendous and exhausting to boot, although Ford managed to stay in good humour throughout. According to Hamill, Ford acted as 'the publicity sheriff. He would give us report cards. "Humility – B. I like what you said about not being in the business for money – A for that." ' When it came round to *The Empire Strikes Back* Ford was too fatigued to grade anyone, himself included. The pace was demanding, particularly one three-day blitzkrieg on New York. 'We met a gross of journalists around a dozen tables, twelve at a time, and moved from one table to another, and so we did about 150 interviews in four hours,' Ford explained in the July 1980 issue of *Rolling Stone*. 'An hour off for lunch and then we came back and did fifteen TV interviews in four hours and then went back to our rooms and passed out.'

Ford's brother Terence is just as much of an enigma. Three years Harrison's junior, Terence has led a colourful and eccentric life. Both were raised in the Chicago suburbs of Morton Grove and Park Ridge, and like Harrison, Terence was a mediocre college student. By the early sixties he had developed a craving for drugs and alcohol which ruled his life for the next twenty-five years. 'Any substance that altered my mind, I took.' Moving to Hollywood in 1968, the freewheeling Terence rented an apartment downstairs from Harrison, before getting caught up in the hippie movement and joining a commune. (While Harrison was horsing around playing fake hippies on TV, his brother was the real McCoy.)

Born with a restless spirit, Terence travelled the world in search of his true self. He lived in Morocco, stayed at a Tibetan meditation centre in Scotland, wandered through India and Nepal and studied film in London. He also married twice, and divorced twice.

Returning to Los Angeles in the late seventies he worked as a commercial fisherman before getting his break in movies. This time it was behind the camera. He once even worked as an assistant on the set of *Blade Runner*. Harrison had nothing to do with the appointment, and when Terence decided to follow in his famous brother's footsteps and become an actor he never received the slightest practical help. You're on your own kid, was the clear message. Just like Harrison, Terence suffered a decade of struggling and hardship, but with the added disadvantage of living in the shadow of his superstar sibling. For years he barely scraped a living doing commercials and the odd bit part in television shows like *Dynasty* and *Beverly Hills 90210*. At one point, when he contemplated quitting altogether, it was actually Harrison who encouraged him to hang on and keep at it. His diligence was finally rewarded when he landed parts in a few continental films, moved to Paris and won a leading role in a trashy pan-European soap opera. He is naturally jealous of his brother's phenomenal fame: 'I cannot begrudge him one ounce of the success he has had. But it has been very difficult for me to watch it happen. Nevertheless, the two have managed to remain close friends and regularly call each other up for a chat. Terence, though, denies there is a family resemblance. 'The family joke is that there were different milkmen,' he told *People* in February 1992. 'But sooner or later everyone does seem to make the connection.'

In the true spirit of the Saturday morning serials, Lucas had deliberately left the fate of Han Solo unresolved at the close of *The Empire Strikes Back*. This and the film's general open-endedness caused consternation among circles of cinemagoers. Some felt cheated into having forked out their hard-earned money for an incomplete movie – with the double blow of having to wait an indeterminate length of time for the conclusion. The reason for such a monster of a cliffhanger was that the *Star Wars* saga had been ingeniously constructed in the form of a classic three-act play. Naturally, there were going to be questions raised in the second act which would have to be resolved in any final instalment. Ford's own defence was typically idiosyncratic. 'I guess it really depends on what you want to go to a movie for,' he told *Starlog* in July 1981. 'I figure that there was at least eleven dollars worth of entertainment in Empire. So, if you paid four bucks and didn't get an ending, you're still seven dollars ahead of the game.'

There may also have been a more sinister reason for leaving Solo/Ford in a state of suspended animation: Lucas's desire not to compromise himself by making the actors feel they were indispensable, particularly, it seemed, Ford. As Mark Hamill observed at the time. 'Look at what's happening to Harrison. He wasn't at all sure whether he wanted to repeat his role and he's not at all committed to doing it a third time. So George has left him in limbo and given himself the option. Solo is not vital to future stories. It's up to Harrison, I guess, as to whether Han comes back into the saga.' Fans were then treated to a repeat performance of the 'will he or won't he' fiasco that preceded *Empire*. Publicists were not letting on; the fate of Solo was clearly to be a closely guarded secret right up to première night. Leaving *Star Wars* purists to idly speculate that the space pirate survives his carbon freezing ordeal because he is the 'other one' of whom Yoda spoke, meaning a second budding *Jedi* warrior (actually this turned out to be Leia, who also happened to be Luke's twin sister. Note how this blood tie neatly cleared the way for the consummation of her romance with Solo), a deduction based on Solo's continuing personal growth in the series and undiminishing popularity. No one really expected Han Solo to spend the rest of eternity as a coffee table in the palace of galactic brigand Jabba the Hut and his rescue is the first order of business on *The Return of the Jedi* menu.

Ford was amused by all the rumour-mongering. 'Such contemplation', he mused, 'illustrates the value of the Star Wars concept'. However, the actor's personal views on the subject were ambivalent to say the least; and even his public pronouncements serve to illustrate his quiet antipathy towards the role by this stage. 'I just work here. I'm so confident in Lucas' control of the story that I really don't spend a second thinking about what direction Han Solo should go in.' Well at least for the next six months. After the blood and sweat spilt making *Blade Runner* Ford announced he was taking a half-year break, more time off from films than he could remember since quitting acting to be a carpenter. He wanted to spend it with his family, relaxing and pottering about at home. For Melissa and himself it was the first time in two years that they'd been able to spend any real 'quality' time together. 'It would take an act of congress to get me to work before Jedi,' he declared.

Morally Ford was committed to seeing the trilogy through to the bitter end. Professionally he was bored sick of Han Solo. The thought of playing him a third time was not at all appealing, given his loathing for safe, repetitious, formula acting. Granted he owed Solo a great deal, and *Star Wars* had launched his career, but whereas his return in *Empire* was a welcome opportunity to salvage something from a particularly bleak period in his life, an appearance in *The Return of the Jedi* would only be a backward step. Perhaps out of a sense of loyalty to Lucas Ford finally agreed to don his blaster one last time. 'If I hadn't made other movies in between,' he conceded, 'I might have felt differently about coming back, but as it stands I'm delighted to be in on the third act. In any case, I. don't condemn sequels when they're done with the pride that George brings to them.'

Nevertheless, Ford's involvement in yet another comic-strip extravaganza hung over him like a black cloud throughout production. Under these circumstances, it is perhaps not surprising that Ford's major contribution to the plot was to insist that Solo be killed off. He gave credence to his argument by concluding that Solo's death would lend the trilogy some desperately needed depth. Lucas needless to say, was against the idea. One suspects that Ford's real motive was to bring an end to the past, close the chapter on Solo forever and press on with new challenges. In any case, Ford's general attitude resulted in his giving what is unquestionably the worst major performance of his career. He is simply terrible in *Jedi*. Those cute faces and mischievous grins he pulled in the two previous films are here embarrassingly irritating. After his superb achievement in *Empire*, which showed that a cardboard character like Han Solo could be made real and believable, this wooden, lazy portrayal is a big let-down. 'Harrison Ford gives a shallow performance that mostly consists of grotesque mugging,' wrote *Cinefantastique*. 'It's his most bone-headed performance ever.' For the first time in the series Ford was out-acted and outclassed by a maturing Mark Hamill.

Filming began on *The Return of the Jedi* on 11 January 1982 at the usual place, EMI's Elstree studios, earth base of the *Star Wars* saga and Ford's home from home. This time Lucas funnelled his ideas through new boy Richard Marquand. (The Welsh-born director was reportedly selected after a nine-month search, after David Lynch turned Lucas down.) Once again, all nine sound stages were fully exploited, filled to capacity with a variety of eye-popping sets. Throne chambers and rebel briefing rooms rose phoenix-like from the debris of other sets, torn down and discarded once work on them had been completed. The real superstructures were housed on the $600,000 *Star Wars* stage: Jabba the Hut's gargantuan Tatooine desert palace, succeeded by the gleaming docking bay of the new improved Death Star.

Seventy-eight fervid days at Elstree were followed by a stressful period of location work. Lucas's decision, welcomed by Ford, to make use of American sites for the first time in the series called for near-ludicrous security arrangements. First stop was Buttercup Valley in the Arizona desert, where sand dunes, stripped clean of vegetation to attain the barren, arid look of Tatooine, stretched as far as the eye could see. To deter reporters and curious citizens everyone masqueraded as players in a bogus film project entitled 'Blue Harvest'. Crew members wore T-shirts sporting the banner 'Horror beyond imagination'. Midway through the second week the ruse was discovered by the *Los Angeles Times* and crowds began to gather. Fans of Harrison Ford caused the most nuisance, and would scream incessantly whenever their idol came into view.

Battered by sixty-mile-per-hour sandstorms, which disrupted the shoot for two days, the unit left the heat of Buttercup Valley and moved on to its final live action port of call. This was Crescent City in northern California, resplendent with towering forests of Redwood. Among these awesome trees Marquand staged the triumphant climactic battle between the imperial stormtroopers and the rebels on the moon of Endor.

For everyone concerned, the filming of *Jedi* was akin to senior year in high school. This was particularly so for the three leading principals, who approached the final chapter with mixed emotions. On the one hand they were relieved to be finally finished with it all, but at the same time they lamented the loss of friendships and working alliances built up over six years. When production wrapped up on 20 May there were no regrets, only bright hopes for the future. *The Return of the Jedi* closed the book on Han Solo once and for all. 'I had great fun doing it,' Ford said at the time. 'I'm glad I did all three of them. But, as well, I'm glad I don't have to do any more'. The first to admit that Solo was a one-dimensional character, Ford had the enviably more stimulating film persona of Indiana Jones to fall back on. Judging from the fan mail he received, Indy was amassing an even bigger following of hero worshippers than Han Solo. 'Solo is no longer the only stamp in my professional passport,' he joyfully declared. 'But somehow he has become part of me.' The *Star Wars* series had been a firm grounding for Ford to build from. Its success enabled him to pick and choose from among a greater variety of high-quality scripts. Today he admits to not particularly liking the Star Wars trilogy. 'And my son Malcolm is more of an Indiana Jones buff.'

Ford has remained on good terms with both his co-stars, particularly Fisher, and they share many of the same friends. 'In any encounter he's always the senior and you're always the freshman,' Fisher told *North Shore* magazine in May 1990. 'I think he always felt I was too loud, a little out of control, and he's the kind of guy who'd kick me under the table or fix me with a withering look to let me know it. I respect Harrison. He's well read, thoughtful. Just don't wear the wrong clothes around him, because then he'll get you. At times like those, he turns into your dad.' Hamill, in an interview for *Prevue* in October 1983, spoke of his admiration for Ford's professional qualities. 'He has still not received the recognition he deserves as an actor. He's a very funny guy, witty and spontaneous. It's difficult for me to separate my admiration for the character of Han Solo and for Harrison Ford. Maybe, because in our relationship, it's very easy for me to look up to him. That's part of Lucas's genius, casting actors who are close to their characters. Harrison has always been very strong and supportive. "Hey kid," he'd say. "Your part's much tougher than mine." He's very gracious that way.'

Fortunately for Ford the *Jedi* shoot proceeded relatively smoothly. In London the pace was frenzied, at times beating Spielberg's *Raiders* record for the number of camera set-ups in one day. Like Kershner, Marquand was very much an actor's director, having once trod the boards himself. This was a factor much appreciated by Ford, and the two got on well. 'Ford is a pure cinema actor,' said Marquand. 'He works beautifully with the camera. He doesn't suffer fools gladly. If you don't know what you're going to do on the day he gets a little confused and upset. But he's terrific as an ally, someone who understands the craft of being a movie actor.' Four years after the release of *Jedi* Marquand died of a heart attack, aged only forty-nine.

Dispelling the murky, sombre mood of *The Empire Strikes Back*, Marquand was determined that the third and final chapter would be a return to the simple fairy-tale elegance of *Star Wars*. But like the last of the Indiana Jones trilogy, *Jedi* simply reeks of creative fatigue. The sterility of repetition has replaced inspiration. The final *Star Wars* film has all the emotional warmth of a dollar bill. Even the script by Lawrence Kasdan – lured out of retirement from the series by Lucas is an inferior pastiche of all the earlier classic cliff-hanging stuff. The sail barge is an elaborate update of Luke's landspeeder; the alien cabaret at Jabba's lair is a re-run of the famous cantina scene; and there's another Luke *v*. Vader light sabre duel. The most blatant piece of imitation is the rebel attack on the new Death Star. While admittedly a marvel of special effects and a breathtaking visual feast, it's nothing more than a replay of the climax to *Star Wars*. Everything in *Jedi* is bigger and more spectacular than before, but not necessarily better. Critically *Jedi* was the worst received of the three, and justly so. 'Resoundingly hollow and rootless' – *New Statesman*; 'a draggy epic, the least entertaining of the series' – *Evening Standard*. The *Sunday Telegraph* referred to it as 'muppets in space'. Lucas does have a bad case of 'the cutes' in *Jedi*. Teddy bears and other equally unconvincing nursery-room creatures contaminate the screen in nauseating numbers.

Public enthusiasm for arguably the most eagerly awaited sequel in film history was predictable and incredible. On opening day, 25 May 1983, $6 million worth of movie tickets were sold, then an all-time industry high. By the end of the first week *Jedi* had grossed an amazing $45 million. The film soon rocketed up the all-time charts to third position, behind *ET* and *Star Wars*, relegating *Empire* to a lowly fourth. By 1984 then, the *Star Wars* trilogy occupied the second, third and fourth spots on the list of the ten most lucrative motion pictures in history, while the Indiana Jones movies were nicely settled in at eighth and ninth place. This meant that George Lucas had his name attached to five of the ten most popular films ever. And for that matter so did Harrison Ford. He was now the most successful actor that had ever lived.

With *Return of the Jedi* the variety of dangling plot threads which had kept audiences bewitched, bothered and excited for six years were finally resolved, to the satisfaction of some, to the dismay of others. It was the big finish and, as expected, Lucas settled for the easiest and simplest solutions. No major twists or surprises. As in all traditional fairy tales everything is brought to a neat and logical conclusion.

Since then, nothing. His promise of two further trilogies has not been forthcoming. The first, chapters one to three of the saga, would chronicle the Clone Wars with a young Obi Wan and Darth Vader. Both Spielberg and John Milius have expressed interest in directing segments, but the project remains dead on the drawing board. Instead Lucas has chosen to churn out rubbish like *Howard the Duck* and devise theme-park attractions. He is apparently happy to wash his hands of the enterprise that made him a very rich man. In doing so he has let one of the greatest merchandising bonanzas in motion picture history peter out and ignored the pleas of loyal fans, who have been waiting patiently for the next instalment. Is it a lack of interest on his part or, as is more likely, a lack of vision. *Star Wars*, after all, is not so much a Lucas invention as it is a synthesis of standard science-fiction themes. Behind all that hi-tech razzle-dazzle lurk some pretty old-fashioned themes to do with sacrifice, self-mortification and redemption. Good always triumphs over evil in Lucas's universe, and even the worst sinner (Vader) can be redeemed. Such simple optimism perhaps no longer has a place in these cynical and corrupt modern times.

The whole *Star Wars* saga evokes and promotes the romance and adventure of space. It is probably a pointless exercise to criticize the trilogy, with its illogical plots, simplistic ideas, stereotyped characters and insufferable cuteness. For one cannot help but admire the films sheer bravura and dazzling pyrotechnics. I have no doubt that the two remaining trilogies will eventually surface, in some form or another. 'Star Wars IV' has not been completely ruled out, though even the most diehard optimists can't see anything happening until 1997/8 at the earliest.

'We've been together for four years,' Ford told the *Daily Mail* in September 1982. 'But I won't even be quoted on saying that I don't know whether we'll get married or not.' Six months after making this statement Ford tied the knot with Melissa Mathison. It was his idea. Both were content merely living together until thoughts of starting a family of their own were raised. Ford then felt it proper that they should marry. 'Harry's old fashioned that way,' said Melissa. The ceremony took place in Santa Monica on 14 March 1983 behind closed doors and in the utmost secrecy. The whole ritual lasted just fifteen minutes and was carried out by a judge in his chambers. The couple presented one another with white roses, exchanged vows, kissed, then sped away in Ford's black Porsche.

This was a perfect match. 'We respect each other considerably,' Ford said, 'both as professionals and as people.' Ford had no intention of blowing it a second time. It helped that Melissa was herself an extremely highly-regarded professional and, unlike Mary, had grown up in a showbusiness environment. She was used to operating in the industry and so was sympathetic to its foibles and the enormous pressure brought to bear upon those in the front line. One of five children, Melissa was raised in the old, undeveloped Hollywood Hills, where jackrabbits and coyotes once prowled. 'It used to be a great town,' she remembers. 'My mother used to let us off on Hollywood Boulevard to play! Now you'd never see your child again.' Although heralding from the West coast, Melissa can scarcely be described as the model Californian citizen. She's athletic looking without being glamorous – with a fine sense of humour. She is also as bashful as Ford can be about success. It was while she was visiting Ford on the Tunisian location for *Raiders* that Spielberg asked Melissa to write *ET*. Actually he had pitched the idea to her a month or so before over dinner in London, having been impressed with the writer's work on Francis Ford Coppola's *The Black Stallion*. Melissa thought the story sounded charming, but declined the offer. 'I've just decided never to write again,' she told him. 'I've just read through some of my recent stuff and decided it's time I looked for another line of work.' Back in Tunisia the subject of *ET* was raised again one afternoon, and this time Melissa said yes. According to Spielberg, Mathison was eighty per cent heart and twenty per cent logic. 'It took her sensitivity and my know-how to make ET.' She began work on 10 October 1980 and within eight weeks a first draft was ready, one of the best Spielberg had ever read. The rest came comparatively easily, and on finishing typing the final page she was overcome with emotion.

With the phenomenal success of *ET* Melissa suddenly found herself in the position of 'celebrity writer'. But although this new status was not welcomed by her, Ford claims that Melissa is better at dealing with fame than he is. Both have often ruled out the possibility of ever collaborating on a movie together, although they have come close to doing so on a few occasions. Ford admits that starring in a film scripted by his wife would be tempting, but is afraid that working so closely with her might cause friction. It is easier, he believes, to maintain working relationships with professional associates. If you start to bring your private life into your work life there's a danger you might muddy the waters. Instead husband and wife prefer their separate careers, occasionally seeking one another's help and counsel. When Melissa goes to a press show for one of Ford's films she goes as his wife – not as a screenwriter. 'But if she doesn't like me in something, she's usually got a damn good reason. And usually she's right.' Equally Ford prefers not to intrude on her career as a writer, though he takes Melissa's opinion into account with every script that he seriously considers.

After a decade of marriage Ford credits Melissa as having helped him to become a better person. 'Melissa probably wouldn't say that I was easy to live with,' he told *Redbook* in a rare moment of candour in August 1989. 'But I think she'd say that I'm easier to live with now than when she first met me. And I certainly give her some of the credit for my change. She sets a good example. She's a happy person. I don't express happiness, perhaps, as much as I should. There was a time when I was worried about losing my anger, worried that losing that edge would hurt my work. But when I married Melissa, I found that it was such a pleasure not to be angry and not to have that bitterness running around in my system.' No longer was he so prone to those bouts of moodiness and aggression that conspired to bring down his first marriage. 'I don't get crazy anymore.' With Melissa's help Ford managed to work out most of his emotional kinks.

Even before pen had touched paper the plan was to make *Indiana Jones and the Temple of Doom* a 'prequel' rather than a sequel and, in many respects, unrelated to *Raiders of the Lost Ark*. Ford would be the only actor in the new picture to repeat his role. Behind the scenes, though, there was little change. Most of the creative team who had worked on Indy's inaugural adventure were back for this one. Executive producer Frank Marshall and producer Robert Watts had worked in similar capacities on *Raiders*. Marshall was also involved on *ET*, while Watts cut his teeth on the *Star Wars* trilogy. Britain's master lensman Douglas Slocombe was back, as were the best stuntmen in the business: Glen Randall and Vic Armstrong. And there was David Tomblin, acknowledged as the best first assistant director working today (his credits include stints with *The Prisoner*, *Superman* and James Bond films), who was ecstatic about the new venture. 'I think it'll be seen in thirty, forty years time as one of the cinema classics.' Spielberg had earlier turned down the offer to direct *Temple of Doom*, saying that he would instead seek some minor peripheral role. However, he changed his tune dramatically after a four-day brainstorming session with Lucas in which the basic concept of *Temple of Doom* emerged. 'I can see it already,' the director enthused, 'and I'd hate to let it slip through my fingers into someone else's hands. I won't be involved in the third or fourth ones [prophetic words indeed], but I really want to do the follow-up.'

Ford felt much the same, although he had hoped to take a year off between the two Lucas blockbusters. But the endless promotional tour for *Blade Runner* added several months on to his schedule. Ford was also disturbed to learn that Lucasfilm was planning three more Indy films after *Temple of Doom*. 'They must be talking to Roger Moore then,' he quipped. 'One at a time for me.' Ford was fast developing an enviable problem: every film he starred in spawned sequels faster than *Rocky*, in spite of his desire not to end up as 'king of the sequels'. And most of these follow-up movies seemed to turn into trilogies – *Star Wars*, Indiana Jones and now even the unworthy Jack Ryan (in the *Patriot Games* series).

With Ford and Spielberg safely contracted Lucas had to find himself a writer. Lawrence Kasdan's absence left a gaping hole. His debt paid with the *Jedi* script, Kasdan was now embarking upon a directorial career, happy to consign his association with the fantasy world of Lucas to the cupboard drawer marked 'past'. Dipping into his own past Lucas turned in February 1982 to his old *American Graffiti* colleagues, Gloria Katz and Willard Huyck. Their preliminary briefing took place over a long weekend at the Lucas ranch. In the first hour George told them exactly what he wanted. *Indiana Jones and the Temple of Doom* was, by its very title, to be a darker tale, containing frightening elements of black magic. The story was to begin in Shanghai, moving then on to India, where Jones comes upon a dying village with tales of stolen magical rocks and children forced into slavery by an evil cult. All hogwash, of course, but that was the basic outline: Katz and Huyck's job was to fill in the gaps.

To help them there were a couple of extraordinary scenes deleted from Kasdan's script for *Raiders*, which the two new writers cunningly grafted on to their own scenario. In *Raiders* the headpiece of the staff of Ra (the key to the location of the lost Ark) was originally broken up into pieces and scattered to different points of the globe. One half was owned by the Karen Allen character (the owner of the entire medallion in the film), while the remainder was kept in the Shanghai museum of an evil Chinese warlord, General Hok. Leaving America, Indy flies direct to the oriental seaport and breaks into Hok's fortress, careful not to disturb a devilish alarm system, part of which is a ten-foot diameter gong. Enter two imposing Samurais, one of whom Indy swiftly shoots; the other he fights, pitting his whip against the warrior's razor-sharp sword. Jones wins, of course, strangling his opponent. Taking the fallen Samurai's sword Indy breaks open the glass cabinet containing the medallion half, setting off the gong alarm. Hok scurries in brandishing a machine gun and begins firing indiscriminately. Our hero quickly manages to push the gong off its hook and rolls it across the floor, running behind it, using it as a shield. The sheer weight of the object cracks the marble flooring. This would have made a tremendous action set piece, but unfortunately was deleted from the script due to time and money problems. Doesn't it sound familiar though? That gong idea eventually wound up in *Temple of Doom*'s clever opening sequence set at the Obi Wan nightclub in Shanghai.

Another rejected *Raiders* idea was reworked more extensively by Katz and Huyck. On leaving Shanghai Indy takes a DC-3 to Nepal to locate Marion. On board there's the usual complement of passengers: a few tourists, a little old lady, some Asians *en route* home. But it's all an elaborate trap and while Indy sleeps everyone on board grabs every available parachute and jumps out of the aeroplane. Indy wakes to discover the cockpit locked and the aircraft on a collision course with a mountain range. Pulling out a rubber life-raft, he wraps it around his body, leaps from the plane, pulls the inflater cord in midair and lands safely on the snowy Himalayan peaks. Using the raft as a sled Indy rides down the slopes all the way to Marion's bar. Preposterous, but exhilarating.

Katz and Huyck wrote the first version of their script in a breathless six weeks, and the next two drafts were completed within three months. Following revisions, the screenplay was handed to Ford who wanted to see more humour and character refinement. Both writers were grateful to him for his help and assistance. 'We did go through the script from Indy's point of view with Harrison and he made many fine suggestions; he wanted a rationale behind every scene.' Ford was relatively satisfied with the extent to which Katz and Huyck had tried to humanize Indy. Hitherto unrevealed aspects of his nature are explored in *Temple of Doom*. Generally speaking, he's less selfish in the prequel, and more considerate towards others. From conception there were continual questions about how much of a scoundrel to make Indy – for example, whether he pursues his archaeology for profit or for the enrichment of science. In this respect *Temple of Doom* is very much a test of Indy's will: Should he take the sacred stone back to the States with him as booty or return it to the villagers, who obviously need it more than him?

It was Lucas's intention to open *Temple of Doom* in mid-action, like the first film, almost as if the audience had stumbled onto the last reel of a previous adventure (a clever steal from the 007 series). But unlike *Raiders*, *Temple of Doom* begins not in some steamy jungle, but a glamorous night club. Here Indy – decked out, uncharacteristically, in a white tuxedo – clashes with a gang of Chinese mobsters in a brilliantly choreographed fight scene that starts off the film in blistering fashion. It also serves as an introduction to the two important new characters who share in this adventure. Kate Capshaw's hysterical dumb blonde Willie Scott is nicely played, but must rank as a major disappointment as a character. Compared to Karen Allen's spunky firebrand, she's a real wimp, screaming and whining at each and every horrific encounter.

Infinitely more appealing is 'Short Round', Indy's young Chinese sidekick, played by twelve-year-old Ke Huy Quan, who was plucked out of hundreds of hopefuls by Spielberg. Quan had never seen *Raiders of the Lost Ark* and was unfamiliar with the men who brought the Indiana Jones myth to life on the screen. He hadn't even heard of Harrison Ford, although he had seen *Star Wars*. 'I had heard of Han Solo before, but I didn't know his real name was Harrison Ford.' Ford took the young Quan under his wing during filming, personally coaching him and even teaching the youngster tricks with the bullwhip. But it was Spielberg's magical touch with children that ensured a winning performance. Short Round is a wonderful creation, a miniature Indiana Jones, unfearing, resourceful and totally loyal. A virginal young princess was originally proposed to interact with Indy but gave way to the charms of this oriental street urchin. Short Round is named after the writer's dog, a fifteen-year-old Sheltie, and since Lucas got to name Indiana Jones after his pet Malamute, it seemed only fair. Spielberg too got into the act, naming Willie Scott after his Cocker Spaniel. Doubtless the namers found the joke a good deal more amusing than the named!

From the nightclub Indy is chased through the crowded, narrow streets and back alleys of a pre-war Shanghai, in reality the city of Macao, on China's southern coast. Managing to evade his pursuers Indy, Willie and Short Round arrive at the Pan American terminal of Shanghai airport. There to greet the weary archaeologist is Dan Aykroyd, just one of numerous cameo appearances sprinkled throughout this scene. Frank Marshall, who played the pilot of the flying wing in *Raiders*, pops up again, this time as a coolie pulling a rickshaw. And look closely next time at the two missionaries waiting for the aeroplane; none other than messrs Spielberg and Lucas.

The main bulk of location filming was carried out in tropical Sri Lanka, formerly the British colony of Ceylon, and home of science-fiction novelist Arthur C. Clarke, whom Spielberg and Ford made a point of visiting whilst guests on the island. Chosen for its beautiful foliage and picturesque terrain, one of *Temple of Doom*'s major set-pieces, involving a rickety rope bridge spanning a deep gorge, was filmed here. Indiana Jones is trapped in the middle of the bridge, while fanatical followers of Mola Ram, an evil priest, guard each end. As there is no other possible course of action Indy cuts the bridge in half, clings tightly to the vines, bounces off the cliff opposite like a rag doll and clambers to the top in defiance of all probability. The scene called for Ford, who declined the use of a stunt double, to walk on to the suspension. Asked by one of the crew how he intended summoning up the courage to stand on the precariously swaying bridge with a 250-foot sheer drop, Ford rubbed his stubbly chin, cracked a rakish grin and paraphrased a *Raiders* retort that is characteristically Indy. 'How should I know? I'm making this up as I go along.' Ford had convinced a nervous Spielberg that there was no danger involved. 'So before anyone could do anything I just ran across it. In fact, it was dangerous as hell.' By sheer good fortune a British engineering team was constructing a massive hydro-electric dam further down river and were more than willing to lend a hand building the 300-foot suspension as a diversion, thereby saving the production money and precious manhours.

Although conditions were more tolerable than those in Tunisia, both the cast and the highly efficient, mostly British, crew of 120 worked a punishing six-day week, filming from 7.30 am till dusk. Lucas, the film's guiding light, visited the location for a short time; otherwise he seemed content enough to leave everything in the capable hands of Spielberg, though he did act as a catalyst to his director's wild imagination. In any case, he was far too busy putting the finishing touches to *The Return of the Jedi* and so was never around quite as much during shooting as he was on *Raiders*.

Once again the perils facing the stunt team were hair-raising and, as was the case on *Raiders*, Ford ended up being the main casualty. Undeterred by his previous narrow escapes, he continued to handle most of his own stuntwork. 'As long as I can still fall down with some reasonable assurance that I'll get up again, I don't worry,' he told the *Sunday Telegraph* in May 1984. But nagging doubts did surface about whether his tired old body could continue to withstand such beatings. Were his days in heavy action roles numbered? 'I'm almost looking forward to getting older parts that won't call for me to be bounced off walls every ten minutes.' (This was a prophetic statement, since, after *Temple of Doom*, Ford made six non-action dramas in a row, breaking out of his new suit-and-tie persona only once during that period, and then to play Indiana Jones one last time.)

The problem in Tunisia had been stomach bugs; in Sri Lanka it was elephants. The four wild elephants acquired from a nearby animal 'orphanage' proved unwilling collaborators and were hard to ride, as Ford discovered to his cost. Astride the beasts for hours at a time, when the camera finally stopped rolling he would drop from the animal's neck and collapse in a heap under the nearest shady tree. 'Those brutes are harder to ride than camels,' he told the writer William Hall.

Exertions of this kind aggravated an old back problem, and by the time the unit returned to wet and windy Elstree Ford was in such pain that Spielberg had no alternative but to send him back home for urgent attention. The Centimela Hospital in Los Angeles, sports injuries specialists, immediately diagnosed the problem as being a ruptured disc, a complaint normally treated by a painful operation known as a laminectomy. Instead doctors tried a revolutionary new technique, involving an enzyme derived from Papaya fruit. When injected into the body it eats away at the disc, like an acid. Remarkably it worked, although Ford was ordered to rest – which resulted in the near closure of production and an insurance bill in excess of $1 million.

A month later he was back in the studio, thankful that all the elephant riding was over, but aware that some of the most strenuous stunts of all were still to come. 'They'd saved up all the good bits until last.' Much of the strain fell on his stunt double. Vic Armstrong, who bears such an uncanny resemblance to Ford that the actor once told him: 'We could go home to the wrong wives and they wouldn't notice!' Even Spielberg used to get the pair muddled up on the set of *Raiders*, and on location for *Indiana Jones and the Last Crusade* Ford's youngest son Malcolm sometimes referred to Armstrong as 'Daddy'. 'We really are spitting images,' Armstrong said to American journalist Tim Ewbank. During the years of working together (Armstrong has doubled for Ford on all the Indy movies as well as *Blade Runner* and *Jedi*), a friendship has grown. 'Harrison's a really super guy. The man you see on screen is the man you see in real life. He's an absolute perfectionist. When you go to his house he'll spend the first hour showing you the new furniture he's made and how perfect the dovetails are.' Ford acknowledged that he could never have done [*Temple of Doom*] without Armstrong.

On his return Ford's grit and sheer professionalism in the face of adversity won him much admiration. It was evident as he tackled the complex fight routines that he had not fully recovered from his wrenched back and was in great distress. Yet he forced himself to continue in painful circumstances without displaying an ounce of self-pity. According to Pat Roach, who in *Temple of Doom* plays the head guard who comes to grief in a rock crusher, Ford just got on with the job at hand and never complained. In an interview for the June 1988 issue of *Starlog* Roach revealed that in order to lighten the mood on set the crew played a practical joke on their star. Chained to a rock and about to be flogged, Ford's mouth fell open when he saw Barbra Streisand stroll in, dressed in kinky black leather and holding a whip, which she proceeded to unleash upon his unprotected back. 'That's for *Hanover Street*,' she bellowed. 'The worst movie I ever saw.' Then she whipped him again for making *Star Wars* and earning all that money. Suddenly in rushed Carrie Fisher who flung herself across Harrison shouting, 'No, no, no!' Enter Irvin Kershner who sauntered up to Spielberg and in deadpan fashion said, 'Is this the way you run your movies? I would never let this happen on one of my sets!' Playfully, Spielberg ordered Kershner out of the studio. 'They filmed it,' said Roach. 'And I think they sent it back to Hollywood. It was hilarious.'

Fortunately Ford suffered no permanent damage to his spine, primarily because he was in the peak of physical fitness. As the character of Indiana Jones was younger in *Temple of Doom* (the tale is set a year before *Raiders*), Ford underwent a three-month period of training and muscle building with 'Body by Jake' (Jake Steinfeld), at Spielberg's request, to get his 'old man's body' into shape. It needed to be, for *Temple of Doom* was certainly Ford's toughest film ordeal thus far. Ford liked to joke that the hardest thing about playing Indy was 'keeping that hat on the whole time'. They would actually use double-sided tape to keep the fedora from slipping off.

With principal photography completed by early September 1983, after eighty-five days on the Indy trail, post-production work continued at a frenetic pace at Lucasfilm's Marin County facility. The film had to be ready in time for its scheduled Memorial Day opening, by now the traditional date for the annual Lucas/Spielberg blockbusters. Ford, too, was rubbing his hands in anticipation. 'George is a very practical and conscientious filmmaker and Steven is one of the best directors alive today,' he told *Prevue* in August 1984. 'They are my allies. I have no fear they'll muck it up. The only anxiety I feel is like … like I'm waiting for Christmas. I want to see the finished film as much as anyone else.'

Rather predictably *Indiana Jones and the Temple of Doom* was the runaway hit of the year. 'Exuberantly tasteless and entertaining, endearingly disgusting and violent. Ford gives an exceptionally skilful comic performance' – *New York Times*; 'When it comes to thrills this is easily the best sustained idiot-adventure movie in history' – *New York*. Thirteen million Americans happily surrendered to Spielberg's manipulative extravaganza in its first week, more than had attended *Jedi* in the same period the previous summer. What no one expected was the furore over the film's allegedly gratuitous use of violence. Anxious parents and moral groups complained that the horrors on show, including human sacrifice, scenes of torture, flogging and cruelty directed towards children, were too strong for its PG rating. The British board of film censors was quick to agree, demanding that some cuts be made before the movie could be shown to family audiences in the UK. On the defensive, Spielberg admitted on live television that the temple sequences, in particular, were unsuitable for ten-year-olds and under. Running scared over the issue, Paramount put out a warning: 'This film may be too intense for younger children.'

When told of Paramount's decision Ford commented, 'I think that's fair enough'. Moreover, he was keen to put the violence in context. 'This is a completely moral tale and in order to have a moral resolve, evil must be seen to inflict pain. The end of the movie is proof of the viability of goodness. But I do not like films that use violence in a reprehensible way. I do not seek out movies that are bathed in blood.' Deep down, however, Ford did feel that the violence went too far, an opinion shared by Spielberg. Lucas, on the other hand, remained unrepentant. It was always his intention to make *Temple of Doom* a frightening, malevolent experience. If *Raiders* was the jungle ride at Disneyland, the prequel was a trip through the haunted house. Today he feels it might have worked even better had more comedy been employed, 'but we set out to make a scary film and I think we succeeded'.

While there is clearly a sadistic undercurrent at play – the camera does seem to linger on all the torture and abuse – the accusations of depraved violence were exaggerated. Everyone knows that children love being scared out of their breeches and are probably more capable of differentiating between real violence and fantasy violence than we give them credit for. One also tended to forget that *Raiders* was just as savage, with its graphic fight scenes and mounting corpses; but it was cartoon violence whereas *Temple of Doom* was darker and more acute. A story showing children in jeopardy was always going to create a greater emotional reaction than a story featuring Indy knocking seven bells out of the Third Reich.

What some critics found inexcusable, especially in a film aimed at a massive youth market, was the frankly racist treatment of ethnic minorities. Much humour, for instance, is made of the unspeakable delicacies that Indian wallahs serve up at a banquet, like monkey brains. Even the honourable village folk, who are made to look like lepers from hell, force our brave white hero to gulp down inedible slop. Indy's exploits in the Third World reek of the xenophobic and sexist pieties paraded in Hollywood films of the *Gunga Din* era. *Raiders* had worked so perfectly because it mainly avoided the pitfalls of sexism and racism inherent in the old imperialist serials it was parodying, and Ford was most apologetic when challenged at a London press conference over the prequel's 'Boy's Own' stereotyping. 'I have absolute sympathy with those criticisms. If that was so it's regrettable and to be guarded against next time. I don't want to be outwardly racist but movies are dependent on stereotypes. But I'm sorry that occurred and I'll use what power I have to make sure it doesn't happen again'.

While less memorable than *Raiders*, and less pleasingly light-spirited than *Crusade*, *Temple of Doom* is nevertheless a brilliantly crafted technical masterpiece. Arguably, the movie was on a losing wicket even before the Paramount logo hit the screen. Not only was this a prequel to one of the most successful films in recent times, but Spielberg and Lucas had been placed in the unenviable position of having to outdo their past glories with each new release. It was a problem the Bond series faced: each action set-piece and fancy gadget had to be better and more incredible than the last. And so it was with Indiana Jones. Audience expectation was so impossibly high that all of *Temple of Doom*'s flaws were magnified. While Ford's engaging performance helps to transform a feeble script, he cannot carry the comparatively daft and uninvolving plot. Whereas in *Raiders* he used his wits in an archaeological hunt, here Indy stumbles upon the treasure almost by accident and basically strong-arms his way through a succession of obstacles and villains placed conveniently in his path. Indy never has to use his brain in *Temple of Doom* as he was forced to in *Raiders*, just his fists. And where *Raiders* partially succeeded in suspending disbelief in unprobable surroundings, in *Temple of Doom* the boundaries of credulity are dangerously stretched. Indy jumps out of an aeroplane with only an inflated rubber raft to cushion his fall of several thousand feet; and a mine car leaps across a missing section of track and lands with a precision no space shuttle crew could achieve on the rails opposite. Both examples sum up the kind of derring-do served up. Yet it is all done with such dazzling bravado that we can't help but find ourselves swallowing everything.

10

Beyond the Edge of Comfort

The peaceful folk, heads bowed in humility, and dressed in plain, dark clothes, process silently over the green hills to attend the wake of a young colleague. Through wheatfields and shimmering meadows, alive with the colours of the season, the wind sends a languorous wave that might be the dead man's passing spirit. Horse-drawn carriages traverse the frame, passing the mourners as they steer their inevitable course down a sloping dirt track towards an outcrop of humble farm buildings. A cunningly delayed subtitle informs us that the place and year is 'Pennsylvania – 1984). We are not looking at the past, but the present. So begins *Witness*.

This carefully orchestrated opening deliberately serves to echo the days of the early settler in the land of opportunity, for the people depicted are Amish, a rural fundamentalist community who emigrated to America from Europe in the 1700s. In their secluded world time has literally stood still. Here, the hollow materialism of 20th-century life has been contemptuously rejected, along with all its modern inventions. Amish farms are relatively self-sufficient; each home is free of telephones, televisions, washing machines, and all manner of goods that we find so indispensable. They even speak their own language, a form of low German, administer their own law, wear a peculiar mode of dress and still refer to all outsiders as 'English'. It was to be this very exclusivity that brought the Amish into conflict with modern Hollywood.

The rather unfortunately named town of Intercourse is situated in Lancaster County, Pennsylvania, on Route 340. Tourists flock every year to this charming region just to have their postcards hand-stamped at Intercourse post office or pay exorbitant prices for a T-shirt which proudly proclaims 'I love Intercourse PA'. Seeing such vulgarity at close quarters one would be forgiven for thinking the gentle, God-fearing Amish have the right idea in shutting out the modern world. The tourists are viewed with disdain here – a necessary evil. In time the Amish have reluctantly grown accustomed to having their privacy

121

invaded by busloads of daytrippers, who arrived to gawp at their 'quaint' customs and who help to feed a $287 million-a-year tourist industry.

But patience with the outside world snapped when a Hollywood film unit arrived in Lancaster County with the expressed intention of using the Amish as the backcloth to a violent movie thriller. A feeling of anger underpinned by fear and suspicion began to spread through the Amish community, whipped up to a fever pitch by the local press, which gleefully painted Hollywood as a vile ogre bent on exploiting Amish culture. More controversy followed. Afraid their way of life would be mocked or misrepresented the Amish elders warned their flock to stay away from the location sites and to give no assistance in the making of the film. From day one *Witness* was condemned by the very people it sought to understand and portray with objectivity and dignity.

A living past coexisting with a decaying present was the kernel from which the story of *Witness* grew. The picture mirrors a conflict the Amish face every day: the confrontation of disparate cultures. For although the sect has little to do with our society, they do not hide from it either. The Amish of Lancaster County, for example, live just sixty miles from Philadelphia. Ford immediately responded to the unique qualities of the scenario. In truth, and Ford knew this to be so, the script didn't really have an original bone in its body. The basic premise – innocent child witnesses brutal murder, police corruption and so on – was straight out of the television cop show cupboard. 'It was a stupid, overly violent script,' Ford told *Moviegoer* in December 1986. 'I would never have done it if Peter Weir and I hadn't been given the chance to rework it.' But what raised the film above the average thriller was the novelty of its setting. In protecting the child witness, a young Amish boy, and his mother Rachel (Kelly McGillis), Ford's city cop John Book seeks sanctuary in a cloistered, arcadian farming community. The culture-shock experienced by his character lends the film a spiritual quality and a moral context, 'something that few films bother about these days,' sighed Ford. Without the Amish serving as a kind of civilizing force, *Witness* would have been the usual indulgent mix of excitement and bloodletting.

The actor was in the midst of filming *Temple of Doom* when producer Edward Feldman sent him the script for *Witness* (then provisionally entitled *Called Home*), by the television writers Earl W. Wallace and William Kelly. Deliberating on whom to cast in the lead role of John Book, a tough, hard-bitten detective, Feldman was reminded of Gary Cooper in *Friendly Persuasion*, William Wyler's classic western of 1956. 'I thought of Cooper wearing that Quaker outfit,' Feldman joyfully mused to the *New York Times* in February 1985, 'and I asked myself, who today is a reactive kind of actor who would also look funny in an outfit like that?' Ford immediately sprang to mind and was duly offered the part.

Now a *bona fide* superstar, Ford's enthusiasm for the project persuaded

Paramount, the distributor of his two previous Indy outings, to finance the $12 million production. Other studios had voiced reservations about whether Ford possessed the necessary acting weight or presence to carry the whole film. Such fears, ludicrous today, were genuine enough in 1984. Because of his winning performances as the valiant Han Solo and the swashbuckling Indiana Jones, Ford had become stereotyped as a comic-book hero. He had the dangerous good looks and terrific screen presence of a Gary Cooper or Clark Gable, not to mention a bank balance bigger than just about any actor around. But when it came to casting the role of a serious male protagonist Ford's name was always embarrassingly low on the list. In Hollywood, where producers love to pigeonhole actors, Ford carried the 'action hero' label like a millstone around his neck. After *Star Wars* Ford's career nose-dived. As good as he was, people in the industry argued that audiences only queued up to see the special effects. His burgeoning talent was overlooked so he fled to Europe, where his brief forays into dramatic territory – *Force Ten*, and *Hanover Street* – were unsuccessful. Even *Blade Runner*, his first important starring role outside Lucas's sphere of influence, flopped at the box office. It was looking as if Ford couldn't get a hit film unless he was at the controls of the *Millennium Falcon* or brandishing a whip.

Then along came *Witness*. After the massive, predestined success of *Temple of Doom*, Ford sensed that now was a propitious moment to change gears, to manoeuvre his career into another arena of work altogether. So he began searching for 'adult' roles in more mature movies which would appeal to a whole different audience. Because of his early television experiences and lack of formal theatrical discipline, Ford feels he doesn't possess the patience to do methodical, safe, repetitive formula acting. There was also the awkward question of artistic aspiration: merely being stinking rich and top of the credits was no longer enough for Harrison Ford. Despite the great riches, he had been feeling the pangs of disappointed ambition. *Witness*, then, was a calculated departure, a gamble almost, from an actor so firmly entrenched in the fantasy genre – and there were a smug few who reckoned and hoped he would lose his way. Close to the opening night of *Witness* the chat around Hollywood was something in the order of: 'Now we'll see whether he can cut it as an actor.' 'When I heard that talk, I couldn't believe it,' Bonnie Bedelia, later to play the spurned, twisted wife in *Presumed Innocent*, told the *Philadelphia Inquirer* in July 1990. 'What did they think he'd been doing? Do you think that's easy, what he does? He wasn't just riding horses and cracking whips. There was major acting going on in those movies. You'd have to be an idiot not to see that. I was really surprised at the business for thinking that way, as though in Witness were any more difficult than what he'd done before.'

While critics continued to dismiss the Indiana Jones trilogy as strictly kids' stuff, in the role of John Book they hailed Ford as a complex actor of untapped potential. 'People started saying, "He's really good," ' Fred Roos remembers. 'But he was always that good.' *Witness* was a major breakthrough for Ford, in nearly every respect a landmark in his career. It gained him respect from his peers, an Oscar nomination, and finally established him as a serious actor and a legitimate box-office draw on his own merits. One of the reasons why *Witness* holds such a special place in Ford's heart is indeed due to the long-overdue recognition he received. 'The reviews were among the first I'd had as an actor, although that's what I'd always been doing.' The *Sunday Express* said – 'No one I can think of has lately transmitted sheer manliness so well and so gently as Harrison Ford'; *Time Out* – 'The film offers a performance of surprising skill and sensitivity from Ford, proving that he can do more than just scowl lopsidedly for the benefit of Lucas and Spielberg'; *Village Voice* – 'what surprises most about *Witness* is Harrison Ford's extraordinarily creative performance'; the *Observer* – 'Ford's a tough, tender hero in the tradition of Bogart, Lancaster and Eastwood and gives his most appealing performance to date'; and *New York* – 'In Witness Ford has become a real movie star in the old-fashioned sense.'

At last Ford had graduated from one-dimensional cartoondom; henceforth he would concentrate all efforts in the pursuit of serious drama and challenging and compelling characters. He would finally break with his blockbuster image once and for all. To date, Ford has not made another fantasy epic (save *Indiana Jones and the Last Crusade*, which one could argue he was morally obliged to do). Audiences, perhaps for the first time, were able to perceive in John Book not only Ford's understated charisma, but his potential as a mature romantic lead. Thanks to *Witness* Ford finally hit the A list of stars who get first crack at the quality scripts. This was a far cry from the days when scripts went to Nicholson, Redford or Beatty first, and if turned down then, maybe, they were passed on to Ford. Now Harrison Ford got them first.

He also played a significant role in the selection of Peter Weir, one of the rising stars of a resurgent Australian film industry, as director. Exercising his by now established prerogative of choosing his own director, Ford, along with Feldman, came to the intelligent conclusion that a non-American film-maker would be able to bring a fresh perspective to bear upon the patently exhausted thriller genre. Ford admired Weir's ability to create a sense of mood and tension on screen. After years of carefully vetoing American film projects, Weir was effectively obliged to accept the first halfway decent offer that came along, when finance for his long-cherished plans to make Paul Theroux's *The Mosquito Coast* fell through at the eleventh hour. His agent mailed three scripts to him, 'and Witness was half way decent, so I took it'.

Weir flew to the States to discuss matters further and to meet Ford, whom he was eager to team up with. The director had genuinely liked his work, the way Ford managed to present a believable presence amidst all the playground antics in the *Star Wars* and Indiana Jones movies. He considered him to be 'one of three or four actors who are simply capable of being a leading man, who have all of those qualities that the screen loves'. Then it was just a matter of whether the two personally got on, which they did immediately. There was a strong mutual affinity brewing even from that first meeting; both shared similar concerns about the script and were committed to making a film of the highest possible quality. Weir was the man most responsible for Ford's cinematic evolution, sensing in him as yet unplumbed depths and a hunger within for more challenges. Ford was indeed desperate to take some risks as an actor, tired as he was of pandering to the masses. Ford was too complicated a chap to fritter his life away in simplistic action movies. And Weir knew it more than anyone.

Like his star, Weir was intrigued with the clash of cultures the story presented and was determined to make the Amish part of the fabric of the film, not merely a backdrop for the action. With just eight weeks' preliminary time – daunting for a man who had normally taken up to two years of preparation before filming – Weir set to work on the script. Courageously, he stripped the narrative virtually bare of all its marketable clothes (violence, action) and replaced them with his own uniquely haunting brand of cinema, which has been so vividly stamped on our subconscious in those early films: *Picnic at Hanging Rock*, *The Last Wave* and *Gallipoli*. All three were variations on the same theme: an emotionally vulnerable outsider struggling to survive in a hostile, alien environment. And this motif was again central to both *Witness* and *Coast*. Weir wanted more emphasis placed upon the tranquillity of Amish life, and swiftly edited out such savage scenes as a man being brutally kicked to death by a mule.

The celebrated raising of the barn, for instance, was drastically rewritten by Weir. In the script there was just an establishing shot of the barn going up, followed by a scene where Book, working high up on the roof, loses his footing, falls and is saved by Daniel (Alexander Godunov), his handsome rival suitor for the charms of Rachel. Weir threw out this contrived piece of action and replaced it with a magical scene of warmth and wonder. The barn raising is lovingly chronicled in a series of arresting tableaux, and accompanied by Maurice Jarre's rousing score. There is little dialogue: men hammer and plane and clamber precariously over beams, while bonnet-topped women gossip, sew quilts and pass round refreshing glasses of lemonade. There is no action to speak of beyond the rhythmic pace of construction. The scene is wonderful and acquires remarkable beauty and significance. (Most of

Weir's photographic images for *Witness* were heavily influenced by Flemish paintings, and the director took Ford to an exhibition of paintings from the Flemish school at the Philadelphia Museum of Art shortly before filming began.) In both *Witness* and *The Mosquito Coast*, Weir fixes on the simple pleasure of watching Ford at work, sawing or welding. The barn scene was not contrived for his benefit, but Weir did decide to make Book a better carpenter than Godunov's character to take advantage of Ford's skills. The barn was one of the biggest construction jobs Ford had ever contemplated and he insisted that it was a technically correct representation of the real thing (although to save money the building was made of spruce rather than oak).

Weir concocted several other scenes – such as an appealing five-minute breakfast sequence – to show audiences the slow pace of an average Amish day. He refused to sentimentalize either. In another scene Rachel is threatened with expulsion from the community because of her romantic feelings towards Book. Weir judged it important to highlight the darker side of the Amish cult – the gossip and the shunning – in order to avoid romanticizing a way of life that, in some ways, is just as oppressive as it is harmonious.

Working on his first American film the Australian *auteur* was forced to tailor his style to the demands and constraints of the genre. His producer, who originally envisaged *Witness* as a kind of western, was always on hand to remind Weir of his obligations. *Witness* was intended for mainstream consumption, not the art-house circuit, and Weir was persuaded to shoot a more action-orientated finale than he first had in mind. The resulting hybrid, while unable completely to disguise the rather hackneyed plot, brilliantly managed to juxtapose urban life at its crudest and pastoral life at its most innocent. Thanks to Peter Weir, a routine studio production had mutated into something significantly better than anyone had any right to expect.

As filming continued throughout May and June 1984, simple curiosity began to take over from overt displeasure among the local Amish. Many families, taking heed of their church leaders' advice, were dutifully keeping their distance and suffering in silence. One couple declined Paramount's tempting offer of $700 a day for the use of their dairy farm as the main setting. But many others were happy to extend advice and hire out their farming equipment. To achieve greater authenticity, John King, a former Amish churchman, was hired as technical adviser and coached the actors on the various tenets of the Amish religion. The younger generation, particularly, started taking a keen interest in the film being made practically on their own back-porch. Occasionally they could be glimpsed lying in the long grass and following the action on the set through binoculars. Sometimes they would wander down from the hills in search of souvenirs. One Amish woman, following developments in the paper, told of how her children loved to cut out pictures of Harrison Ford, even though they had no clue who he was. 'Somebody told us he was in Star Wars, but that doesn't mean anything to us,' she said.

Strange as it may seem, Ford never once came into social contact with any Amish. 'I very carefully kept my naïvety about them. Part of the character is that the Amish culture is foreign to him.' The opposite was true of his co-star Kelly McGillis, who lived for a short time with a genuine Amish family. Instead Ford's preparation took him into the brash city and the world of murder and vice. To hone his characterization, Ford spent a fortnight prior to filming with the homicide squad of the Philadelphia police department, under the personal tutelage of Captain Eugene Dooley, observing proper police procedure and the everyday routine of a detective. Too often the actor was exposed to the harsh realities of crime. Not only was Ford invited by the coroner to see slides of the week's gruesome unsolved murders, he was also privy to the real thing. 'The first corpse was shocking and the fifth was just as shocking.' He also joined Dooley on a couple of raids to serve warrants on murder suspects, dressed in the required bulletproof vest, 'shotguns and all. It was a little scary. In fact it was damn scary'. The objective was to try and stay with his patrol through the night. 'What a lesson.' When asked by a journalist from the *Daily Express* whether his screen persona got in the way out on the mean streets Ford replied with typical bluntness. 'Listen, when you are a citizen in distress or you're standing there with a cop's pistol pressed against your head, you are not looking to see if there are any movie stars present.' Ford was, however, 'nailed', as he puts it, by a small child. Travelling in an elevator with five hardened detectives the star was spotted by the youngster, who pointed a finger up at him and shouted, 'I know you.'

Before embarking upon his sojourn with the police Ford's confidence was low. But he was quickly made to feel at ease by his hosts at homicide and even downed a few beers with the men. In the end the journey was worth it; Ford's short stay had proved to him that, if need be, this was a job he could capably deal with in real life. Apart from Book and his partner, all the cops featured in *Witness* are corrupt, willing to kill anyone who threatens to expose their narcotic racket. Ford wondered what his new friends at the Philadelphia police department would make of this lamentable picture of themselves. When he finally got around to telling them about the 'bent cop' scenario Ford was relieved when none of the officers took offence. Everyone he met shared his personal revulsion towards police corruption, which was then rife and on the increase. As if to confirm the point, just as the shooting of *Witness* began a deputy chief in the force was dismissed and later sentenced to fifteen years for corruption.

Ford's commitment to *Witness* did not end after the fifty-one days of shooting. Although exhausted, he and Weir continued to mull over the material during the editing stages. 'He's an enormously likeable man,' Weir commented in *The Times* in May 1985. 'I was impressed with his lack of interest in showbusiness and power and status. He is for me in the great tradition of Hollywood heroes – the strong silent type.' Compared to many other films, *Witness* progressed smoothly and everything clicked perfectly into place. Everyone was happy on location, giving rise to much good humour and mischief-making. Both Ford and Weir are wonderful jokesters and together they cooked up some of the impromptu comedy on show in *Witness*. For example, Book and Rachel's dance in the barn to the strains of a love song playing on the car radio is classic romantic comedy; and the wonderful breakfast-time sequence, in which a smug Ford points to his cup and says, 'Honey, that's great coffee,' stems from a television commercial audition the actor once failed. 'Peter lets me interpret ideas intellectually rather than kinetically,' Ford revealed. 'Before Witness all directors ever seemed to want from me was the forward propulsive action and the sly wink.' It is ironic that it took an Australian to bring out to the full Ford's very American blend of humour, honesty and idealism. 'My relationship with Peter worked more than it ever has with a director before.'

So pleased was Ford with his work for Weir that he went out of his way to publicize *Witness*. At one huge press conference Ford was asked, among other equally dumb questions like, Had Witness changed his life? whether the scene on the farm was the first time he'd ever milked a cow. 'No,' Ford replied. 'Well, it sure looked like it,' persisted the journalist. 'Yeah, well, that's what we call acting.' Ford even attended a gala screening of the film at Cannes. Sporting an unattractive crew cut, Ford looked distinctly uncomfortable among the chaotic crowds jostling outside the theatre as he made his way through the crush and the throng of international photographers. 'I felt sorry for the people being elbowed and pushed around,' he said afterwards. 'That's no way for human beings to treat each other.'

Director and star were amazed at the quite unexpected public enthusiasm for their film. Released in February *Witness* was one of the surprise hits of 1985, grossing $4.5 million in its first weekend, then an exceptional figure for a picture that boasted no special effects or superfluous violence. What it did have, though, was Harrison Ford. Weir had worried that Ford's participation might work against the film in the sense that cinemagoers, expecting Indiana Jones-type thrills, might react against the movie. Weir's nightmare scenario was realized at the first preview screening. When the director arrived two hours early he saw, to his horror, a line of Ford fans stretching for several hundred yards, noisy with expectation. 'The anticipation for a Raiders mark 3 was

An early studio portrait. Those boyish looks hide the seething hatred he felt during his apprenticeship as a Hollywood contract player

Ford's roguish personality and laconic comic air made him ideal casting for Han Solo in *Star Wars* (1977)

The gang are reunited in *The Empire Strikes Back* (1980), Ford's personal favourite of the *Star Wars* trilogy

An odd amalgam of Errol Flynn, Humphrey Bogart and James Bond, the Indiana Jones image will forever be indelibly linked to Harrison Ford

Ford in one of cinema's true cult films, Ridley Scott's pyrotechnic masterpiece, *Blade Runner* (1982). But Ford clashed with his director on the set and has since distanced himself from the work

The 'playboy' side of Indiana Jones is briefly glimpsed in the thrilling opening moments of *Indiana Jones and the Temple of Doom* (1984)

The haunting closing tableau of *Witness* (1985) showing Harrison Ford and Kelly McGillis. This is one of Ford's most popular and revered films

The quixotic Allie Fox, Ford's most ambitious creation, in *The Mosquito Coast* (1986), Peter Weir's grandly tragic, multi-layered and minutely observed examination of American madness

Ford on a rare social night out with
his wife, successful screenwriter
Melissa Mathison

Ford with his third and youngest
son, Malcolm, born in March 1987

The auspicious pairing of Ford and Roman Polanski in *Frantic* (1988), a Hitchcockian thriller, was a curiously muted affair and a box office failure

A deleted sequence from *Indiana Jones and the Last Crusade* (1989)

Guilty or not guilty? Harrison Ford as Rusty Sabich in the adult melodrama *Presumed Innocent* (1990)

Ford's quirky performance as the man-child Henry Turner is a delight, but the film, *Regarding Henry* (1991), was a disappointment

Ford's latest screen hero, Jack Ryan in *Patriot Games* (1992), America's answer to James Bond, a 007 for the responsible, caring 90s, a family man rooted in reality, but with that indestructible movie hero streak

Ford finally consents in 1992 to join the ranks of movie immortals by placing his hand and footprints in cement on Hollywood's walk of fame

terrifying,' Weir told *Screen International* in June 1985. 'At first, one could sense that they were puzzled because they were expecting more action; but, by the middle of the film, they were loving the humour. Whether that became some sort of substitute for the expected shootings I don't know, but they got lost in the story and were obviously entertained'.

The public immediately took the new-look Harrison Ford to their hearts and minds. But the actor was right when he admitted that John Book was not a huge departure from his other characters, merely an extension. Ford's screen reputation had been founded on his portraits of loners without roots or responsibilities. Book casts a solitary shadow, and like Deckard in *Blade Runner* he's searching for an identity, a place to belong; like Indiana Jones he begins and ends the movie on his own. But Book's attraction for Rachel, a slow-burning love that violates Amish tradition, changes him forever. Their tender romance, which hovers on the brink of consummation, is the film's heart and thankfully never degenerates into a graphic sexual tussle. 'I don't think that watching how the plumbing works is what people really want,' Ford said. The brief nude scene, where Book watches Rachel bathing, beautifully captures the electrifying sexual tension between the two characters. The finale, when Book leaves the farm and Rachel, is one of the most haunting in recent cinema. His new-found sensitivity to the values of the Amish has made him aware that he can never really belong within the community. Weir's observations on the gulf between the peaceful, old-fashioned way of the Amish sect and the violent, abrasive world into which Book must return won him much critical acclaim. 'A gem. If Hollywood comes up with a stronger film this year it'll be a surprise' – *Time Out*; 'An outstanding drama, one of the year's best' – *Mail on Sunday*; 'One of the most originally conceived and gracefully made suspense dramas of recent years' – *Time*.

With *Witness* Ford finally managed to cast off the fantasy-film straitjacket. An Oscar nomination for Best Actor was, perhaps, the ultimate veneration. 'When I got the nomination, my friends told me I should feel vindicated for all the critics who said I walked through the Spielberg/Lucas movies. Well, I don't feel vindication,' Ford told the *Dallas Morning News* in December 1986. 'It's just not in my repertoire. Besides, no one could criticize me as harshly as I do myself.' On Oscar night Ford lost out to William Hurt for *Kiss of the Spider Woman*, but was neither bitter nor frustrated in defeat. 'It's a high honour, I don't disdain it, it's just not the most important thing in my general scheme.'

As Book Ford gave a skilful and seductive portrayal of a haunted man trying desperately, but unsuccessfully, to build a new life for himself. It ranks amongst his greatest achievements and *Witness* as arguably his finest film. 'I feel that we are yet to see his best work,' predicted Peter

Weir. *Witness* also marked the culmination of the most remarkable half-decade in the career of any film actor. From 1980 to 1985 Ford didn't put a foot wrong, making some of the most popular film entertainments in screen history. While some critics said that he had now reached the pinnacle of his profession, Ford preferred to think of it as a plateau. 'From a peak, there's no way but down.'

When Paul Theroux began to write his Conradian novel *The Mosquito Coast*, a grandly tragic, multilayered and minutely observed examination of American madness, he intended the central character to be the son, Charlie Fox, who is also the narrator and innocent victim of his father's fated crusade. As the novel progressed Theroux became inexplicably drawn to the father, Allie, a brilliant inventor who dreams of creating a utopian paradise in the untamed Honduran jungle. Allie gradually took over the novel, and when he died the tale was finished. Theroux had planned more chapters, depicting the long-voyage home of the remaining family members, but without the dominating figure of Allie Fox there seemed little point in continuing.

Shortly after the book's publication in the States in 1982 the film rights were snapped up (for $250,000) by producer Jerome Hellman (*Midnight Cowboy*). Seduced by the spirit of the original, Hellman rebelled angrily against plans to shoot in Jamaica or Mexico to save money. He insisted that the film be made on the Mosquito Coast itself, which follows a jagged, snakelike course from Belize to Nicaragua. This picture was going to be done right, whatever the cost; no one was going to cut any corners. Paul Schrader was drafted in to write the script, and Peter Weir, who had been intrigued by the book ever since Sigourney Weaver gave him a copy while they were making *The Year of Living Dangerously* together, gratefully seized the directorial reins. Everything seemed rosy, but for one vital missing ingredient: a backer. Over the next four years Hellman flew from country to country and visited nearly every major studio in Hollywood in an effort to raise cash, but the double disadvantage of a $16 million budget and Weir's then poor track record at the box office worked against the picture getting made. Then, out of nowhere, in early 1985 producer Saul Zaentz (on a high after his Oscar-winning *Amadeus*), agreed to finance the project. By then Weir was a hot property, thanks to the success of *Witness*.

Numerous actors were mooted for the part of Allie Fox, Theroux's dictatorial, flawed idealist. Immediately one thinks of Jack Nicholson, who was indeed producer Jerome Hellman's first choice. When the star's pay demands grew exorbitant the package was handed over to Harrison Ford, eager to reacquaint himself with the director who had steered him to one of his greatest performances. Ford was really the logical choice. Not only had he proved himself as John Book to be a fine and subtle actor; but to play Allie Fox in the jungles of Belize would require great physical and emotional strength. 'Harrison had it all,' Theroux told *Vanity Fair* in December 1986. 'Even the quietly smouldering gaze and the serious grin. He was Allie to his fingertips.'

Ford has always been extremely selective in his choices of project. No more so than after *Witness* when he was deluged with scripts, most of which he wasn't interested in enough to finish reading. He was content to wait until the right story came along. Primarily Ford was looking for something that would contrast with his performance in *Witness*, but another project with some degree of originality. After a year of dodos Paul Schrader's radiant and ambitious *The Mosquito Coast* arrived with the best role he'd read in ages. An actor's dream, Allie Fox is full of complexity and contradiction, with a sharp tongue to match. 'Allie says more in one scene than characters I've played said in the whole film.' Both clown and monster, fool and genius, this was a man living on the edge – a man who is willing to crush his loved ones in his dash for Nirvana. Naturally the part would be controversial, which merely added to its appeal; and the fact that Allie Fox was so unlike anyone the actor had ever played was as good a reason as any to take it on.

There was also an element of thrill in the risk-taking and a certain pleasure to be derived from playing against type. There was, too, the gamble of portraying an unsympathetic person, a loser. In the Hollywood scheme of things big-box-office film stars are generally unwilling to risk their reputations by taking on the role of such fatally flawed heroes. But Ford's sympathy for this self-styled prophet, a grudging admiration for his energy, imagination and strong moral sense, hooked him. 'There's a lot to commend him. But he's also a pain in the arse.' As a fanatic visionary who leads his defenceless family on a disastrous personal odyssey Ford was to shed his customary fantasy persona more daringly than in *Witness* and stretch his talent yet further.

The opportunity to work again with Peter Weir was a further inducement. After *Witness* they had remained good friends, with a keen respect for each other's abilities, and often talked casually about making another film together. 'Peter and I have a special relationship,' Ford told *New Idea* magazine in December 1986. 'I enjoy working with him enormously. We think the same way, our approach to work is the same.' Like Paul Theroux, Weir too saw something of Allie Fox in Harrison Ford. It first occurred to him to cast the actor when they were filming *Witness*. 'He evokes a very American quality – strength, leadership – just by walking onto the screen,' Weir told the *Chicago Sun Times* in December 1986. 'All of which made me believe we would follow him to the jungle and believe what he said.' The Australian saw the irony of

Fox, this bombastic and ultimately pathetic figure who rejects all of American society, being played by an instantly recognizable American cultural icon.

While others saw him as the near-personification of Allie Fox, Ford did not. Some similarities existed, to be sure. Both were fathers, sons, husbands, working men, Americans. 'For me, the film is most exciting as an investigation of fathers and sons,' the actor explained in the *Chicago Tribune* in December 1986. 'I have been a son and I have been a father. I deeply understand the relationship between Allie and his eldest son, Charlie. Allie is popular with his son and I'm proud of the relationship I've had with my sons. But even though I haven't been nearly as tough on them as Allie is on Charlie, I know I have been close to the loss of control that Allie exhibits. I've seen it in my father too.' Moreover, as a man who rarely accepts things the way they are, Ford also related to Allie's antagonistic criticisms of modern America – a fear that his country is fast becoming a decadent wasteland, a junk-food emporium peopled by morons addicted to a diet of phoney religious evangelism and television game shows. 'I understand his criticisms of America,' Ford told a packed London news conference before the film's British release. 'He complains about hypocrisy, lack of ambition, mediocrity. Most Americans identify with that and we're particularly adept at looking at ourselves critically and facing the facts.' Wrong in this case. *The Mosquito Coast*'s frank anti-American stance goes some way to explaining the poor reception it received Stateside.

But do all the parallels end there? Ford doesn't attempt to create a character hugely different from himself – to censor those parts of his personality that are inappropriate to the character and to invent those parts where there is no overlap. 'There's Harrison Ford in everyone I play,' he revealed to the *Morning Advocate* in January 1987. 'I have nothing to work with but the experience of Harrison Ford, the psychology of Harrison Ford. You have to translate it into another character. You have to make that character predominate.' Part of the challenge of playing Fox was to transform himself inside and out, confronting themes he had never faced in a role and, for the first time, going out of his way to change his physical appearance. Personally supervising the overhaul Ford deliberately deromanticized his hero image. Onscreen he looks ten years older and although he didn't put on any weight, as Allie he seems distinctly paunchy. The unruly, sun-bleached hair is slicked back off the face, hanging long and greasy over his shoulders; his eyes hide behind gold-rimmed glasses too small for his face; his skin is the tone of a freshly backed brick; and his garish Hawaiian shirt is cut off at the bottom and too tight in the sleeves, making his body look more ungainly. Ford also adopted an entirely different walk and physical attitude, which gave Fox the outward appearance of a world-weary, weather-beaten beachcomber. Ford was pleased with his creation, although for a time he had considered taking Fox in completely the opposite direction, turning him into an even older man and shaving off his hair.

Weir cast the supporting players carefully. As Mother, Fox's long-suffering wife, he chose the highly respected Helen Mirren. Noted for her Shakespearean performances and having worked with such stage luminaries as Olivier and Gielgud, the actress was, none the less, starstruck when she was first introduced to Ford. 'It's stupid,' she admitted in the *Los Angeles Times* in October 1986, 'but I'm scared of people who are famous. I went absolutely to pieces when I met Harrison Ford'. Fifteen-year-old River Phoenix brought a convincing combination of hero worship and disillusionment to the role of Charlie. During filming a bond developed between Ford and Phoenix, partly because the teenager never once treated his senior in an overly reverential fashion. 'Harrison was very down to earth, a very logical man. A very smart man. Practical. He's sturdy, a real father figure. In control. Very centred.' Later to play a young Indiana Jones, critics and public alike noted the striking likeness between the two; they could almost have been father and son in real life. Whilst in Belize the star passed on some homespun wisdom to the youngster. 'Keep your head on your shoulders. It's just a job.' Nothing better encapsulates Ford's philosophy on movie stardom.

The familial rapport between the cast began to develop almost from the beginning. Prior to filming Weir organized a picnic lunch. Everyone crowded into a van: Weir sat in the back, Ford drove and the rest of the actors stayed up in the front with him. 'It was the first time they were all together,' Weir told the *Chicago Sun Times* in December 1986. 'And I didn't say anything; I just listened and watched them. Then I noticed Helen and Harrison starting to use the dialogue and ideas from the movie.' The twin girls would start playing around and Helen would have to calm them down. 'Don't distract Harrison,' she'd say. 'He's concentrating.' Sometimes Mirren would turn to Ford and ask politely, 'Are you lost?' To which he'd reply, 'I'm never lost.' Right from the off the casting worked. 'It was almost Mother and Allie,' Weir said.

Very evident in *The Mosquito Coast*, as it was with Quan in *Temple of Doom* and Lukas Haas in *Witness*, is Ford's beguiling affinity for working with children. Allie's exchanges with his four children – a kindly slap on his teenage son's shoulders or the strong clasping of his young daughter's hand to betoken love – are moving and thoughtful, and make his subsequent mistreatment of them all the more terrifying. Allie's daughters walk towards Weir's camera. Ford stands nearby, takes the hand of one of the twins and comically salutes Weir. 'Action team ready, sir,' and Weir acknowledges with a wry smile. Time passes before the take, and the girl begins to fidget, as would any bored 8-year-old.

Looking down at her Ford says, 'I want a finger. I collect fingers from all the kids I work with. How about this one.' The girl giggles in mock fright, her twin notices and runs over to check out what's happening. As one reporter on the set noted, 'The children then began to play over Ford as cubs would play over a grizzly.'

The jungles of Belize were hot, bug-infested, loud and beyond most people's comprehension. Whether prior to filming Ford exhibited Allie Fox-type characteristics is open to debate. What is certain is that once he arrived on location he began to display some of the qualities of his fictional host. Watching his creation made flesh from the bylines was Theroux himself, in Belize to lend moral support and jot down the odd observation into a diary. During his stay Theroux got to know Ford quite well and wrote of him, 'Harrison is a brilliant mimic; he is funny and physical and full of ideas, a kind of embodiment of Allie.' Nowhere was this better demonstrated than in the actor's disturbing attitude to the subject of where he was going to stay while resident on the island. Ford's first visit to Belize was a real eye-opener, and the state of the accommodation horrified him. 'I looked at the houses and looked at the hotels. Jesus, those hotels. They said, "Where do you want to stay?" and I said, "Get a cargo plane." ' Wrote Theroux – 'Without any apparent effort Ford had turned into Allie Fox. The beaky cap, the flapping shirt, the pushed-back hair, the I-know-best eyes, and the gently manical voice explaining his brilliant plan.'

'One of these C-130s,' Ford expounded. 'I told them, a big mother. Fill it up with a prefab house in lots of sections, all the plumbing, all the wires, maybe a helicopter too. Drop the whole thing into Belize in one package and bolt it together. That's where I'll live.' It was an idea that soon lost much of its initial appeal. Theroux asked Ford what had made him change his mind. 'Because I had a better idea. I didn't have to live in Belize City – I didn't have to live in Belize at all.' This again, observed Theroux, was 'pure Allie'.

Ford ended up hiring the 122-foot *Mariner II*, a fully restored air-conditioned fantail motor yacht of mid-twenties vintage, with shiny teak decks, lead-crystal windows, wood and brass furnishings, a gourmet cook and a crew of five. For someone who so publicly proclaims his aversion to the material trappings of stardom, this was decadence on a grand scale. Ford anchored the vessel offshore and commuted to the set each morning by speedboat, leaving Melissa, who was working on a teleplay about General Custer, onboard during the day. In his spare time Ford would go scuba-diving around Belize's majestic 150-mile-long Lighthouse Reef. He had learned the art while vacationing in Hawaii and was now a keen warm-water diver. In the crystal-clear seas of Belize Ford swam to depths of up to 125 feet, deeper than he had ever attempted before.

The *Mariner II*'s excessive opulence obscured the fact that the boat was a vehicle for escape. Ford's charter of it was, selfish or otherwise, an act of privacy, a rare enough commodity in the life of a movie star. It served as Ford's sanctuary away from the rest of the crew, who crowded out the city's only two hotels. 'I had the feeling that if I didn't get away from it all, I would go quite mad after a while,' he told the *Independent* in January 1987. 'Also, the noise of the city. The boat offered me some control over my environment.' He was right in many ways. This steamy, former British Caribbean colony was like something out of a Graham Greene novel: a desperately poor country, decaying and miserable, and the fourth-largest grower of marijuana in the Western hemisphere. For even the hardened traveller Belize City is difficult to digest. The wooden shacks and tottering houses of this nondescript town are mostly raised seven feet above the muddy earth on stilts – a protection against tidal waves and regular swamping. You'd be hard pressed to locate a typical Belizean, for all races intermingle here: Indians, Chinese, *Mestizos* (persons of mixed European and Amerindian ancestry) and a good smattering of West Indians. When Ford first came to Belize on a scouting trip with Weir he ended up personally clearing a plot of land with a machete, leading a local workgang. To him the place was pretty bizarre, 'very Third World,' and far removed from his normal support systems; but he understood the value of filming in a real jungle environment. 'If you've got tropical heat and mosquitoes, you don't have to bother to act them.'

Ford still had to act Fox though. This time round he relied less on research; rather he fed off the original book, the Belize location and, above all, Weir. The role of Allie Fox was to cripple Ford physically and mentally. He was a tough character to be with for fourteen- and sixteen-hour days, six days a week. Once, desperately worried about his performance, he confided in Theroux. 'You shouldn't worry,' the author told him. 'You're doing everything right. You're Allie Fox. Listen, that's from the horse's mouth.' Unimpressed, Ford retaliated. 'Don't tell me not to worry. I worry all the time. Does Allie Fox worry? right. That's why I worry.' The jungle too finally got to him. What with the heat, the bugs and the boredom, after three months he was totally drained of energy and patience. On the last day Ford ransacked his trailer, ripping open cupboards and throwing unwanted magazines and cassettes onto the floor with all the speed and urgency of a man late for an important appointment. The appointment was his return flight. 'I'm never coming back here!' he raved to a gathering of onlookers. 'Never!'

While no method actor, Ford is undeniably affected by his characters after he leaves the set. Allie Fox was harder to shake off than most, and it took Ford months to come down from 'a period of personal reflection,' as he chose to call it. The film made him ponder the father-and-son

relationship in an 'oblique way'. Both Ben and Willard saw the film and
were deeply moved by it. 'I know that our discussions about the movie
will go on for the rest of our lives. Ford disclosed to the *Chicago Tribune*
in December 1986 that his sons' reactions went well beyond reminding
him of the times he was as stubborn or as harsh as Allie Fox. 'They say
that much with the arch of an eyebrow. Let's put it this way, I know what
they're thinking about Allie and the movie, and they know that I know
what they're thinking. One thing that did amaze them, is just how
personal the process of being an actor is. I think they were surprised to
see me use so much of myself on the screen.'

Gracey Rock was little more than a piece of raw jungle on the Sibun
River when the bulldozers moved in to transform it into the town of
Jeronimo, Allie Fox's vision of heaven on earth. The whole site was
erected from scratch, and built to last. When *The Mosquito Coast* team
flew back to the States some of the buildings of the fictional Jeronimo
were turned into community centres, while others were taken over by
the homeless. At one point, a bulldozer hit a twenty-foot-high mound of
rock which turns out to be an unrecorded Mayan temple site, an
archaeological discovery of which Indiana Jones would be proud.
History, then, supplied Weir with the perfect camera platform. One
might question the ethics of an environmentally conscious film, whose
makers behaved in roughly the same reckless manner as the character it
sought to reproach. Like Allie Fox, rallying against the materialism of
modern America, but destined to duplicate in his virgin paradise the
flaws of the very society he deplores, Weir's crew arrived in Belize and
proceeded to wreck it.

Ford is used to filming in far-off, underdeveloped countries like
Tunisia and Sri Lanka, and is familiar with the problems which occur
when Hollywood crews work abroad. 'One of the great disappointments
in my life is that I go to these fascinating places, but don't have very
much time to see them. Also, by going there, you sometimes change the
place so much that you don't get a chance to see it as it really is. Making
a film is a very technological event to impose on an unsophisticated
environment.' While Belize may have been exploited,there was a plus
side too. Weir's road show employed nearly three hundred locals out of
an entire city population of just 148,000, and brought in some $7 million
in foreign exchange, making the film's producer, for a time anyway, the
third largest 'industry' in Belize, after sugar and pot. Despite
government assistance the logistics of the production were mind-
boggling: roads needed to be built into the jungle and supplies flown in;
an entire hospital had to be maintained; and a team of couriers were
hired to shuttle film back and forth from a Miami laboratory for dailies
(unedited footage).

Despite the obvious strain, Weir's crew, a motley band of Britons,

Australians and Americans, many of whom had worked on *Witness*, were able to keep a tight, happy ship. They all appreciated Ford's lack of snobbery, his common touch. When not floating in his ivory tower, Ford would occasionally drink a few beers with the electricians and carpenters, and was sufficiently at ease with the technical people for the Australians among them to describe him as 'matey'. Always willing to pitch in, to share the workload, Ford rarely came on the big-shot movie star. 'I'd rather help than stand around and wait for them to do it themselves,' he explained to *USA Today* in December 1986. 'If I can't stand in front of the camera until all that crap gets moved to the other side of the river, I grab a box. To everyone's absolute amazement and amusement. I'm just used to being part of a working group of people. The collar around my neck is blue.' Producer Saul Zaentz's nephew, Paul, saw this at close hand. 'I took Harrison on a recce in Belize before shooting started and he was always the first guy to come forward to carry the bags.' Spielberg, in particular, has noticed this admirable characteristic of Ford's. 'Harrison will always be Harrison,' he told *News Extra* in November 1991. 'On more than one occasion I've seen him pick up a hammer on the set and fix something he didn't like. At that moment, he looks like a simple carpenter. Inside, I think that's what he really is: no superstar – just a craftsman who's proud of what he does, and does it well.' Ford is a man of pride, but not of vanity or ego. There are no delusions of grandeur about him.

Ford described his working relationship with Peter Weir on *The Mosquito Coast* as immeasurably different from the one he experienced on *Witness*. 'It was much more difficult. On Coast I wanted very much to be directed,' he told *Photoplay* in March 1987. 'I wanted not to have control of the situation. I wanted to be able to give in to the excesses of the character, to be pulled back from the brink by Peter when he thought it was necessary, or encouraged to go close to the edge when he thought I should. I've been a servant of the story and of the director on Coast to a greater extent than I've ever been before.' Although partly true, in many other areas Ford was more collaborator than servant. Peter Weir would later speak highly of his sparkling inspiration on the set, remarking that he was one of the few actors he would ever involve in a film's creative process. As a team they were well-matched: both essentially saw themselves as storytellers; and Ford, the logical thinker and self-described 'technical' actor, was the perfect complement to Weir, the improvising visionary. 'Harrison is more than just an actor,' said Weir, 'he's a filmmaker. He has a good head; he's worth listening to. And he's the exception.' Weir remembers Ford inspecting the set of Allie's workshop before filming was due to start and remarking, 'This is the wrong kind of lathe; Allie would have a metal lathe not just a wood lathe.' Weir took his criticism on board, and a metal lathe was brought in. Ford even went as far as to design a couple of Allie's inventions himself, including the delightful pedal-driven washing-machine. He had become Allie Fox, no question.

The general antipathy shown in the States towards *The Mosquito Coast*, by public and press alike, upset the actor greatly and almost certainly robbed him of a second richly deserved Oscar nomination. Normally, though he does read reviews, he doesn't pay an awful lot of attention to them. However, he took the criticisms of *The Mosquito Coast* very much to heart and rallied behind Weir's film in a way he had never hitherto done, urging people to go and see it and make up their own minds. So appalled was Ford by the film's shabby treatment that he wrote in protest to a number of national newspapers. 'I have never seen a serious film treated so badly by the critics,' he complained to the *Philadelphia Inquirer*. 'And I think they're wrong. The picture is well worth seeing. It's a very complicated and ambitious piece and I would like people to see it. I would like to do whatever I can to help that happen.' He was backed up by Paul Theroux who, writing to *Newsweek*, said: 'Peter Weir's film is gripping, powerful, brilliantly realized and true to the novel. It is a great pity that your readers have been misled that it is otherwise. That is from the horse's mouth.' The author delivered a similarly worded letter to *Time* magazine, who had also given the film a big thumbs-down.

Fox is a case of the American dream gone wild, a man who carries the seeds of his own destruction. Ford bravely rose to the challenge of exploring the dark side of leadership and heroism, documenting his deterioration into madness in a subtle, chilling performance, the most ambitious of his career. Of course one could criticize it for being too operatic in scale. Ford begins at an incredibly intense pitch as Fox and then blasts through the movie on the same note – there are few furrows or valleys in the performance. It is all rather self-indulgent, and takes up so much emotional space that Mirren and Co. can do little but tag along in his wake. *The Mosquito Coast* is a one-man film and this is both its strongest suit and its greatest weakness.

But, in any case, it wasn't the Harrison Ford the public adored. In the 1980s the actor had almost single-handedly revived the old-fashioned American hero, extolling virtues like honour and decency. Then along came Allie Fox. However much Weir tried to tone down some of the uglier aspects of Theroux's protagonist, for fear of alienating cinema-goers, his cruel and unsympathetic nature still repelled the audience. However intelligent, provocative and hypnotic Weir's tale, in the end it was too unsettling and nasty for mass consumption. The world was not ready for a movie in which the immortal Indiana Jones ends up lying in a river boat with a bullet in his back. But those critics who were dismissive of the film itself approved of Ford's involvement in meatier roles. 'Ford's vigorously uncompromising performance confirms that he's an actor of real substance' – *New York Times*, '... the masterful work of a highly competent actor with a range that almost exceeds imagination' – *Brandon News Weekend*; '... a central performance that shows Ford's acting range steadily increasing' – *Independent*; 'He is an actor of greater depth than he was ever allowed to be in his adventure films. His performance is a near masterpiece' – *Pottsville Republican*. Ford too was proud of his own achievement but, like all perfectionists, saw in it faults and areas for improvement. 'I tend to be hard on myself. I'm never completely satisfied. But I do think it was a worthy effort.'

11

Virgin Land

By Ford's own reckoning he drives into town only about '0.3 times a week'. The locals generally respect his privacy and have grown accustomed to his presence, but still view him as something separate and different. There is, too, a lingering suspicion about why he would choose to live among them. Early on, some treated his arrival as a big joke and Ford as a novelty item. They would catch fleeting glimpses of him cruising around in his Chevrolet pick-up truck or sipping a glass of beer in the resident saloon. Was he playing at cowboys, this tall, quiet man from Hollywood? 'I think they'd prefer it if I did behave like a film star because then I'd represent something exciting. As it is I'm ordinary, totally comprehensible to them.'

This image of Ford as urbane cowboy is one the press have exhausted ever since his celebrated move from the smog of Los Angeles to the snow-capped Rockies. Off duty, Ford invariably wears 'Marlboro Man' clothes: blue jean jacket, denim shirt and dirty Levis. If it weren't for the sunglasses, protection against chance recognition, he could be mistaken for just another ranch hand coming into town to stock up on provisions or a clerk at the local ironmonger's on his lunch break.

Jackson Hole, population 4,500 is nestled on the brim of the Grand Teton National Park, 310,000 acres of mountains, lakes and forests. The town, at first glance, resembles an old western set from a film studio lot, and the surrounding majesty of the Rockies merely adds to the illusion. But despite the old-style storefronts, wooden plank sidewalks and saloons with saddles for bar stools, Jackson Hole has sadly gone the way of most mountain resorts. The main square boasts Benetton and Ralph Lauren factory outlets, there are a good few real estate offices and a fair sprinkling of ski shops.

Like most people raised in the suburbs of a big city Ford would dream of escaping to a pastoral setting, to live off the land as a farmer or perhaps work as a forest ranger. His most extravagant childhood daydream was to become a marine biologist. Steven Spielberg, one of

140

the privileged few who know Ford intimately, has described how the actor seems to drift above all the false glitter of celebrity. He could just as easily be a contented farmer, an observation Ford readily acknowledges. Since he could remember, Ford had always wanted to own a place in the country, somewhere secluded and peaceful, far from the grime and noise of city life. While growing up he carried with him a little postcard image in his head of the perfect idyllic place with woods, open water and wildlife. Never one to attach much credence to planning ahead, after ten years in Los Angeles Ford was losing patience with all the cheaters and the phoneys, and from this resentment grew a desire to get out as quickly as possible. Two things were holding him back: he'd have to wait until he had reached a certain plateau of success, until Ben and Willard had finished their schooling.

By Ford's harsh reckoning Los Angeles is a failure as a city and 'one of the most hostile environments known to mankind'. He enjoys working there, but that's where the love affair ends. Moreover, he has made no secret of renouncing all the showbusiness hype that pervades the movie capital. 'I absolutely despise the Hollywood social life,' he told *People* magazine in May 1990. 'I hate all of it – the gossip, the drug use, the plastic surgery and the rush to buy over-priced real estate.' It is as if Ford was determined, once he had reached a certain status, to be the antithesis of a movie star. He simply refuses to play the game by Hollywood's rules, shunning the shallow chat-show circuit, dismissing the publicity hoopla of premières, and rarely eating out at such high-society eateries as Spago and Chasen's. Needless to add, he wouldn't be caught dead at a Hollywood party. Ford prefers his company in ones and twos; he abhors nightclubs – his private vision of hell is of being confined in a disco for twenty-four hours a day. He just makes his films, does his obligatory press tours and then vanishes to do what he wants with his life. 'So many people in Hollywood are discontented, despite any success or money they may have acquired. They're so busy exercising their thighs that they have no time left to read a book or learn something about the world. I've never been a part of that scene. That's why I left.' Once his older children had gone off to college and were properly settled in their own lives the need to be close to them was diminishing. Nor was direct contact with Hollywood necessary any longer. The need to sweet-talk Hollywood deal makers over lunch evaporated, and today Ford conducts most of his business from Wyoming via the telephone. It is a fallacy, as far as he's concerned, that attending fancy parties and hustling for attention in the right Hollywood circles helps your career. 'I think you can take it or leave it, and I choose to leave it.' It helps, though, when your closest colleagues in the industry are George Lucas, Steven Spielberg and Francis Ford Coppola. After spending the best part of two decades in Los Angeles, Ford described leaving as 'effortless'.

Harrison and Melissa first inspected properties in California and later spread their net wider to encompass Colorado, Idaho and Wyoming – 'anywhere I don't have to be known as anything but a distant neighbour'. All the time Ford was searching for that childhood picture of the American Eden: woods, streams and clear mountain air. Then he found it, seven miles from the town of Jackson Hole, Wyoming: a vast tract of virgin land on the banks of the Snake River, beneath the comforting, watchful gaze of the Teton Mountains. In the beginning all they were looking for was a hideaway, somewhere to escape to when the need arose, but it soon became their first home.

Surrounded by cattle ranches, the 800 acres of evergreen trees and cottonwood bought by Ford included no buildings of any description and prior to his arrival had been used mostly for pasturage. So remote was it that Ford had to build a road, bring in electricity, water and other amenities and bury septic tanks before construction could even begin on his dream home. Painstakingly designed by Ford and built in six months during 1985/86 by himself and a number of helpers, the final product was a simple two-storey white clapboard farmhouse which stands in the refreshing shade of an immense 150-year-old Engelmann spruce. Architecturally plain – 'a Shaker mansion' – the Ford country homestead wouldn't look out of place amongst the Amish farmhouses of *Witness*. Yet in spite of the building's considerable size, the only outward signs of wealth are a black Mercedes in the driveway, a tennis court and a satellite dish near the garage.

Those few mortals fortunate enough to have been granted an audience inside Ford's inner sanctum have come away from the experience surprised by his frugal lifestyle. His home is modestly laid out with functional wooden furniture, some of which he makes himself, and lightly furnished with simple decorations. Like his home in Los Angeles, there is no trace of chintziness of unnecessary ornament. The house becomes a metaphor – form follows function.

That Ford cherishes his privacy is clear enough. The property is surrounded by fences with large signs bearing the one word which above all others defines the personal world of Harrison Ford: 'PRIVATE'. 'No Trespassing,' they warn; 'Private Drive. No Access. Keep Out.' But they don't work. Despite rigorous efforts to keep the whereabouts of his retreat a secret, Ford was unintentionally to become Jackson Hole's biggest tourist attraction. People would now pass through the town merely on the off chance that they might bump into him doing the shopping. They would literally stop Ford in the street and gush, 'We heard you were here. Would you just stand still for a minute while I get my camera.' Or they'd pull into the local gas station to enquire, 'Where is he then?' And half the time the attendant told them. Yet stubbornly, Ford continued refusing publicly to name the town where he now lived, even though by this time it was common knowledge. He was beginning to receive mail addressed simply to 'Harrison Ford, care of his ranch'. Earlier he had been reluctant even to mention in which state he lived. He was worried, apparently, that he would be trapped in Wyoming, which is, after all, only about twice the size of England. No one begrudged Ford his right to claim a little peace and quiet; what came across as being needlessly defensive was the fact that when journalists arrived in town none of the articles could mention the location and nobody was allowed within a stone's throw of his front door. 'You cannot see the backstage part of my life,' he told them. 'You cannot come to my ranch.' When he is not working or busy promoting a movie Ford is not in public view. Apart from the odd tiresomely necessary trips to Hollywood, home was now Wyoming and he intended to be blissfully unreachable there. Accusations that Ford had become an insufferable hermit soon followed.

Ford's defection to Wyoming from the goldfish-bowl environment of Los Angeles was partly precipitated by the problem of losing both his privacy and anonymity, a tragic but inevitable side-effect of fame. He was not in flight from civilization, nor running scared from Hollywood; he was merely using his enormous wealth to, in effect, buy back his privacy, to create some artificial freedom. The house in Wyoming represented 'the major reward so far'. Hence when people showed up near his home bearing Wisconsin plates and with zoom lenses on their cameras he didn't care for it very much. Such intrusion, he feels, denies him a real life. 'And I don't want to be denied a real life'. His theory is that he can keep trespassers and snoopers at bay by keeping a very low public profile and objects to being branded a recluse. He doesn't even think he is particularly obsessive about his privacy; he simply chooses to maintain strict control over it.

By the close of the decade Ford had sufficiently softened his attitude to begin accepting the inescapable conclusion that his whereabouts were a secret no more. 'For a long time I just said we lived somewhere in Wyoming, leaving it vague,' he told the *Los Angeles Times* in October 1989. 'Now, every story about the foreign minister's summit in Jackson Hole seems to have a sidebar saying Harrison Ford lives nearby. I guess we're not a secret anymore.'

When he began looking for land in western Wyoming, Ford had no intention of becoming what effectively he is today, a public benefactor. He originally sought no more than ten acres, but ended up with 800. Due to the pressures of increasing development on neighbouring properties his land has become a refuge for wildlife. Today sixty-five species of mammal live there: a permanent elk herd of about forty; deer and moose roam freely; and otters and beavers play on the banks of the river. Trout shoot through the creeks, while overhead bald eagles hover;

ospreys nest nearby and there is also a great blue heron rookery. When a real-estate agent informed the actor of the Jackson Hole Land Trust, a non-profit-making organization dedicated to preserving the terrain in spruce and cottonwood rather than in industrial parks and shopping centres, Ford took the bold step of giving over his sequestered nook to nature conservation. There was now a feeling more of stewardship of the property than ownership. By deeding his land to the trust Ford won a guarantee that it would be preserved in perpetuity – as well as a substantial tax benefit (in the region of two-thirds) for what the law treats as a charitable donation. 'I really want to preserve it for my kids, to let them know this is what's dear to me rather than a big pile of money in the middle of the floor.' Granting an easement on the land naturally devalued the property, which hardly bothered Ford. 'I can't think of a better legacy than to do what you can to protect a small piece of wilderness.' In addition to his own home, Ford retains the right to build further houses on every forty acres, although he intends to allow only four more, one for each of his children.

Ford's involvement in the trust (helping them to acquire land that he didn't own), and a dedication to nature conservation (often consulting with biologists and fish and game experts), did much to muffle accusations that the star was living like a hermit up in the mountains. True, he isn't particularly visible in the community, but he is concerned with local issues and prides himself in the number of good causes to which he has lent his name. Late in November 1991 Ford was appointed, with five other town residents, to the Jackson Hole Land Trust board of directors, for a three-year term. He joined fellow actor James Stewart in supporting the first Jackson Hole wildlife film festival, and appeared at the twenty-eighth Grand Teton music festival. He narrated Aaron Copland's Lincoln portrait.

As a rule Ford now appears in only one film per year. The reason he does fewer than he would perhaps like is because his concentration is so intense that he can stand the pace for only three or four months at a time. When he is working Ford is totally absorbed in the task at hand. Nothing else matters: he doesn't want to go out to dinner, and he has no energy left for weekends and, by the same token, his children. When his chores are over he needs to patch up everything and get his life back on its feet again, to retreat into the private world of his home in Wyoming and spend time with the family. 'My life is much more important to me than any one film.' Once described by Ford as 'a refuge for animal animals and human animals', over the years the ranch has become a haven, an antidote for the burden of showbusiness and the media spotlight. It is somewhere where he can relax and recharge his batteries after the exhausting demands of film-making.

Too much exposure to Hollywood make-believe and Ford urgently requires at least a six-month 'fix' of real life. While some of us go to the movies to escape from humdrum existences, Ford loves nothing better than temporarily abandoning the actuality of being a film star to become one of us, a faceless member of the public. The things we find so tedious about our lives Ford wallows in; those little household errands we try so desperately to avoid are what he most enjoys doing when not working: unblocking the sink, polishing his shoes, keeping a tidy sock drawer. The paradox is intriguing. 'The pleasure of my life,' he told the *Palm Beach Post* in December 1988, 'is that, however long it takes to make a movie, when it's over, I'm back to reality, back to the banal tasks where I belong.' Talking of banality, Ford is a notorious list-maker, constantly jotting down little jobs that need to be done, sometimes inking them straight on to the palms of his hands. It's an obsession that derives from having a mind like a sieve.

Most of these tasks take Ford outside into the sprawling majesty of his wilderness estate. Rising early to enjoy breakfast with his family, Ford is usually out of the house by nine o'clock and tinkering in his workshop. Or he might be out in the fields mending fences, repairing equipment, checking on damage caused by beavers and chasing the odd stray cow off his land. The harsh winter months are the busiest: there's snow to be ploughed and the road to keep open. While this all sounds rather arduous, it is a rugged, yet satisfying life which the Fords cherish. Granted that Ford feels most alive when acting, living out the fantasy of being someone else, the best thing of all is to be able to hang up his actor's clothes at the end of the day and be normal again. It is a satisfying change of pace. 'When I finish doing a movie,' he told the *Daily News* magazine in November 1986, 'I can't wait to get back home where I can go grocery shopping or go to the hardware store. When I'm working, I miss driving my own car and cooking my own eggs.' Ford sees it as vitally important to preserve this contact with reality. Once you glibly give it up you can never get it back, and you are no longer much use as an actor. He knows the kind of life he leads is far from the average, so he clings to normality as if it were a life preserver. A well-adjusted family life and conventional relationships with colleagues keep Ford in touch with reality. 'Being normal is a kind of victory. What I really like is peace and quiet.'

Ford is ferocious about his right to lead a life that is at least a credible facsimile of the one he led before fame claimed his soul. The amazing thing is that Ford has managed to succeed. His home life is, in many respects, indistinguishable from millions of fellow rural Americans. Ford is never more happy than when he is pottering about the house, and would never be tempted out to see a movie. 'Out of sloth,' he admits. 'I'm really very embarrassed by my lack of knowledge about film.' At first this was to avoid imitating other actors, and then it became a habit. 'My wife would like to see a lot more movies than we do, but she finds it hard to drag me out of the house. I'm a real bore.' Socially Harrison is an invisible animal and when in public he's a nondescript, hesitant figure. Arnold Glimcher, producer of *Gorillas in the Mist* and a friend of Melissa, told *Vanity Fair* in August 1990: 'Mike Nichols was being honoured at the Waldorf by the Museum of the Moving Image in New York and Harrison had to come [the actor was just beginning to work on *Regarding Henry* for Nichols]. And he was in excruciating pain. He just detests going out.' In Hollywood Ford is a fish out of water. At the post-première party for *Working Girl* held in Los Angeles, fans and *paparazzi* swarmed around Melanie Griffith and other star guests while Ford made his way through the crowd virtually unnoticed.

While appreciative of good music and fine literature (holed up in Wyoming his main contact with the outside world comes from reading the *New York Times*), time spent with his family is assuredly the most precious. When Ford's third son Malcolm and daughter Georgia were very young each evening, naturally, revolved around them. 'Until they're tucked in at 8.30 or 9, the evening is all about them. They're up at 5.30, so for Melissa and myself there's not a helluva lot left, except a little exposure to radiation in the form of television. And then sleep.' For relaxation Ford and Melissa ride their property on horseback or hike it or travel down the tranquil river in a canoe. Sometimes they ski. He also loves to fish. Ford has never hunted on his land but does partake in a spot of fly fishing, although it's all catch and release. As with everything he does, it is the craft and mechanical skill of the sport that first attracted him, the challenge of getting the fly in there under the branch and setting it down quietly in the water. The trout streams on his property were restored by the actor himself. 'I particularly like to fish alone. I just walk out the door, walk five or ten minutes and I am at the stream where I know the fish by name.' An actor renowned for his action roles, Ford surprised even himself by the pleasure he found in rural tranquillity. Wyoming has played a significant part in bringing calm and peace into his life.

In his teens, despite an admirable physique, Ford showed no interest in sport and was a self-confessed 'powder-puff' on the college football fields. Once in a while he would go camping, but he was never the big outdoorsman. During the keep-fit boom of the eighties Ford was a proud non-participant, and he delighted in informing journalists of his hatred for jogging and general exercise. 'I'm a founder member of the underground of anti-joggers,' he'd quip. At that time Ford was possibly the only celebrity in Hollywood not indulging in some form of keep-fit regime and not a member of a fancy Bel-Air sports club. Ford has never followed the herd. 'I'm just an ordinary creaky bag of bones. The only way I ever keep fit is by acting,' he once said.

It is ironic, then, that Ford should have taken up sport in middle age. Competitive games and keep-fit exercising are still viewed with disdain, although he now enjoys playing tennis. But the kind of physical activities which Ford really prefers go hand in glove with the great American outdoor life he cherishes so much. It began with cross-country skiing and fishing in the foothills of the Rockies near his home, both of which are contemplative hobbies perfectly in tune with his solitary personality. Then a harder edge crept in when he took up downhill skiing, rock climbing and scuba diving, risky pursuits involving trust and dependence on others. Did this possibly mean that Ford's isolation had given way to sociability? No chance.

Carpentry also helps Ford to relax. Near to the house stands a series of outbuildings, a hay barn, a tack shed, an office and the nucleus of Ford's inner sanctum, his workshop. Like the house nothing here smells of pretension; it is orderly, clean and obviously well used and loved. To get to the workshop one passes through the garage, passing by two Harley Davidson motorcycles under covers, one of which is a beautiful 1990 black and cream heritage model. High above, suspended on hooks, is a canoe. A large machete in a scabbard hangs menacingly on the wall. The workshop itself would be the envy of many a professional carpenter. 'I still do a lot of carpentry. It's something I've always done, always enjoyed doing. I wouldn't actually call it therapy, but it is a very valuable part of my private life.' One of Ford's friends, the novelist Jim Harrison, was once a carpenter himself and says, 'I'd hate to work for him. He'd be incredibly demanding. I think he has an exquisite gift for carpentry. That Wyoming house is just a marvel. In terms of details, people don't build houses like that, for obvious reasons.' Speaking in a local Jackson Hole magazine he continued, 'Ford's a very non-Hollywood human being. He is, by far, the least show-biz person of anyone I've met in show business. I'd say the focus of his interest is the woodworking shop.' Although he spends a lot of time slaving over a lathe, Ford doesn't make nearly as much furniture for his ranch as people surmise. His proudest achievement in recent years was constructing son Malcolm's bed. 'He watched me make it. But I'm sure he thinks that everybody's dad makes their bed.'

12

The Reluctant Star

Ford has been dubbed 'the reluctant star', a hermit, an enigma, self-protective, withdrawn. Hollywood's most impenetrable figure. It irks the man to hear himself so described. Refer to him as a superstar and he can get very shirty or politely attempt to laugh off the suggestion, depending on his mood. Generally, though, he prefers the term of 'working actor' to describe the job he does. 'When I look in the mirror, I don't see the highest grossing movie star of all time ... I see his idiot twin.' The whole idea of being a star holds no interest or meaning, save purely a commercial one. Few contemporary stars have Ford's power or influence, and he certainly doesn't begrudge his coveted status or the trappings of fame which serve him so well. The ambition of every actor is to achieve success, after all. It is simply the whole sordid industry of celebrity – the business of promoting oneself as a fascinating personality – that disturbs him. 'I don't consider myself unique. I just work in the movie business.' Ford has always maintained that the most interesting thing about him is the work he does. 'I am more revealing on the screen than I am in ordinary life. I'm not as exciting as the parts I play.'

Ford is keen to promote this Mr Ordinary image. It is part calculated move, part a legitimate predilection for privacy. Ford is naturally reclusive, which makes the fact that he chose one of the most public of professions almost an absurdity. It simply never occurred to him that he would achieve the degree of success which he enjoys today. Ford never became an actor for fame and fortune, nor to gain attention, and certainly not to be heralded as a sex symbol. The idea of women lusting after him is something he finds unpalatable. Cool, lean and ruggedly good-looking, with perpetually tanned skin, his swashbuckling action roles of the past have fuelled passions around the globe and resulted in creating one of the sexiest men alive, the thinking woman's heart-throb. Inevitably an actor's audience tends to think of him in terms of the parts he plays, but while some stars pander to this Ford dismisses it out of hand. He doesn't find himself particularly attractive. 'I wake up in the morning and hate what I see.' Women, in his opinion, fall for the image on the screen, not the real man. 'Believe me,' Ford told the *Orange County Register* in December 1986, 'they'd walk right past me on the street without looking at me twice if it weren't for the roles I've played in the movies.'

Still Ford remains embarrassed by the attention he receives in public. In the past incessant fan adulation really got on his nerves. He would be walking along a street and hear people whispering his name out of the corner of their mouths or he would wander into a shop and feel heads turning to watch him. It drove him crazy. In recent years, though, Ford has learned how to deal with his fame. Those fans have made him one of the richest of all entertainers and Ford is smart enough not to seem ungrateful. 'I have a responsibility to them for having invested in me. I try to think of those people as satisfied customers and that's why they're approaching me.'

Admirably, Ford hasn't allowed fame to change him. To a large extent he is the same modest and diligent man who drove into Laguna Beach thirty years ago. He knows he isn't a regular guy, that he left his regular life behind the moment he signed along the dotted line for Columbia. But he would prefer neither to apologize for his wealth and status nor to wield it. 'Harrison just hasn't changed,' Spielberg told *Vanity Fair* in August 1990. 'In real life, he's a very plain and simple person. Harrison only became a movie star because Thomas Edison happened to invent the movie camera. I've seen him pick up a hammer and fix a set when the construction man's not there. I've seen him, during a shooting day, drift off – he already knows how to play the scene, and I think he's just drifting away from all the fakery. He's planting a crop, or building a bookshelf in Wyoming.'

It was edging towards Christmas, 1986. Melissa had for some time been working on a script about Tin-Tin, the famous Belgian cartoon hero, for Roman Polanski, to be produced by Steven Spielberg. A story conference was taking place in Paris and Melissa was invited to attend. She was pregnant at the time, and because Paris had recently seen an upsurge of terrorist activity, Ford was naturally concerned for her safety. Not wishing her to go alone, Ford decided to tag along. He had never met Polanski before but there was a strange and instant rapport between them and on the second day the two men started talking movies. Polanski suggested that Ford might be interested in reading a script he and Gerard Brach had just completed, a Hitchcockian psychological thriller called *Frantic*. The actor couldn't read French so Polanski obliged by jumping on a table and acting out the story himself in an hour-and-a-half-long bravura performance. 'He played everything but the weather,' said Ford. 'And he was great.'

The tale was an especially gripping and compelling one. Richard Walker is an American surgeon in Paris, combining a conference with a second honeymoon. No sooner is he unpacked than his wife is kidnapped. Forced out of complacency he begins a desperate search to find her. Because of Ford's own concern for Melissa's safety the story hit especially close to home. 'I was very receptive,' he told *Premiere* magazine in March 1988. 'I'm always worrying about her. That pretty much defines my reality.' While watching Polanski act out the plot line Ford suddenly realized that these horrors, which for many of us are only dormant nightmares, were for the director appallingly real. Many of *Frantic*'s details – the disappearance of a spouse and alienation in a foreign place – mirror aspects of Polanski's life. Polanski is a man who has suffered more tragedy in his life than anyone should have a right to bear. In 1969 the crazed followers of Charles Manson broke into the director's Bel-Air home interrupting a small party of rich and glamorous denizens of Hollywood. They butchered everyone in sight, including Polanski's then pregnant wife Sharon Tate. Having lived through this ordeal, Polanski lent elements to the story that Ford could never begin to imagine. 'It was clear that this was deeply emotional for Roman. To think how I'd feel if the circumstances had happened to me was, well ... When it was over, I said, if that's what it's going to be like when it's written down, I'll do it.'

This must surely rank as Ford's most bizarre route yet to securing a film role. Famous for his long ponderous deliberations over scripts, this was indeed an injudicious leap into the dark. What made *Frantic* so different? Why did he accept in so devil-may-care a fashion and in such abnormal circumstances? The answer lies in the man who was offering the job, Roman Polanski, for whom Ford was openly keen to work. With the possible exception of Ken Russell, Polanski ranks as the most infamous director of our time. He is cinema's poet of the sinister and disturbing. Though of Polish extraction he was born in the Bastille section of Paris in the year of Hitler's rise to power, 1933. Raised mostly in the ghettos of Krakow, Poland, the infant Polanski managed to escape the brutal Nazi suppression there, but his mother perished in Auschwitz. Meanwhile his father, who survived the tortures of Mauthausen, the Austrian concentration camp, subsequently died of cancer. Polanski's first feature, *Knife in the Water*, made in 1962, shortly after leaving film school, established him as one of the most original of the young generation of Polish film makers. After a mid-sixties stopover in swinging London which resulted in three minor classics – *Repulsion*, *Cul de Sac* and the underrated Hammer spoof *Dance of the Vampires* – Polanski came to Hollywood. There he secured his place in the annals of film history with two genre pictures of outstanding depth and quality: *Rosemary's Baby* and *Chinatown*.

Unfortunately, in recent years Polanski's predilection for underage girls has detracted heavily from his obvious film-making talents. His arrest in 1977 for the statutory rape of a thirteen-year-old model whom he was photographing for *Vogue Hommes* in the mansion of Jack Nicholson resulted in exile from his beloved America. His life in tatters, Polanski jumped bail and fled to Paris where his nationality protected him from subpoenas. In the eighties he directed just three movies: *Tess*, one of his most haunting works; *Pirates*, an enjoyable but grossly miscalculated flop; and finally *Frantic*, his first Hollywood-backed feature since *The Tenant* in 1976. A broadly commercial venture, less overtly Gothic or perverse than standard Polanski fare, *Frantic* was a plea for Hollywood respectability and an attempt to re-establish his flagging reputation after a decade in the wilderness. Which all goes some way in explaining his unlikely appointment of the very American Harrison Ford as star.

The idea for *Frantic* was hatched during the filming of *Pirates* in Tunisia. After spending a little over two years location hopping around north-west Africa, Polanski yearned for the sanctuary of his swanky apartment on Paris's Right Bank. He was also eager to make a film in the city he knew so well, to peel back the beautiful skin of the French capital and reveal its sometimes shocking underbelly, to dispel its postcard image as the city of light, lovers and tourists. This was to be a film about the Paris of today, a strange, bewildering place of freeways and highrises, slums and Arab bars, 'not that romantic Irma La Duce bullshit you get in American movies,' proclaimed Polanski.

As star vehicles go *Frantic* was second to none, providing Ford with the kind of part leading actors pray for. The entire plot centred around Dr Richard Walker, and hardly a frame of film passes without Ford's panic-stricken face imprinted on it. The responsibility of such a role was enormous, for the success or failure of the movie hinged entirely upon the believability of the performance. To capture the essence of the man Ford, as he does with practically all the characters he inhabits, borrowed heavily from himself. This time, however, it was rather more than usual. Richard Walker may be the closest we'll ever get to glimpsing the real Harrison Ford.

One of Hollywood's most frequently interviewed but circumspect stars, as far as Ford is concerned a personality profile begins and ends with his films. By the very nature of his job, acting, Ford believes he has already revealed everything that anyone should reasonably want to know about him. 'I just can't imagine how much more you can expose yourself than what I've done on screen. You can't know a person better. Who the hell do you think that is up there? Some total stranger? That's me. The way I see it I've revealed everything. I've gone stark naked in public for fifteen years.' Looking back over his repertory of characters, a little bit of Harrison Ford exists in all of them. In an interview for CBS in June 1987 the actor was put on the spot and asked to reveal aspects from some of his key characters that reflected the true man. He started with Bob Falfa from *American Graffiti*. 'I think that there's a bit of a smart ass in me, I think that's the smart ass. Han Solo is a cynical kind of guy with a heart of gold, if you will. There's a little of that in me. The character in *Hanover Street*, I played a real romantic, there's a touch of that in me. The Frisco Kid was basically a person that couldn't turn somebody down. A guy who just wasn't too smart, but was generous of heart. One thing that I think was most prominent in Indiana Jones was his tenaciousness, his unwillingness to give up, and I am tenacious. *Witness*, he's again a sentimental person who wants very much to be a part of life, a part of a community, but he's an outsider, a loner.'

Which brings us neatly back to *Frantic* and Dr Walker. What did these two men have in common? It wasn't until after Polanski had come to know Ford extremely well that he hit upon the idea that Walker should be a specialist in cardiology – a job that requires absolute meticulousness. In life, Ford is peculiarly obsessed with tidiness. He's the kind of man who continually straightens all the piles on his desk. Ford's wardrobe is a shrine to order. Suits and socks are placed in neat rows strictly according to colour, and he cannot begin to function properly if such details are not observed. It is a routine repeated everywhere in the house, and most strikingly in the workshop in which Ford's carpentry tools and hammers are arranged by size. Woe betide anyone who tampers with the layout, anyone who puts a hammer back in the wrong place. 'My wife and kids think I'm nuts – and people in the film business indulge me.'

This behaviour also extends to the workplace. 'I am a great nuisance to art directors and others when on a film set. I am always asking questions: "Why and where?" It is the only way I can be really happy at home and at work,' Ford explained to the *Today* newspaper in September 1992. 'I only do my best work when I consider the surroundings to be absolutely correct.' This obsession for detail, which his family and work colleagues have learnt to tolerate, is, according to Ford, the key to his success. Filming *Patriot Games*, Ford rebelled against the choice of Jack Ryan's American home. The art department had selected a modern house, whereas he felt Ryan would buy into the American dream with a more traditional, old-fashioned home. He argued his case strongly and ultimately won the day. 'If we could represent my character's feelings with such a house, then I would not have to act that part of me. A small detail? Sure. But that is the way I can bring out the best performance.'

Some psychiatrists agree that near-obsessive behaviour, like Ford's, is frequently hereditary. It is unclear whether Christopher Ford ever displayed similar compulsive tendencies or whether Harrison has suffered from this annoying complaint throughout life. He blames it partly on the fact that he is a born worrier. 'My brain does not easily relax. I am always trying to keep myself from obsessive behaviour, without much success.' It can also be triggered by stress or changes in lifestyle. Certainly fame and fortune can be very unsettling. Is this then another price Ford has paid for stardom?

Polanski recognized this flaw in the Ford persona, his meticulousness, crankiness and coiled anger, and exploited it. Walker is established as an ordinary enough man, one accustomed to functioning in an environment of minute detail, and is then dropped headfirst into a dangerous underworld of which he has no knowledge. Early on, Ford shows Walker as a professional used to wielding authority within his own sphere. Later as he becomes steadily more 'frantic' about his wife's abduction that sense of calm resolve erodes and Ford began to rely on 'shadings of anxiety and degrees of frustration' to illustrate a man now forced to trust his instincts in order to survive.

The only clue Walker has to his wife's whereabouts is a suitcase she picked up by mistake at the airport. The trail leads him to the beautiful Michele, the casual author of the mix-up, a junky *femme fatale* and smuggler, who is played by 22-year-old Emmanuelle Seigner, then Polanski's girlfriend. Tempted by the provocative, nubile body of this street punk, almost young enough to be his daughter, Walker never falters from his faithfulness to his wife. It made a nice change for the hero not to give in to that 'fatal attraction' and was one of the themes Ford found most appealing about the film. With Michele's help Walker confronts the kidnappers, who turn out to be buffoonish Middle Eastern terrorists trying to get their hands on a nuclear bomb triggering device hidden somewhere in the suitcase. Polanski's handling of the shoot-out denouement is boring, even inept.

Ford's performance was made easier by the fact that his penchant for taking control over his own dialogue was, for the most part, encouraged. In the Hollywood blockbusters he's used to everything is pre-planned to the smallest detail months in advance. There is little deviation from the vision of the writer and director. Whereas Polanski, in the typical European style, was much more creative and loose. If he saw a scene working before him he didn't care as much as other directors Ford had met that the scripted words were being delivered verbatim. And there was a fair amount of improvisation – for example, Walker's sweet gesture of leaving two roses on his wife's pillow was Ford's own concoction. These little creative ideas found favour with Polanski and there developed between director and star a healthy working

relationship, which later blossomed into friendship. (While filming
Patriot Games in London during the winter of 1991, Ford made a point
of hopping over to Paris with Melissa for a weekend break to visit
Polanski.) They are a mutual appreciation society too. Ford calls
Polanski one of the finest directors he has ever worked with, one of the
great film-makers; Polanski, returning the compliment on Italian
television, described Ford as a 'fantastic actor' in the tradition of the
Hollywood greats. 'As a human being, he's interesting, very
straightforward, very direct, very honest.' Another factor which bound
them together was a diehard perfectionism for their craft which borders
on fanaticism. 'Je suis un enculeur de mouches' (I'm a buggerer of flies)
is Polanski's way of saying that he is a stickler for details.

   Polanski is renowned for driving his actors to the brink of exhaustion,
and Ford, while rejecting accusations that he was exploited by Polanski,
conceded that he was made to work as hard as he'd ever worked for
anyone before. But he enjoyed the experience none the less and was
always made to feel part of the action, almost a partner in the
collaborative process. On set both men worked as a closely knit fighting
force. Theirs was certainly an odd relationship, as the producer, Thom
Mount, noted. 'Polanski's this mischievous little Polish devil and
Harrison's a thoughtful American guy. And so you had a kind of creative
and philosophical Mutt and Jeff.' Both threw themselves into their work,
sometimes at risk to life and limb. Ford, as usual, handled most of his
own stunts, including one hair-raising scene. Filmed in a studio, Ford
dangled precariously near the edge of a sloping Parisian rooftop
thirty-five feet above a courtyard. 'The whole crew held its breath for
twelve hours at a time,' recalled Mount. Ford's insistence upon
performing this sequence himself stemmed from a belief that no stunt
man, however proficient, could realistically duplicate the movements
and mannerisms which he had invested in Walker. This brave decision
led to six perilous days. 'Polanski and Harrison were up on that steep
roof climbing around like a couple of ten years olds, trying to work out
the shots,' *Frantic*'s editor Sam O'Steen recalled to *Premiere* in March
1988. 'Had either of them slipped, they would have been killed. I
watched three takes and had to leave the set, it was so scary.'

   Ford later described *Frantic* as the most physically and mentally taxing
film he had ever done. 'The frustration and anxiety I had to create had a
serious residual effect on me,' he told *Prevue* in March 1989. 'I took it
home with me every night in a way I never had before. I usually get that
out of my system, but this one was unremitting, relentless.' It was
Melissa who caught most of the flak when Ford returned to the hotel at
the end of the day's shoot. He still carried with him the frustrations and
suppressed hysteria of his character, instead of leaving them behind at
the studio as he normally does. 'So it felt good to stop being Dr Walker.

It was more of a strain than I thought.' The pressures of filming were temporarily lifted when everyone flew out to Ibiza to celebrate Ford's forty-fifth birthday. A secret party was organized in his honour at a local nightclub. Putting aside, for one evening at least, his hatred of discos, Ford was visibly pleased and touched by the gesture.

There was no one to blame but himself for the fact that he was required on the set every day, having failed to recognize on his first read-through of the script that Walker was in every single scene. It was hectic, and what little spare time the Fords had was taken up with looking after their new son Malcolm. Every night Ford took the toddler in with him to view the dailies, where he would often fall asleep. 'He used to come all the time,' Ford told *Redbook* in August 1989. 'But now that he's older he wants to talk back to the screen, so we don't bring him as much. So far he hasn't made any critical comments about my work.' During their spring/summer sojourn in Paris, Ford and Melissa mostly stayed indoors. Regrettably Ford never really got to grips with the language, though his inadequate French was never a real handicap. Indeed much of *Frantic*'s humour lies in the actor's fumbling attempts to speak French to pompous public servants.

En route to Los Angeles from Paris Ford reflected on the four months he had spent working with Polanski. Personally he was uncommonly excited about the film and confident of success. The flight certainly provided plenty of spare hours for internal cogitation. The Warner Brothers chartered plane, which Ford was sharing with Clint Eastwood, ran into landing-gear trouble over Maine and the two stars were forced to bed down at the airport hotel while a second plane was hurriedly dispatched to pick them up.

Ford's high hopes for the film were not reciprocated. Warner disliked the original ending and the new, chastened Polanski obliged them by reshooting it. Furthermore, after a glut of disastrous preview screenings the director cut fifteen minutes off the running time – this in spite of Ford's insistence, upon viewing the rough cut, that Polanski 'not change a fucking thing!'. But no amount of last-minute tinkering could halt the inevitable. *Frantic* bombed badly and met with frowns of disapproval from even the staunchest of Ford's admirers. 'A plodding rip-off of Hitchcock' – *Philadelphia Inquirer*; 'Lacklustre and mechanical' – *Chicago*. Some critics applauded the film as a return to form for the turbulent Polanski. *USA Today* called *Frantic* 'the most underrated '88 film to date'. On the plus side Ford won some of the best notices of his career. 'Ford makes you realize what a movie star really is – someone whose every on-screen move is totally enjoyable, an indefinable synthesis of his own personality and the role he's playing' – *Newsweek*. 'Ford is superb, with an intriguing blend of innocence and guilt, and a watchability that brings to mind none other than James Stewart' –

Philadelphia Daily News. 'There's a naturally ironic, self-mocking quality to Ford's work as an actor. He isn't an actor of any real depth, but he's turned into an enormously likeable star performer' – *Washington Post.* 'Ford is sensational. There aren't many Hollywood stars around with the kind of eye-grabbing projection of a Bogart or a Gable. Ford has it in spades' – *Insight* magazine.

Swept up in a torrent of international skulduggery, Ford runs the gamut of emotions as Walker, from exasperation to paranoia, and desperation leads to some stupefying attempts at heroism. While no Indiana Jones, Walker is a typical Ford hero – an honourably ordinary everyman figure, whose unexpected depths of courage spring from his love for his wife. Ford brings credence to the familiar role of the hapless American abroad, managing even to make his own crankiness look endearing. But his limited dramatic range is sometimes woefully self-evident here. That perennially bewildered expression and rubbery face of his looks tired and irritated even before the story gets underway. Perhaps the actor hadn't quite dispelled the overbearing surliness which he had developed for Allie Fox. Ford's expressive limitations are particularly noticeable in a tear-filled telephone monologue to his son. Clearly Ford is giving his all in *Frantic*, and perhaps it is churlish to wish he had more to give. Ultimately it is a dour, monotonous performance, though sufficiently believable to prop up an otherwise mediocre thriller. He makes a compelling, if rather uncomplicated, hero. There is but one amusing scene in which Ford appears from a bedroom doorway naked, his embarrassment covered by a conveniently placed stuffed bear. Punched on the nose by a bad guy he deftly maintains his grip on the cuddly toy as he tumbles to the floor.

Ford admitted defeat gracefully. Famous director, big star, glamorous location, promising storyline. What went wrong? Perhaps *Frantic* was never going to have much appeal to non-European audiences. Polanski's leisurely direction, with its slow-burning suspense, never quite grips or twists or enthrals and the sparse thrills are curiously muted, belying the picture's title. 'I always knew calling it Frantic was a mistake,' Ford said later. 'The script never had a frantic pace. I told Polanski we should call it "Moderately Disturbed". He was not amused.' Anticipation of a tight eighties-style thriller with trademark Polanski dark undercurrents – say, *The Tenant* meets *Lethal Weapon* – were dashed. Oh well, the actor sighed, 'It's a film I think will hold up in years to come.'

In March 1987, not long before the couple were due in Paris, Melissa gave birth to Ford's third son. Christened Malcolm, this white-blond bundle of joy was Melissa's first child. His arrival was awaited with an excitement tempered by caution. While Melissa embraced motherhood, selflessly putting aside two years of her career to raise him, Ford displayed a father's fierce protective feelings, and they shared the fear that their child had been born into a world already in decline. There were concerns too about the age gap between Malcolm and himself. Ford was now in his mid-forties – not quite Methuselah, but old enough to worry about being a father all over again. 'I started adding up ages in my head, thinking how old I'll be when Malcolm's eighteen. I must admit, I find it a little daunting.' Such fears, however genuine, were overshadowed by the prospect of a second chance at fatherhood. And this time around Ford was intent on getting it right.

Ford's sons from his previous marriage were now entering their twenties and neither contemplated a career in showbusiness. Neither had enjoyed being forced to perform in school plays. Benjamin, the eldest, ended up at the California Culinary Academy studying to be a chef, while Willard was determined to teach high-school history and enrolled at the University of California, Santa Cruz. Both have successfully managed to avoid the public eye and are comparatively unaffected by their father's fame. 'They're not fan types,' Ford explained to *Insight* magazine in March 1992. 'They're not impressed by what I do at all. They see it as just the job that I happen to have. They don't display much enthusiasm for my work. I'm just another dad – somebody's dad who's got this odd job!' Ben and Willard were on the scene when Ford was just a struggling actor trying to make ends meet. When *Raiders* made their father a famous and wealthy man they were already teenagers. Both have known poverty as well as riches. Malcolm, on the other hand, was being brought up in a completely different atmosphere and wouldn't have that perspective. The chance of him growing up as the spoilt and jaded son of a Hollywood star is Ford's greatest worry. Determined that Malcolm be aware of what his job entails and be capable of divorcing the man he sees in the movies with the man who tucks him up in bed at night, Ford takes the boy with him whenever he leaves home to make a film. It works. Aged three, Malcolm was sitting watching television one afternoon when a clip of Indiana Jones came on. 'Who is that?' someone asked. Malcolm answered without hesitation. 'That's my other daddy.' On another occasion, during the filming of *Regarding Henry* on a Manhattan street, Ford introduced Malcolm, then two and sitting in his father's chair, to the writer. 'This is Jeffrey,' he said. 'He wrote this movie.' Malcolm looked up and nodded. 'I like your work,' he said.

That his family always accompany him on location and are properly provided for is something Ford insists upon. 'If I can't bring them with me, there's no deal.' It is a decision based on bitter experience. When Ben and Willard were kids Ford wasn't paid enough money to be able to take them along on filming trips. 'I didn't miss years on end, but I did miss some very important times in their lives.' It's something he now deeply regrets. Blessed with this new lease of family life Ford vowed to himself that he'd not miss a single moment of Malcolm's formative years and would try to be a devoted father to make amends for the mistakes of the past. Perhaps, back in the sixties, Ford had become a father too early in life. The problem about having kids when you are young is the loss of freedom – a loss that Ford particularly resented. 'I wasn't prepared either by experience, maturity or disposition to be a good father the first time round. I've learned a lot since then – not just about being a father, but about being a human being.'

Families and family values are important to Ford; he believes solidly in couples, monogamy and procreation. 'I have to have children,' he told *USA Today* in December 1986. 'And I have to have a place of my own. Those are two primordial needs.' Not many of us are given another opportunity to be a better parent, and Ford seized this second chance with both hands. He had become a more stable, patient and mature person, which made it easier to deal with all the frustrations and anxieties of raising children. Moreover, his success would allow him to spend more time with his future offspring. The results were treasurable. Ford credited the birth of Malcolm for making him a happier person. 'He's remarkably self-possessed,' Ford said of his son to *Redbook* in August 1989. 'And I mean from the time he was born. After the birth, he just rested on Melissa's chest for about seven hours, while she and I talked to him. And he kept looking back and forth at us. It was strange – not how you expect a newborn to act.' Ford embraced parenthood again with all the vim and vigour of the nineties 'new man', changing nappies and the like. He wasn't the one to get up in the middle of the night, however. 'I don't have the required biological mechanism to soothe him.'

Harrison Ford had come a long way from the fresh-faced, shy, anxious man who swept to fame in *Star Wars*. Shrewdly, he made sure he was on the other side of the globe, filming *Frantic* in Paris, when tenth-anniversary celebrations seized America. He did, however, allow *Starlog* magazine to reprint his own personal salute to Lucas. It read:

> George Lucas.
> Maker of myths.
> Champion of the innocent.
> Defender of the faith – or force – if you will.
> My colleague.
> My friend.
> Let's face it – my mentor.
> Best wishes on the 10th anniversary of Star Wars
>
> Love, Harrison.

Ford had changed relatively little in those ten years. At forty-five he still retained his boyish, clean-cut good looks and trim figure. Life's tribulations (the break-up of his marriage, loss of privacy) had in no way marred his temperament, and, indeed, he acknowledged that the '77 Ford model, the sometime sourpuss, had mellowed considerably. 'I'm much more mature,' he told *Hello* magazine in January 1989. 'I still have the same moral values as before, the same few friends and I basically think the same old thoughts. I'm a bit older and wiser. Nothing more.'

Ford maintains a select coterie of companions, from the singer Jimmy Buffett, who appeals to the 'shit kicker' in Ford, to Los Angeles gallery owner Earl McGrath, who satisfies the actor's longing for intellectual debate. Arnold Glimcher attests to Ford's liking for highbrow stimulation. 'Harrison's a very urbane man, and one of the funniest people I've met. Conversations with him are provocative and fun. It's not talk about the movies – I want to talk about movies more than he does. He wants to talk about art.' (Ford is a modest collector of Impressionist paintings, like his friend Jack Nicholson.) Ford has few celebrity chums: the last thing he wants to do in his spare time is talk shop with movie types.

With maturity came the suspicion that Ford treated his fame as if it were a mildly amusing joke or mistake. In his acting Ford occasionally signals to the audience that there's something hilarious about his being a star – that if he's a star something must have gone horribly wrong. Having established himself as a pulp hero to millions, he was now successfully carving out a new career, playing challenging and sensitive roles in theoretically deeper and more artistically worthwhile projects. He no longer wanted to keep repeating the same winning formula, that was a recipe for stagnation. Although Ford has never had a focused ambition and refuses to think or plan far ahead, this change of tack was a calculated move, related, perhaps, to the onset of middle age. As he himself confessed, his days of playing 'young, vulnerable types' were truly over. 'I mean Star Wars was over ten years ago. I am ten years older. There's no sense denying it. In fact, I revel in it.' *Witness* was the breakthrough, and moviegoers steeped in his fantasy epics discovered a more complete Harrison Ford: introspective, cerebral, multilayered, and infused with humanity and vision. Next came Allie Fox, a thousand psychotherapy sessions away from Solo and Indy. Such a taxing role, coming so soon after his Oscar-nominated work as John Book the previous year, highlighted the skilful and deliberate way Ford was turning audience attention away from his swashbuckling to his burgeoning dramatic talents. And he was visibly improving with each performance. 'An actor must constantly change the public's perceptions of what he can do, constantly expand those perceptions.'

Luckily the audience Ford had gained in the early eighties had grown and matured with him; their interests and tastes had broadened too. No longer did they feel betrayed if Ford wasn't dragged behind a speeding truck, imperilled by snakes or lethal aliens. He could afford to indulge in a little quality and if the popcorn crowd didn't like it and turned instead to the antics of Cruise or Schwarzeneger, so be it. 'Raiders III', quietly lumbering into pre-production provided the perfect backstop. The kids would flock like sheep to see that one, wouldn't they?

Ford never did like cities very much. Growing up in Chicago he came to resent the noise and filth of a teeming metropolis. He now prefers the serene meditation of country life, and that ranch in Jackson Hole provides a haven for a man whose definition of madness is Los Angeles, where he still maintains a modest home. At first the Fords divided their time between both homes, as the winters in Wyoming were prone to be long and harsh. 'My wife and I came up here because we wanted a private place with four seasons – three of them winter,' Ford liked to joke; but temperatures can often dip down to minus twenty degrees Fahrenheit, and unprotected cattle have been known to freeze to death. Connie Pasqual, one of the local helpers at the Ford ranch, told *Sunday* magazine in May 1989 that Jackson Hole was the kind of place where people get snowed in for weeks on end during the cold months. 'Anybody who spends winters in the highlands of Wyoming was either born there and probably has no choice – or they're nuts.' After years of settled contentment in Wyoming Harrison and Melissa became more and more rare and reluctant visitors to the West coast. Now, when life becomes too quiet and Ford feels the brief need for the jazz and excitement of city life, the family head east for part of each year. New York is the antidote to Wyoming's rugged calm; there, the crowds give him some anonymity and he can indulge his love of Japanese and Thai food. Ford surprised even himself when he fell under the spell of a city he once despised. 'I rather enjoy New York now. It's a great contrast to Wyoming. My little boy, strangely enough, loves it. It's very exciting for him.' At one time both parents seriously contemplated raising Malcolm in New York.

It all started when Ford was filming *Working Girl* in the big Apple in 1988. Two more pictures, *Presumed Innocent* and *Regarding Henry*, were also shot in the city, obliging him to buy an apartment in Manhattan to house his brood. In the summer of 1989 Ford successfully bid $3.5 million for a twelve room Central Park West apartment. All the paperwork seemed in order and the deal was closed. Only it wasn't. Out of the blue came a Wall Street tycoon who upped the asking price by a cool $100,000. Ford responded in kind, but not enough to oust the businessman who claimed the apartment for the eventual sum of $3.7 million. Ford tried again the following spring, this time successfully purchasing a $2 million-plus apartment overlooking Central Park from the actress Debra Winger, who decided to sell while in Nairobi filming *The Sheltering Sky*. The two stars made the long-distance deal over the telephone.

With his puckish grin, Ford has always shown a delicate touch for comic inflection and timing. The humour he instilled into characters like Han Solo and Indiana Jones will be fondly remembered. Even during the heavyweight drama of *Witness* the actor had his wry and light-hearted moments. And yet, save for *The Frisco Kid*, when he was landed with the role of straight man to Gene Wilder's manic rabbi, Ford had no out-and-out comedies on his CV. This in spite of the fact that he is a natural comedian. Humour is a major clue to Ford's personality. Colleagues delight in his bone-dry, terse and ironic wit, a mixture of irreverence and put-on, with a hint of self-deprecation. 'I'm always doing comedy,' he once said. 'It's a point of view about life.' Bonnie Bedelia swears that Ford has a genuinely warm and inspired sense of humour. 'He's very funny, but he doesn't horse around. He's not a silly person,' she informed *Inside Hollywood* in November 1991. 'He's a very bright, astute man with an impeccable sense of form and a huge star, so it's obvious that he would feel guarded. Considering the magnitude of stardom, he's the most real person with the most wonderful dry sense of humour.' One day on the set of *Presumed Innocent* Bedelia didn't feel her make-up was quite right. 'So I rushed back into the dressing-room and Ford was sitting with his feet up. I turned to him and said, "Do I look unfinished to you?" He waited a beat, then he said, "Yeah, you could have been a little taller." '

On every set Ford likes to keep a sense of humour. One day during a break from shooting the pivotal trial scene in *Presumed Innocent* Ford overheard one of the stagehands on the telephone, struggling to convince his girlfriend that he'd be working late. 'There's nothing I can do,' the man pleaded. 'There's been a delay.' The voice on the other end was sceptical. Walking over, Ford grabbed the receiver and said, 'He really has to stay, sorry,' then promptly went back to his waiting, with a broad, mischievous grin on his face.

Ford was disgruntled that critics were surprised to find him so eager to play comedy, since he had always been of the opinion that most of his films were comedies, in the sense that he played larger-than-life characters. Indiana Jones, for instance, would be nothing without a sense of humour. 'And I thought Star Wars was comedy. I look for comedy all the time.' While aware that he has a good sense of humour Ford doesn't feel it comes across on screen. 'I've seen myself and deduced that when I go for laughs I come across as kind of wooden.'

Even so, from as early as 1982, Ford was keen to try his hand at light comedy as a change of pace, but nothing moronic. 'I'd like to do sort of Cary Grant-type roles, you know, screwball comedies.' A prophecy, perhaps. Plenty were offered (he turned down the chance to play opposite Barbra Streisand in 1982), but the majority of them were too lightweight, 'eminently disposable'.

Then along came Kevin Wade's smart script for *Working Girl*, which seemed ideal in every respect. The storyline was excellent: a feminist fairytale about a girl-Friday secretary, betrayed by her boss, who begins an earnest assault on the corporate ladder, stealing her superior's boyfriend (Ford) into the bargain. The screenplay had a firm dramatic structure and an emotional context which had Ford glued to the page. 'It had a lot of serious things to say about modern male–female relationships, and how women are treated in the workplace. I found it all very interesting.' The primary attraction was the choice of director. Ford had always wanted to work with Mike Nichols, whose list of achievements include *The Graduate* and *Catch 22*, whom he had known for years and greatly admired. (They came close to making *Silkwood* together, but their schedules didn't match.) Indeed, everyone involved was of a very high calibre.

Sharing the limelight with him were two gifted actresses: Sigourney Weaver, who like Ford had made her name in fantasy films, and highly touted newcomer Melanie Griffith. Ford had a lot of fun working with these two women, although it grieved him when Weaver went on the warpath over sex discrimination in Hollywood, citing his wage packet as a prime example. Both she and Griffith were paid about half of what Ford received, in spite of the subordinate nature of his role. 'I'm slightly embarrassed,' he confessed to *Maclean*'s magazine on hearing Weaver's complaint. 'It's not within my control, but I'm certainly sympathetic to her point of view – she's right.' To play second fiddle to the women, far from denting his superstar sensibilities, was precisely what Ford craved. He took delight in what was essentially a secondary character. 'The girl's part, the love interest,' as he described it, since usually two men are vying for the charm of the same woman in such films. After his last couple of pictures, which were real killers in terms of workload, it was a relief to have two other people to share the burden. He didn't, however, want to make a habit of playing supporting roles. 'I'd rather be home. If I'm going to leave the ranch at all, I would prefer it be for a big piece of work in a successful film,' he told the *Anderson Independent Mail* in May 1989. 'I certainly didn't mind taking on a secondary role. Sometimes the secondary roles are where you find really interesting characters who might not have a whole movie of their own.' Ford concedes that some of his best early work is on show in small roles; he cites *Heroes* and the television special he did for Stanley Kramer as the best examples.

Ford plays Jack Trainer, a high-powered Manhattan broker. His preparation included immersing himself in the unfamiliar world of Wall Street, spending time at brokerage houses around New York and mixing with a few authentic investment bankers. Ford even attended a few meetings with their clients, until he realized that his 'star' presence was affecting the reality of the situation. 'We wanted a guy who looked like he could be a winner on Wall Street, but who also had the look of burnout around the fringes,' producer Douglas Wick told the *Philadelphia Inquirer* in November 1988. 'Harrison has that funny warmth and softness that goes against the grain of his personality.'

Ford breaks new ground as Jack Trainer, a former whizzkid now on the slide, complete with expensive designer suits and a rough-edged urbanity. Despite only being in his mid thirties Trainer fears his job may be grabbed by some new hotshot broker. Parallels with Hollywood are tempting, but Ford shares none of Jack's middle-age anxiety. He scarcely worries about competing with up-and-coming actors for the year's coveted roles. 'I'm not competitive with other actors in any way. I have never felt that way. I don't think I'm a competitive person. I've never been one to want to win at games that much.' Indeed, Alec Baldwin, some years Ford's junior, had earlier been touted to play Trainer, but lost out once Ford declared an interest, ending up instead as Tess's unfaithful boyfriend. Baldwin took it well. 'The minute Harrison Ford shows up you drop everything and you sign up Harrison Ford.' He was less charitable when Ford later robbed him of the coveted role of Jack Ryan.

Once cast, the character of Trainer was altered to suit Ford's persona and, during a hectic fortnight of rehearsals, was beefed up to exploit his enormous box-office appeal. Ford succeeds brilliantly in the role, bringing an unusually likeable dimension to a universally loathed profession. In one hilarious scene he strips off his shirt, washes his armpits in a pitcher of water before putting on a fresh one. But he has forgotten to draw the office blinds and his staff of giggling secretaries applaud the routine. Far from embarrassed, Jack takes a bow as if on stage. Ford's performance is stylish, self-mocking and wonderfully deadpan. 'He displays a comic talent never previously explored' – *Hollywood Reporter*; 'Ford gets to show his finesse as a suave, romantic comic' – *Newsweek*; 'Ford is marvellous. He's so identified with action movies that it comes as a small shock to see him doing tremendously interesting work in a romantic comedy with a coat and tie on. He's put on a coat and tie a lot lately, and he's been getting more impressive with each film' – *Buffalo News*; 'Ford's comic abilities are a total surprise; he's been so good recently that a critical re-evaluation is due' – *USA Today*.

Critically, then, *Working Girl* was well received: 'It's the most entertaining American comedy of 1988' – *New York*. Many saw the film as a fond throwback to the Hollywood screwball comedies of the past. 'You haven't seen Harrison in a sophisticated comedy of this type,' executive producer Robert Greenhut bragged to *Premiere* in October 1988. 'He's the closest thing we've got to Cary Grant in the talent pool these days.' Such talk was lost on Ford, of course, who hadn't seen many of those classic comedies of the thirties and forties. But he was flattered by the press reviews and proud of the public's response to the movie, which amazingly garnered six Oscar nominations, though nothing for Ford.

13

The Last Crusader

The idea of a trilogy featuring Indiana Jones was discussed by both Spielberg and Lucas from the outset. When production began on *Raiders* the two men had shaken hands and agreed that if the first one worked they would do three of them. But a suitable story idea for the third instalment proved elusive. It took five years to come up with a script everyone could agree on. Early scenarios, one involving ghosts and children, were ultimately scrapped on the orders of Lucas, although a few elements, including a tank chase, were retained.

Ford was not contractually obliged to do a third Indiana Jones movie but there was no question, when the time came, of him refusing to don that battered fedora once again, if the script was good enough and Spielberg was holding the reins. Any doubts might have been allayed by the reported $5 million fee, plus a minimum of 5% of the profits. But no, he was actually looking forward to it. Ford makes no secret of the fact that he loves making these films and working with Spielberg. 'Playing Indiana Jones is fun, it's every boy's dream. It's like having the best toy box in the world.' He decided to go ahead in spite of only having had one month's rest after *Working Girl* – which was rare for him. However, there had been no decent work around in 1987, and he was worried that he hadn't had a movie out in over a year. Ford therefore decided to make *Working Girl* and *The Last Crusade* back to back, then take the whole of 1989 off and sink back blissfully into his family life.

Like Ford, Spielberg had also diversified as an artist since *Raiders* (*The Color Purple* and *Empire of the Sun*) but was just as keen to complete the trilogy. In part, he wanted to atone for the perceived sins of the second adventure, which many had criticized on release for its inadvertent racism, sexism, brutality and general sensory overload. In the years since, Spielberg has virtually disowned *Temple of Doom*. Ford feels much the same, 'but I haven't been as vocal'. Personally Ford had liked the idea of taking Indy for a walk on the dark side, and had seen it as a valiant attempt to deepen the myth. But the result wound up being too dark and unbalanced, with too much emphasis on pseudo-mystical bunkum. 'It was unnecessarily graphic,' says Ford. The actor sensed that things were going wrong on the set, but his warnings went unheeded. 'Occasionally I rose to protest, but moviemaking is a collaborative effort and while my attitude was noted, it did not prevail.'

To bring Indiana Jones to life on the screen Ford invested himself in the character, bringing to bear his taciturn nature and sly humour as he had earlier done with Han Solo. 'One invests them with as many aspects of oneself as convenience allows,' Ford told the *Sunday Telegraph* in May 1985. 'You certainly want to take advantage of things you have in common with the character.' *Raiders of the Lost Ark* was very much a discovery process for the actor. He found out who Indiana was in the course of making the movie. 'The character just sort of evolved that way,' Spielberg recalled. 'Harrison brought a lot of his own personality to the part.' *Temple of Doom* was a little more of a cruise for Ford, and he was content merely to play him as written. With *Indiana Jones and the Last Crusade*, however, Ford felt a certain obligation to serve up something fresh to his audience. He wanted somehow to deepen the character, to tease out unseen aspects of his nature and to uncover some of the man's shrouded history.

Finally the concept was born that brought life to the second sequel: give Indiana a father and so add a new dimension to the series. This in turn would allow Spielberg the chance to weave in a meaningful emotional relationship amid all the action. Ford immediately warmed to the notion, not least because, like Lucas and Spielberg, he too had been a recent father. The problem soon arose of whom to cast. Writer Jeffrey Boam envisaged Professor Henry Jones as an elderly man not unlike the crotchety character played by Henry Fonda in *On Golden Pond*. Lucas, on a similar wavelength, had in mind various little-known British character actors. Then lightning struck Spielberg: Who better than Sean Connery? he thought, for Indiana Jones has a spiritual father, it is James Bond. It was an inspired choice and arguably the casting coup of the decade. But Lucas was grieved. Connery was, he felt, too formidable a force to play the bookish professor. Jones senior was supposed to be a much older gentleman, a scholar who is completely out of his element in the chaotic world of his son's adventures. Having Connery in the role completely altered the character. But Spielberg insisted, perhaps in the knowledge that Ford's on-screen aura would smother an actor of lesser stature. Moreover, he wanted Ford to have to rise to the challenge of working against a strong star performer, something that hadn't been required of him in the previous two films. 'I figured Sean would give Harrison a run for his money.' And it worked, Connery brought out the very best in Ford, who ended up giving his finest and funniest portrayal.

Once Lucas's objections had been overcome another hurdle

presented itself. Spielberg was doubtful that Connery would want to get involved in a production so similar in spirit to the Bond pictures. As it turned out he was keen to climb on board. The gimmick of introducing the father and showing Indy as a teenager was intriguing; it was like the three stages of the man. What didn't please him was the screenplay. The presentation of Henry Jones as an elderly, gnomish wise man was at odds with his own perception of how to play the part. He saw the father as a stern Victorian patriarch, a contradictory mixture of action man and quixotic academic. But still very much a traditionalist, in the eccentric mode. The story goes thus: When his mother died Indiana was thirteen and left in the care of his father, who neglected him. Years later, Jones senior continues to treat his son as if he were a child in need of a remedial education, all of which inevitably leads to conflict.

Once accepted, Connery was accorded an unusually generous amount of operating room to mould his role to his own personal specifications. Not only was he instrumental in instilling Henry Jones with his infectious humour, but he also managed to graft on to the old-timer a few tried and tested Bondian qualities. Notable among these was the revelation that Henry has slept with Elsa, the film's *femme fatale*, prior to Indy's conquest. Would the Henry Jones character, as originally conceived, have bedded Elsa? 'No way,' Boam answered, 'but Sean Connery would.'

Ford's initial reaction on being told of Spielberg's brainwave was that Connery wasn't old enough (a concern shared by the latter). Only twelve years separated them, which meant they were closer to being contemporaries. Otherwise Ford, who had the power to veto, was pleased with the choice. 'It was a brilliant idea to bring Sean in.' By agreeing to share the limelight with an actor of such legendary status Ford demonstrated a refreshing lack of ego for a major Hollywood actor. But Ford isn't stupid; he was well aware of how much weight Connery could bring to the film. It was also obvious that the father of a hero like Indiana Jones had to be a figure of substance and charisma. But was he worried about being upstaged? 'I want the best possible support I and the film can have. And anyway I thought I could take care of myself. I think competition on a movie set is a big mistake.' At first there was some concern about the pairing of Ford and Connery. 'I didn't know quite how it would work,' Spielberg confessed. 'But there is the most wonderful chemistry between the two of them; it's a little like the Newman/Redford chemistry in Butch Cassidy and The Sting. It's a real sparkle of screen magic.' The critics agreed, hailing their partnership as one of cinema's most memorable.

Back in the sixties Ford was never much of a Bond buff, although he enjoyed *From Russia with Love*. The rest of the series was, for him, too gadget-orientated. But he was an admirer of Connery's other work.

'When I got to be an actor, I could see that Sean was one of the good ones. I thought he was great in The Man Who Would Be King, Robin and Marian and The Wind and the Lion.' Although neither had met before, both stars hit it off from the start and little rehearsal was needed to perfect their unique, almost vaudevillian, father/son rapport. 'When Sean and Harrison arrived on the set,' Spielberg recalled to Time magazine in May 1992, 'everyone got quiet and respectful. The two are like royalty.' The wonderful chemistry and friendship established during filming owed much to the fact that both men had a lot in common. They always hunt for the most stimulating and challenging material available and their acting styles correspond. Neither subscribes to the 'method' school, where the actor is supposed to 'live' his character; rather, they are heavy on technique. 'We like to work fast and loose,' Ford explained. 'And we like to have fun.' In some respects Connery is just the sort of movie star Ford aspires to be – someone who became famous as a fantasy hero before graduating into a variety of roles that have fed a long and illustrious career. Each has been one of his generation's definitive and dominant men of action. Both have also known failure away from the roles that made them global stars. Yet they have managed to avoid becoming victims of their own success and have gone on to prove their artistic worth.

The pair's anarchic sense of fun was displayed most prominently during the filming of the zeppelin sequence. The temperature was in the hundreds and very uncomfortable, particularly for Connery, wearing a three-piece tweed suit, and Ford, sporting his standard leather jacket. Because the actors were only being shot from the waist up, Connery dropped his trousers. At first Ford didn't quite appreciate this, but soon, his face dripping with perspiration, he followed suit. They both sat there for the remainder of a very serious father/son dialogue minus their trousers. 'Working with Sean was the pleasure that it looks to be. He's a great actor. I've learned from him.' Connery too appreciated both Ford's creative input and his bone-dry wit. 'Harrison's sense of humour is sly and sneaks up on you.'

The Last Crusade is closer in spirit to Raiders than Temple of Doom, what with the desert locations, the return of the Nazi terror and the search for another biblical artefact. However, more emphasis was brought to bear on character development, particularly through Indy's often petulant relationship with his father. Wisely dispensing with attempts to recapture the central romance of Raiders, Spielberg developed the emotional core of The Last Crusade through the sparring relationship of Ford and Connery. Boam's script highlights themes of neglect and reconciliation. In the course of searching for the Holy Grail father and son reacquaint themselves after many years of estrangement. Ford felt that it was a rite of passage to which audiences, as well as himself, could relate. 'I have a father, I am a father, I know it from both sides,' he told *Movies USA* in May 1989. 'I've gone through the process of adjustments with my own father that all fathers and sons have with each other, accepting each other for who we are and not expecting them to be perfect.' Ford used these experiences, common to us all, to shape his performance. At times it reminded him of just how much he was like his own father. 'All those things that always drove me crazy about my father have started showing up in my personality.'

Utah, 1912, is the setting for the opening episode of *The Last Crusade*, in which a young Indy fights a gang of thieves aboard a train full of circus animals. In terms of structure and formula this third adventure closely follows the examples set by its elder brothers, not least in starting with an exciting teaser. Various ideas for a slam-bang beginning were submitted, but all were considered tired and hollow compared with the forerunners. Amid the crunching bone and wild action, these opening sequences had always told us something new about our hero. Therein lay the problem: it seemed the writers had nothing fresh to say. That was until George Lucas came up with the idea of having Indy appear as a teenager. The casting of River Phoenix (who plays the role with all Ford's quirky charm) inevitably led to press speculation that the brat-packer was being groomed to step into Harrison's shoes. When Phoenix played Ford's son in *The Mosquito Coast* their likeness was duly noted. Although consulted, Ford did not influence the decision, but was evidently pleased with the choice.

To help Phoenix with the intonations and physical externalization of Indy, Spielberg drafted in the services of the genuine article. For one week Ford was given a free hand to coach and direct the youngster. 'I wanted to make sure he got the moves right,' Ford commented. The locomotive set-piece, praised by some critics as the most inventive moment in the film, is Spielberg at his best. It is a magical and gutsy sequence, economically and humorously explaining the origins of Indiana's mythic characteristics – his hatred for snakes, that scarred chin, his dexterity with a bullwhip and his trademark fedora.

Filming got underway on 16 May 1988 in Almeria, southern Spain. A dry river bed was the site for an elaborate tank battle, the film's action highlight and Spielberg's attempt to equal the impact of the truck chase in *Raiders*. The ten-minute sequence man-on-horse-versus-steel-behemoth was unbelievably expensive and time consuming: two weeks in the making (it only took ten more days to make the whole of *Duel*), at a cost of $200,000 a day. Once again Vic Armstrong doubled for Ford and supervised all stunt work, the most dangerous of which was a heart-stopping fourteen-foot leap from a galloping horse on to the moving tank. Though this was one stunt Ford didn't even bother to attempt, he did almost everything else, including hanging off a side cannon as the vehicle ploughed through a rocky gorge. He described the ordeal as, 'one of the hairiest stunts I've ever been involved in'.

So eager was Ford to get involved in the physical action that Armstrong sometimes had to restrain him from going too far. One scene had Indy jumping off a sixteen-foot ledge, knocking a villain from his horse, taking the reins himself and galloping off. Ford desperately wanted to do the whole thing himself, but Armstrong feared he might break his legs. 'The only way I could dissuade him was with a little white lie,' Armstrong told the *Sun* in December 1991. 'I dragged him to one side and hissed that if he did stunts he would do me out of money. Harrison was horrified and said, "Sorry Vic, I just didn't realize. Of course, I'll shut up."' Still determined to do as many stunts as Spielberg, Armstrong and the production company's insurance carriers would allow inevitably led to occasions when Ford's life was put in considerable danger, although the set-ups were calculated to reduce the risk of real injury. 'Bumps and bruises go with the territory,' Ford says. 'It's what distinguishes an Indiana Jones movie from another adventure film. You sit there in the theatre and know I'm doing it.' The actor still rigidly believes that there are important opportunities for expression of character in those physical moments. Some of the best nuances of his personality come through during the fight scenes, in which a well-chosen expression after a punch and a shrug after a gag are all part of the panache.

But pushing fifty could his body continue to take such punishment? Ford now regularly works out at home, ever since he sprained his back on the set of *Temple of Doom*. 'He's very strong,' Jake Steinfeld, who has trained Ford since the early eighties, told the *New York Daily News* in June 1989. 'He has a lot of determination and doesn't quit. That's why he looks consistently good year-round.' By adopting a carefully monitored exercise regime, primarily concentrating on building up his abdominal muscles, which strengthen the back, Ford was able to overcome his disability and resume his duties as Indiana Jones. But at what cost? 'He's practically a bag of old, aching bones,' a work colleague revealed to the *Globe* newspaper in January 1989. 'The doctors have told him to stop being so macho, but he likes to do his own stunts and he's in pain often.' Other sources confirmed that Ford was suffering on location, taking a lot of aspirin and complaining about his back. He was invariably worn out after a long day's shooting.

Ford also had to contend with severe accusations of cowardice made by a British tabloid newspaper. The article, published in December 1988 by the *News of the World*, alleged that Ford behaved in an inconsiderate and arrogant manner on location. It went on to say that his cowardice in refusing to do even the simplest of stunts was regarded with contempt by the stunt team. Members of the crew apparently referred to the tightly knit club of Ford, Spielberg and Lucas as the Three Musketeers. But for all the smug camaraderie that implied, Ford rarely spent much of his free time with them. Over the years, as Ford's fame and stature within the industry has risen, those around him have noticed how he has grown increasingly more reserved and withdrawn. A female crew member on the previous two Indy movies told *The Times* that Ford was 'quieter, if anything, and more into himself' on *The Last Crusade*, despite the fact that he was working with a team he already knew well. 'The set is very serious around Harrison,' she continued. 'The leading actor tends to run the floor and the director goes with it. With Harrison there's always a respectful air.' Robert Watts, the film's producer, who has known him since they first worked together on *Star Wars*, agrees. 'If anything, Ford has become a more private person as his success has grown.'

The following May a second *News of the World* 'exclusive' appeared, concerning Ford's activities in his home town, which portrayed him as self-centred and unpleasant. The article alleged that Ford had caused a serious accident when he lost control of his brand-new £5,000 snowmobile, mowing down innocent tourists in the process. Allegedly the whole affair was hushed up, at his insistence, and people paid off. The article went on to say that Ford was a man obsessed with a tough screen image which he could not live up to and that his marriage was on the rocks as a consequence. Ford was also, apparently, bitten by a snake and almost killed. Melissa had bought a snakebite kit when they moved to Wyoming – against his wishes. When he was bitten, she quickly read the instructions, applied the medicine and saved his life. The article was nothing less than a character assassination. So offended was Ford that he took the rare step of suing the paper for libel. In September 1990 the publication admitted that both articles were untrue and agreed to pay damages and legal costs. A vindicated Ford gave a large portion of the five-figure sum to charity.

Leaving Spain far behind, Ford and the Indy crew travelled to Venice, then on to Petra and Jordan, finally settling in Elstree for ten weeks of interiors. These were conducted under a cloak of secrecy, lifted occasionally to allow stars like Michael Jackson to make flying visits. While in London Ford was robbed of £50,000-worth of jewellery. Relaxing downstairs at his £1 million mock Georgian home in Beaumont Gardens, Hampstead, Ford spotted a thief trying to break into a neighbouring house and raised the alarm. It wasn't until an hour after the man had fled that Ford discovered that he too had been burgled, despite the presence of electronically operated gates manned by twenty-four-hour guards. The thief apparently shinned up a drainpipe and got in through an open office window, snatching the gems from a cabinet in the master bedroom. The incident did little to improve Ford's already tarnished impression of London.

Things were scarcely any better up at Elstree where Ford was almost

set on fire and attacked by six thousand rats. During the filming of the
scene in which Jones and son are tied up in a blazing room within a Nazi
stronghold, a stunt backfired. While horrified technicians struggled to
free them Ford and Connery were temporarily exposed to the deadly
flames. For the Venice catacomb sequence, with its leering skulls and
blackened skeletons, some six thousand rats had been bred in captivity
especially for the occasion. Following on in the grand tradition – snakes
in *Raiders*, insects in *Temple of Doom* – it was inevitable that in the third
instalment Indy should meet these, the grossest of all vermin. And, as
had happened on the preceding two movies, at least half the crew hated
rats and had to wait outside the stage until filming was completed. 'Same
thing with the snakes,' Spielberg recalled. 'We lost half the crew on the
first movie, and we lost three-quarters of the crew with the bugs.' Ford,
as always, remained unruffled. 'That kind of stuff doesn't bother me at
all. The rats didn't bother me, the snakes didn't bother me. It's people
I'm scared of.'

Taking a well-earned rest from the rigours of filming, Ford was
somehow persuaded to participate in the Jackie Stewart celebrity
challenge shoot – by Connery perhaps, a long-time friend of the former
racing-driver. The event, in aid of a cancer charity, took place one
Sunday in late June at the Gleneagles estate in Scotland. Other stars in
attendance included Billy Connolly, Nigel Mansell and Kiri Te
Kanawa, as well as Ford's 'Indy 3' buddies, Connery and Spielberg.
The moors were simply awash with the high-born: there were
princesses, dukes, lords and even two kings. This mixture of sporting
event and social happening clearly goes against the grain of Ford's
semi-reclusive nature, yet he seemed relatively at ease. He was even
spied hob-nobbing with King Hussein and Queen Noor of Jordan. But
for the most part Ford and Melissa kept to themselves. Ferried to and
from the shooting area in a fleet of Range Rovers, Ford's team ended up
disappointingly low on the honours list. Both he and Connery (cinema's
two greatest action heroes) had to be coached on how to handle their
weapon and hit the target, and even then failed to score many points.
Ford, in particular, was mocked by the press, who were there in
abundance, for his ineptitude with the gun. The *Daily Record*, a local
paper, wrote, 'And as Harrison Ford missed shot after shot, someone
said, not without cause, "The man may be a Hollywood star, but
obviously can't hit a barn door with a banjo." ' Given that he had not
picked up a shotgun until a fortnight before the competition, this was
unfair. Actually it was Spielberg who surprised everyone with his
shooting prowess, scoring a perfect ten on one event.

Approaching the new decade, the formerly cloistered Ford was
beginning to be conspicuously visible in social circles. He was among
several top star names, including Clint Eastwood and Kevin Costner,

who attended Sean Connery's sixtieth birthday bash at a plush LA nightspot in June 1990. He also joined in the festivities at a party in honour of Warner Brothers, spending much of the night joking in a corner with Steve Martin. In October 1991 Ford attended the wedding of Steven Spielberg and Kate Capshaw in East Hampton, Long Island, and was one of the revellers at the surprise stag party the night before.

One of the year's most eagerly awaited film events, *Indiana Jones and the Last Crusade* was released at the beginning of a summer gripped by sequel mania. Competing with the likes of *Lethal Weapon II*, *Ghostbusters II*, *Star Trek V*, *et al.*, records crashed as *The Last Crusade* claimed the biggest seven-day opening in film history, with receipts close to the $50 million mark. The critics were unanimous in their praise. 'This is a film of which Lucas and Spielberg long will be proud' – *Variety*; 'In this imperfect world, you're not likely to see many manmade objects come this close to perfection' – *People*; 'Probably the best written and most accomplished of the series' – *The Times*. It was the second most popular film of the year in America (the Gothic *Batman* was the surprise winner) with a final box-office tally of $195 million. But even this figure was put in perspective by the international turn-out, yielding a truly staggering gross of $440 million. Though pleased with the enthusiastic response to his latest work, Ford did admit that he was no longer impressed by box-office figures. 'My hope is predominantly for its artistic success, not its commercial success.' Devoted to the idea of making a movie out of *The Mosquito Coast*, Ford was deeply upset when it bombed; conversely, he was proud when *Witness* and *Working Girl* succeeded, having never anticipated they would be so popular. Gauging whether or not a film will be successful is one of the things Ford considers when deciding on a role. But the financial revenue is not the key issue – rather, if one has spent time and energy on a project one wants people to see it. 'That's the payoff.'

Spielberg faced an impossible task in trying to top the great escapism of *Raiders*. There is no way a film could rekindle the sense of joyous discovery one felt at seeing, for the first time, the old cliffhanger serials fused to state-of-the-art technology and dazzling direction. It made adults children again. But on its own terms, *The Last Crusade* was a considerable achievement, and Ford was enormously proud of the finished result. But it is hardly in the same class as its illustrious predecessors. Not even the welcome inclusion of Connery, who practically steals the show, could hide the all-too-evident cracks of formula fatigue. In his haste to recapture the magic and lighthearted spirit of *Raiders*, Spielberg almost succeeded in running off a photocopy. All the familiar elements are present, but the thrills are shopworn; and the action set-pieces, though grandly staged, are curiously flat and uninvolving, with the exception of the glorious tank battle. Where the film does work, and wonderfully so, is in the comic sparring of Ford and Connery. Their relationship is the story's most gripping and charming component. The sight of Indy reduced to snot-nosed-child status whenever confronted by a father who refers to him as junior is priceless. *The Last Crusade* is full of divine lunacy. It is easily the funniest of the trilogy – more campy than *Raiders*, less cynical than *Temple of Doom* – which Ford attributed to Spielberg's magic touch. Some of the new situations Indy found himself were just plain ludicrous and Ford knew it. The most audacious scene was Indy's face-to-face encounter with Adolf Hitler at a Nazi book-burning rally, where he ends up with the dictator's autograph. History meets myth. For all its frothy nonsense, the film works splendidly, and is full of inspired and gleeful moments.

The closing tableau of *The Last Crusade*, with Indy and his troupe riding into a spectacular sunset, is arguably one of the most satisfying emotional moments of the trilogy and brought Indy's cinema adventures to a suitably rousing finale. It was widely known prior to the opening of *The Last Crusade* that this was to be the end of the series. Neither Spielberg nor Lucas had the inclination to continue. Lucas, it is true, returned in 1992 with *The Young Indiana Jones Chronicles* for ABC television. This explored Indy's childhood as he travelled the world, and the events and people that helped to shape his incredible personality – the likes of Picasso, Churchill, Mata Hari, Lawrence of Arabia and Roosevelt. Ford deliberately steered clear of the show, ignoring Lucas's appeals for him to star as the 93-year-old Indy for the narration scenes. He was, however, tempted to make a cameo appearance as 50-year-old Indy in a two-hour special, a one-time stunt which ABC hoped would boost the series' flagging ratings. Entitled *The Mystery of the Blues* and broadcast on 13 March 1993 Ford guests as a middle aged Indy, snowbound, where else but in Wyoming, while searching for a sacred Indian relic. Waiting out the storm in a wilderness cabin he reminisces about his wild adventures as a teenager in prohibition Chicago where he learns about jazz and racism and gets mixed up in the city's bootleg wars with his college room-mate Eliot Ness.

Back in 1989 though Ford had grown tired of Indy's adventures. While he earnestly believed the potential existed for more films, it made better sense to quit while ahead. 'I am happy to have done all three,' Ford told *USA Today* in May 1989. 'But it pleases me just as well to get on to something else.' Almost word for word, this was the attitude he expressed upon the demise of the *Star Wars* trilogy. Likewise, on the close of filming on Indy's final escapade Ford displayed neither sadness nor joy. But his unabashed fondness for slipping back into the familiar guise of the veteran scoundrel led to his lamenting the loss of an old friend and one of cinema's greatest hero figures. 'I'll miss the whole thing,' Ford acknowledged to the *Lucasfilm Fan Club* in the spring of

1989. 'There is a lot of pleasure in this character for me. I enjoy the kind of humour that we have in these films and I love doing the physical stuff. It makes me feel like a kid. I'll miss the particular fun of playing the character but I think three films is enough.'

With each successive year the likelihood of seeing Harrison Ford returning as Indiana Jones diminishes, especially now that he's committed to playing Jack Ryan (*Patriot Games* etc.) in a protracted series of films which should see him comfortably into the next century. And let's face it, he is getting a little old for these 'running and jumping' movies; he is ageing while Indy remains locked in a 1938 time-frame. 'I'll be in my fifties pretending to be thirty-five, and I'm afraid it's going to get to a point where it's too hard to get out of bed in the morning! I just won't be able to do the things I used to do.'

While Indiana Jones has finally been laid to rest, cinematically at least, his legend lives on in television, video games and books. Some of his prized possessions were either given away or sold off. First to go was his brown fedora and battered leather jacket. In a ceremony full of pomp and circumstance they became national treasures when Ford personally presented them to the Smithsonian Institution's National Museum of American History in Washington DC. The event was a publicity triumph, following on the heels of the last film's première. 'I'm flattered to be here,' Ford told the hordes of reporters in attendance, 'and to have these artifacts on display here.' In Christmas 1990, Indy's whip was kindly donated by Ford himself in aid of the Institute of Archaeology in London. Christies sold it on for $24,300 to the owner of Paris's City Rock Café. But Ford did confess to having another at home. 'It's on the top shelf of my hall closet, handy in case I need it.' Earlier in the same year, Indiana Jones passed into American folklore when he became an attraction at the Disney–MGM Studios Theme Park.

The demise of Indiana Jones was a sad loss to world cinema. Spielberg's rousing 'Boy's Own' trilogy was an example of comic fantasy film-making at its most masterful. *Raiders*, like the first of the *Star Wars* series, was an exhilarating resuscitation of cinema's past, and brought a definitive high gloss to a B-movie genre. Ripped from the pages of Rider Haggard and Conan Doyle and the serials of a flickering monochrome yesteryear, Indy is a *bona fide* superhero, ageless and immortal, like Superman, Tarzan and Bond, from whom the series took some sideways inspiration. But unlike the push-button automaton that 007 became, Indy had always to rely on his own resources. He uses no gadgets or gimmicks, just good old-fashioned fists, a bullwhip and a horse, if there's one around. And that's what made him so universally loved by the masses – his tenacity, bravery and good humour, and the way he gets into life-threatening situations and then extricates himself. Additionally irresistible was the combination of romantic and cynical traits. The tension and interplay between these two facets was what originally so fascinated Ford about the character.

Ford was the unchallenged master of this kind of material. Who else could maintain a straight face and a credible presence in the midst of such chaos? With his deadpan charisma he made what he did seem effortless, and that was his genius. Ford's solid and unflashy work kept the whole enterprise tethered to some kind of reality. He gave Indy a daring, soaring spirit without ever losing sight of his flesh and blood mortality. Those fallibilities and imperfections endeared him to a cinema that loves the underdog. The odds are always stacked against Indy but the audience never leaves his side. Time after time, whenever our hero is staring defeat in the face, he musters up that one last drop of courage and snaps back into life with all the suddenness of a spinach-inspired Popeye, usually to the strains of John Williams's classic anthem and our rousing cheers.

14

Regarding Harrison

First-time novelist Scott Turow's *Presumed Innocent*, a literate exposé of American justice, corruption and seedy sex, was the publishing sensation of 1987. The book, composed over six years (Turow would jot down notes as he commuted to his office of attorneys in Chicago), remained on the *New York Times* fiction best-seller list for forty-four weeks, selling over four million paperback copies. It went on to become the object of one of the most frenzied bidding wars in recent Hollywood memory.

What made *Presumed Innocent* one of the hottest properties of the late eighties? It certainly had some of the dense, fast-paced immediacy of a top-drawer Hollywood thriller, with a lead role that could be played by any number of top male stars. There was a feeling, too, that films aimed specifically at teenage audiences were on the wane. Recent successes like *Fatal Attraction* and *Dead Poets Society*, serious drama which appealed to a more mature and discerning audience, pointed irrefutably to a resurgence in adult cinemagoing. It was becoming accepted movie-industry wisdom that ageing audiences wanted fewer pyrotechnics and special effects and more of the sophisticated characterizations that the likes of Alan J. Pakula, Sidney Lumet and Mike Nichols could deliver. The protagonist of Turow's dense psychological thriller is Rusty Sabich, a district attorney and upstanding family man. While investigating the brutal murder of a female colleague, with whom he was involved sexually, he is accused of the crime himself. The hunter becomes the hunted. Is Sabich merely a victim of circumstantial evidence, a political scapegoat or is the man a cold-blooded killer?

The film rights to this intriguing tale were snapped up by Sydney Pollack for $1 million, raising the possibility of Pollack's frequent star Robert Redford – they've made seven films together – in the leading role. But Pollack considered Redford too old. Instead he sent the book to Alan J. Pakula, a serious and sensitive film-maker with a trial lawyer's appetite for telling detail. Pakula had also previously brought two other 'unfilmable' books, *All the President's Men* and *Sophie's Choice*, to life on screen. He found Turow's novel a fascinating read, containing a real insider's knowledge of big-city politics and the legal system. Pakula saw the chance to explore that area of American professional life as he had with journalism in *All the President's Men*. However, because of the book's complex maze of themes and subplots, he was worried about the practicality of translating it to the screen.

Those reservations were shared by Pollack and the screenwriter Frank Pierson, whose main problem was deciding which of the book's two main themes to focus on. First there was the 'justice' theme, the story of a public prosecutor hounded by the very system he religiously upholds – this combined with cut-throat office politics where back-door plea bargaining and old-boy protectionism is rife. Secondly, there was the 'passion' theme, the study of a rational man who abandons his own high ideals for the sake of a mad love affair. Which should take precedence? This was Pierson's dilemma. Pollack, when toying with the idea of directing the film himself, had chosen to go all out for the sex-and-violence angle. Pakula decided to reverse the emphasis, concentrating more on the justice theme and using the love affair as a subplot. Indeed the movie's sexual heat is decidedly cooler than Turow's prose, which was driven by explicit scenes of sadomasochism and anal intercourse between Sabich and lover Carolyn Polhemus (Greta Scacchi). The film does retain, however, the dubious misogyny of the novel. When Carolyn dumps Rusty he's truly lost. A motive for murder?

Pleased with all the advances made on the script Pakula's next obstacle was possibly the most important. He needed to choose an actor who could convincingly convey Sabich's deeply repressed emotions, while at the same time remaining sympathetic to an audience who are pondering on the question of his guilt. When casting, Pakula had in mind someone of the quality of Henry Fonda as he was during the fifties, who seemed to possess a rare kind of decency. He looked like the average middle-class American, and yet one sensed that beneath his graceful veneer there lurked something dark and subdued. Sabich fits squarely in the classic Hitchcock tradition – a hero innocent of the crime for which he is accused but guilty of some other moral malfeasance.

From the beginning Pakula's first and only choice was Harrison Ford. 'We wanted an all-American leading man, the kind that personifies truth, honesty and integrity,' he told *Movies USA* in August 1990. 'Harrison Ford was right up there as someone you don't want to believe could be embroiled in this type of mystery, plus he's an icon.' Filming *Presumed Innocent* without him as Sabich would be, the director said, as unlikely as making *Klute* without Jane Fonda. 'The movie has to have someone you can identify with as a lead,' he explained. 'Warren Beatty is a movie star who happens to be a person. Harrison Ford is a person who happens to be a movie star. The ordinary male viewer thinks he could be like Harrison Ford.' It was this everyman quality which made Ford the ideal choice. He may not own the perfect chiselled features of a film star in the grand tradition, but he does have a unique duality of character, equally at home playing the all-action hero or the American Joe Average. Ford has an instantly identifiable persona: he's the guy down the block. And he was, most definitely, Rusty Sabich – decent, moralistic, vulnerable, flawed.

Pakula was concerned, however, whether Ford would be able to bring out the dark side of a man capable of obsession and murder. His fears proved groundless. 'Harrison has a great depth to his talent,' the director said. 'A depth that people might not be aware of yet. He has an enormous range with a first-rate intellect behind it.' So desperate was Pakula to secure the services of Ford that he personally flew out to Wyoming and spent several days at the actor's ranch discussing the project. Initially Ford had serious reservations. Indeed, several of his colleagues advised him against accepting the role, which they considered limiting, shallow and boring. Their argument was that Rusty was a passive, interior character who held back on his emotions. Although he featured in practically every scene he was invariably reduced to the level of a bystander in his own life. For a man who enjoys challenging himself, raising the stakes, Sabich represented the most serious dramatic test of his career. Ford had to sustain a two-hour suspense drama devoid of car chases and shoot-outs. In the courtroom scenes, which are the focus of virtually the last half of the film, he is reduced to brooding silence as other more colourful and vibrant characters, Raul Julia's defence lawyer and Paul Winfield's judge, occupy the stage. It worried Ford that, as the leading player, he couldn't open his mouth during these crucial moments. His eyes and face had to tell the story. 'I just had to convince him that anyone can say lines,' Pakula revealed. 'It takes a great actor to play reactions.' After long deliberations Ford called up Pakula with his answer. 'It's a scary, complicated role,' he began. 'It's not going to be easy to play this repressed character, but, yeah, let's jump in.'

The first thing that strikes one about Rusty Sabich is that close-cropped haircut. Greatly mocked in the press, it seemed to receive almost as much attention as Ford's performance. 'Never in my life, not since carpentry became such a prominent part of my story, has one item been such a big deal,' Ford complained to the *Guardian* in August 1991. 'People have gone nuts about it. Completely, absolutely nuts.'

The new look was hardly flattering, as some of his friends enjoyed pointing out, but that's exactly what he wanted. Ford strove deliberately to rob himself of glamour, paying particular attention to the way Sabich would wear his hair. The cut was meant to convey a number of clues

about the man. First, that there was no personal vanity or strong ego to
him; if there were, then that would have thrown a whole new light on his
extramarital affair. Secondly, here was a man who was less sophisticated
than the lady with whom he was having an affair – certainly no
womanizer. 'I wanted to create a character who was conservative by
nature, by choice.' And thirdly, Ford wanted to inform audiences that
this was not the typical role played by a movie star. 'I wanted to tell
people to leave their baggage at home,' he told the *Philadelphia Inquirer*
in July 1990. 'Not to expect this to be the Harrison Ford that they've met
any other place.'

Pakula was dismayed when Ford rang him up shortly before shooting
got underway announcing that he'd shaved his hair to a short,
unattractive style in order to psyche himself into the part. 'God,
Harrison, very short?' the director inquired. 'I want you to be true to this
character, but we did hire Harrison Ford. The audience is fond of you
and if we don't recognise it's you ... ' Ford butted in. 'No, no, no – it's
going to be terrific for this. You don't want me looking like a movie star.'
It took Ford a month to convince Pakula that the hair was right, after
that time the director couldn't imagine him looking any other way.

Once committed, Ford applied himself with customary dedication to
the task of painting Rusty Sabich in real-life colours, going to the
unusual length of moving into a DA's office and sitting in on an actual
murder trial. 'Harrison has been extremely involved in keeping it
authentic,' executive producer Susan Solt told *Premiere* in June 1990.
'He took the lead and everyone followed suit in really immersing
themselves in the characters they portray.' Early in June 1989 Ford
spent a week in Detroit to soak up the potent atmosphere in the city's
courthouses. He was given near complete access to all the goings on in
the Detroit and Wayne County prosecutor's office. His guide, George
Ward, chief assistant prosecutor, was amazed by his guest's
commitment. Ford quizzed lawyers at lunch, took files back to his hotel
at night and watched training films. At one particular meeting a question
arose concerning the relative heights of a gunman and his victim which
totally foxed every lawyer present. 'Harrison was the only one who knew
the answer,' Ward recalled to *Time* magazine in June 1990. 'Because he
had studied the pictures of the two persons. He really did his
homework.'

Arriving quietly and unheralded, Ford tried honourably, but in vain,
to keep a low profile. Attired in tortoiseshell glasses and a dark suit he
visited the Frank Murphy Hall of Justice to observe a recorder's court,
'hoping to stay out of the way and see the day to day events'. Despite a
claim that he was 'the least important person in the courtroom,' word
soon spread that Indiana Jones was in the building. Suddenly attorneys
remembered urgent business in the courtroom where Ford was sitting.

The door swung open repeatedly as clerks, lawyers, judges, witnesses and reporters dropped by, some for a quick stare, others to say hi or get an autograph. The scene was so chaotic that once Ford slipped away a sheriff's deputy had to tape a note on the door saying: 'Harrison Ford has left the courthouse.'

In the event Ford was less interested in courtroom behaviour than in the minutiae of a lawyer's life, their grinding daily routine. He observed their clothing, how they conducted themselves with colleagues at the coffee machine or in chambers with the judge. He even studied the way they handled files and papers. 'I needed to ground it in some reality,' he told the *Boston Sunday Globe* in July 1990. 'To see what their offices looked like, how hot it was, how tired they were, what was in their briefcases, what it felt like. I hate it when people just give me a briefcase from props. You have to tell the prop person you want heavy stuff in it because they're liable to take pity on you and take all the stuff out. Feeling that case is heavy is something you shouldn't have to act.'

On his way back from Detroit Ford stopped off at the Chicago home of Scott Turow to meet 'the mind behind this brilliantly constructed text. It was like seeing a magnificent building and wanting to meet the architectural mind behind it.' Turow had been especially pleased with the casting of Ford as Sabich. 'Harrison looks just like Rusty as I envisioned him,' the writer told reporters. 'I don't think anybody could have done it better.' Ford's brief visit was, in essence, a trip back to his roots. Raised in the manicured suburbs on the north side of the city, Ford chuckled at the thought of having been born with exactly the right flat, Midwestern accent for Rusty, 'and a sense of morality that is particularly midwestern'. Ford had returned to Chicago after living on the West coast for the past two decades 'with a different tribe of people' to remind himself of what it was like to be a Midwesterner. 'That feeling of industry, of energy, of living by the lake. I also love the architecture of cities like Chicago, I miss that.'

Filming began during the summer months of 1989, mostly in Detroit and New York, after a three-week cast rehearsal. It was not without its problems. The very presence of Ford anywhere in the public domain is enough to breed considerable excitement, even hysteria. Once the news of Ford's visitation had spread among cliques of ardent followers, most of the location sites lay vulnerable to siege. Extra security was drafted in to prevent fans from crossing police barricades and getting too close to their idol. The crowds had been gathering outside the Detroit court-house building since morning, hoping to catch a glimpse of Ford. Among the muffled cries of 'Where's Harrison' and the shrieks of false alarm, one teenager shouts 'Isn't this the movie where Indiana Jones kills his wife?' The sudden arrival of the film crew at the top of the stone steps heralds a rush of anticipation among the weary throng. There is enthusiastic applause when an immaculately dressed Ford finally emerges through the great doors, and looking poised and calm. 'I'd kill to get his autograph,' one woman says. As Ford leaves the set he politely but firmly declines to stop and sign autographs. Fully in control, he plays the role of movie star reluctantly, but with consummate grace.

After starring in a half dozen of the most popular and celebrated films in history, many sniggered when Ford announced he was leaving his comic-book incarnations behind to pursue a more serious career. But his work in *Witness, The Mosquito Coast* and *Frantic* demonstrated a mastery of acting technique, and with *Working Girl* he displayed a delicate, self-deprecating touch for comedy. Fast approaching his fiftieth birthday, Ford was being hailed as arguably America's most versatile leading male. (Can you imagine De Niro or Hoffman as Indiana Jones or Schwarzenegger as Allie Fox. I think not.) With Rusty Sabich Ford's penchant for taking risks was evident. 'I don't look for star vehicles or commercial success. What counts for me is getting the best material, something I can respond to emotionally.'

Whilst reading Pierson's script Ford was immediately drawn to the story of a moral, dedicated man whose life is destroyed by an uncontrollable sexual obsession with a manipulative woman. Here is someone for whom ideals are important and who falls short of his own standards. Ford could identify with Sabich and sympathize over his plight. Ford believes people need stable relationships, and Rusty aspires to the same thing. Therefore, when he strays from the dictates of his well-developed conscience he is consumed with terrible guilt. That is his ultimate punishment.

Eyebrows were raised when Warner Brothers released the film in July 1990. It was a calculated risk, intended as a bracing antidote to the traditional summer overload of brainless action thrillers. *Presumed Innocent* was scarcely going to appeal to the popcorn crowd, who refused to see Ford as anything but Han Solo and Indiana Jones. Rusty Sabich was a man far removed from any of the characters in Ford's past and presented numerous new challenges. Throughout almost half of the film, he had to convey everything from bemusement to growing outrage almost exclusively through facial expressions. Draining himself of personality, Ford had to maintain tense, repressed and impenetrable body language. In the end, he delivers an admirable, if sometimes morose and droning, performance, displaying a touching vulnerability. Critics were impressed. 'Harrison Ford proves once again that he is steadily developing into one of the most powerful and versatile actors in American films' – *Seattle Post-Intelligencer*; 'Ford gives the best performance of his career' – *Daily Express*; 'Ford is so subdued and solid that at times he begins to resemble one of the big pine beds he probably builds in his spare time' – *Empire*.

Much praise was heaped upon the film itself, although the overall tone was so sombre and demanding that some found *Presumed Innocent* just too joyless a ride. Pakula deliberately sets the tale at a methodical, unhurried pace, the better to enjoy its complexities. Part riveting courtroom whodunit and part evocative character study, the film is intelligent and extremely well crafted. At times unexciting, even dreary and plodding, it none the less manages to hold the viewer in its doleful, powerful grip. The finest aspect of the production was undoubtedly its ensemble acting. Right down the line the supporting players were impeccably cast: Bonnie Bedelia as Sabich's tormented wife, Raul Julia, who begged Pakula to hire him, burly and dependable Brian Dennehy and Paul Winfield. Ford felt honoured to be among them. 'Working with professionals like that is the way you keep on learning.' These actors were quick to return the compliment. Bedelia referred to him as a very interior type of person. 'He keeps his own counsel. But he's also very funny,' she told the *Philadelphia Inquirer* in July 1990. 'Very gentle and generous. A meticulous craftsman. And quite a specimen of the male animal to boot.' Paul Winfield first met Ford in 1964 when they were aspiring contract actors with Columbia. 'Harrison was my only friend, the only one who took me at face value. He was a breath of fresh air, very non-judgemental in his dealings with people. Very open. I don't think he's changed very much as a human being since.'

Ford's real coup is that, despite our sympathies being with Sabich, we simply don't know until the shocking denouement whether he's the killer or not. Ford has refined the comical grimace of Indiana Jones into a mask of guilt and fear that keeps the audience guessing. Avoiding gimmicks or frills, Ford quietly and wholly compels the viewer in a way he has never done before. He seethes and he churns silently, suggesting volumes through the smallest movements of his eyes.

Nowhere was this better amplified than in the film's final scene. While Bonnie Bedelia delivers a moving, haunting speech Ford's silent and subtle reactions put him in the class of Spencer Tracy or Gary Cooper. In one emotionally charged sequence, where his wife pours her heart out to him, the normally unemotional Sabich cannot stem the tide of bitter memories and breaks down into tears. Like Ford this responsible man, who prided himself in looking after his family now realizes that his behaviour is tearing them apart. That scene poignantly echoed Ford's situation during the collapse of his first marriage. 'I found that that tear rolled each time within five words of the previous take,' Ford said. Although each scene was carefully planned beforehand Pakula had no idea Harrison was going to break down and weep. 'But the pain in him was just so real, he totally gave himself to that character's feelings,' the director told *City Limits* in October 1990. 'There's a lot of movie stars/actors who would feel that that's unmanly, showing that kind of vulnerability, that kind of pain. It's not manly to cry and I didn't ask him to cry. To not worry about his image, to just play it honestly as an actor, was a great gift to the film. It took a lot of courage to do and a lot of faith in being his own man.'

Pakula welcomed Ford's partiality for accepting challenges and warmly praised his star's sterling service. 'I don't think this movie could have worked without Harrison. I don't know another actor of his stature who's so willing, so eager even, to take risks. Ford's a remarkable collection of contrasting qualities. He's solid, he's strong, he's responsible. At the same time, he has an outrageous humour. There is an adventurous quality about him, a danger. That's probably responsible for a lot of the sex appeal he has.' On set the two were a well-oiled working machine. They would discuss the script for hours, continually exchanging ideas and striving to iron out every little detail. The atmosphere was amiable and the pace purposeful, which is how Ford likes it. Pakula particularly admired his great sense of storytelling. The actor was always on hand, probing, asking questions, making sure, that each scene in this exceptionally complex story had been adequately explained for the audience. 'He's very bright, very collaborative. I find his instincts very trustworthy.'

Indeed Pakula insists that Ford would make a wonderful director. 'He has enormous technical skill' Pakula told the *Dallas Morning News* in July 1990. 'I've worked with two actors who went on to win Oscars as directors, Warren Beatty and Robert Redford. Believe me, Harrison is in that category.' Mark Hamill is another who agrees that Ford's future may lie behind the camera. 'I think he'd be a great director, because he naturally understands the direction a scene should go in.' Ford proved his directorial competence in his sex scene with Greta Scacchi, enabling the young actress to feel as comfortable as possible. 'I give him the credit for that scene,' Pakula said. 'He really staged it himself. I've told him that if he ever wants to direct, I'll produce.' High praise indeed, but Ford has neither the patience nor the inclination to be a director. Put simply, it's too damn difficult, takes too long and would mean a cut in wages. 'What I love about my job is that I'm able to come on to a project, work intensely for a finite period of time, then I'm off.' Taking up directing would also involve Ford more deeply in Hollywood, and, like his colleagues Lucas, Coppola and Nichols, he wants as little to do, geographically and professionally, with Hollywood as possible.

If you talk of acting as a profession, Ford reasons, there is inevitably a part of an actor that is a businessman. 'I'm responsible for the success of my product. So I think like a businessman. Everything I do on screen, it's all my fault. I make the decisions.' Ford is very good at doing business, wisely insisting on a large slice of the profits from all his films. As a consequence, his personal wealth is considerable, and some sources put the figure well in excess of $100 million. According to *Forbes* magazine Ford's income covering just the years 1989/90 totalled $22 million. In the press, though, Ford likes to play down his affluence. 'Money is really only important if you don't have any. I don't have a room where I go like Uncle Scrooge and roll around in it.'

Ford currently earns around $10 million per picture and studios anxious to secure his signature readily agree to almost any conditions he cares to make. While conceding that he earns more money than anyone has the right to make in one lifetime, Ford does regard himself as value for money, considering the vast sums his movies rake in at the box office. Even *Presumed Innocent*, a doleful, wordy drama with no action thrills whatsoever, still managed an impressive $43 million gross in the States against stiff opposition from *Ghost* and *Die Hard II*. Ford's favourite compliment is 'You're worth the money.' He is prudent with his riches, leaving their investment in the capable hands of a business manager, and has a reputation for being tight-fisted. His own explanation is that he enjoys the simple pleasures and spends his fortune on the only things that truly matter to him, his family and a bit of privacy: 'Money helps me buy back a bit of the private life that fame has stolen from me.'

On 30 June 1990 there was a new addition to the Ford family when Melissa gave birth to a baby girl, Georgia. Ford took every precaution to ensure he was there for the delivery. Promoting *Presumed Innocent* at the time, he carried a bleeper with him to every interview. After three boys Ford was thrilled about becoming the father of a daughter at last.

As varied as his characters and films have been over the last decade or so Ford has selected each of them using the same basic criteria. How he maintains his position in the Hollywood firmament seems largely a matter of good judgement in picking the films he wants to make and in the collaborators he chooses to be associated with. A concern for story above character ensures Ford is an astute reader of prospective scripts. Over five hundred, he reckons, are merely browsed through before a final decision is made. 'I say almost facetiously that if I get through a script, then I'm probably gonna do it.' Ford can normally tell in the first thirty or forty pages, sometimes in ten, whether it is worth continuing. What did surprise him was the discovery that the competition for the rubbish was the same, if not greater, than the competition for the good stuff. 'Learning to read a script for quality and structure – that's what took longest of all.' Usually scripts are sent to either Ford's business manager or agent. 'My car mechanic gets a stack, too!' he once joked. A secretary reads them and then prepares a breakdown of the plot and main character for Ford to peruse at his leisure. If the topic intrigues him and the main character has some depth, then and only then does he read the full script. The primary question always is: 'Do I want to spend four to six months of my life doing this film and working with these people?' After all, the script may be great but the director might not be appropriate for the material or Ford might fear a clash of personalities. All the ingredients have to be just right, and Ford can be an extremely hard judge. He's perfectly willing to wait eighteen months for the right combination of people and story.

His criteria are so exacting that many projects of a high pedigree have slipped through Ford's fingers, including the Jack Nicholson role in *Terms of Endearment*, which he turned down because he felt he didn't have the track record. 'I just couldn't see myself making all those clever retorts to Shirley MacLaine at such a pace. Yet five years later I had very little trepidation about Working Girl which had glib, sophisticated dialogue.' It is a decision he has never regretted, even though Nicholson went on to win an Oscar. Ford also lost out on two of the most popular films of the eighties: Bob Hoskins beat him to *Who Framed Roger Rabbit?* and with *Beverly Hills Cop* Ford refused on the grounds that it read like an ordinary police drama. 'Of course, you can't tell how something will turn out. When I first read the script for *Witness*, it read just like an episode in a television series. But I knew we could make something really fine out of it if we rewrote it.' Roland Joffe had also desperately wanted Ford to play Oppenheimer in *Fat Man and Little Boy* (a.k.a *Shadow Makers*), his flawed but arresting film about the development of the atomic bomb. After reading through the script three times Ford decided to leave it alone.

One of Ford's pet hates are projects written expressly with him in mind. These, he feels, tend to be tailored only to his strengths and avoid his supposed weaknesses. 'And that's not fulfilling.' Unlike the majority of Hollywood stars he doesn't develop or produce his own projects. 'One of the major problems of developing a property for yourself is that it tends to be made for you, when who *you* are is what you want to change.' Ford is far more attracted to films that have been developed for someone else – to wear, if you will, another actor's custom-made suit and hunch his shoulders a bit to make it fit. 'I want to be surprised when I open a script, to read it and say, "Jesus that's it, that's a movie. I'll do that." '

This was precisely his reaction upon receiving Jeffrey Abrams's *Regarding Henry*. Emotion, according to Ford, is the true language of film, the coin of his realm. One can have the most brilliantly constructed story, but without the emotional connection between the audience and the events on screen, it is worthless. Ford's emotional response to the central character of hot-shot lawyer Henry Turner, was immediate and strong. This man's career is abruptly truncated by a store hold-up which leaves him with a bullet in his brain and his mental faculties severely impaired. Ford was touched by the character's sudden tragedy, his struggle through rehabilitation and eventual success. Again we see Ford tackling a showcase role with complex and diverse ingredients – and he got to play the hero and the villain.

College graduate Abrams had thrashed out the script for *Regarding Henry* in an astonishing seven days, and it showed. Privately sure it wouldn't sell, producer Scott Rudin convinced Paramount to fork out $450,000 for the property and then had it sent to Ford, one of his favourite actors. 'The script had an incredible humanity to it,' Rudin told the *Dallas Morning News* in July 1991, 'and Harrison was the first actor I thought of for the role. He is one of the few guys I know who could pull it off, who could make you believe that he was both a shark lawyer and a diminished adult. When I saw the finished result, I knew I had made the right choice. It's rare that you get the film on screen that you envision in your head, but Harrison did it. It was a beautiful, subtle performance.' Ford read Abrams's script the night it arrived and was amazed how someone so young, only twenty-three, could have such insight into human nature. He thought it was a remarkable piece of work, 'very smart, very emotional and good enough to attract the kind of people that I would want to work with.'

First on the list was Mike Nichols. Since *Working Girl* Ford had been scouting for projects the two might want to do together. He rated Nichols as particularly appropriate for this film's combination of humour and pathos and telephoned the director one afternoon. Abrams's script, Ford assured him, was the most interesting that he'd read in five years. Nichols duly browsed through it and called Ford back the following day. 'I agree,' he said. 'I want to do it.' Both men recognized that there was much fine-tuning still to be done, but loved the central idea. A man loses his memory, is therefore forced to re-evaluate his life through the eyes of a stranger and is revolted by what he finds. Henry sees his old world of wealth and power with the outsider's perspective of a Frank Capra hero and sets about undoing the mistakes he made in a misspent life which he cannot remember. A case history of a head injury it isn't. This is a fable about redemption.

Many industry insiders were surprised at the speed with which Ford and Nichols pounced on the *Regarding Henry* project. What fed their eagerness? Jeffrey Abrams had his own pet theory. In 1988 Nichols had had the opportunity to make *Big*, but turned it down. 'He and Harrison wished that they had made that film,' said the young screenwriter. 'Well, here was another film about a man's body that was essentially being filled by a child.'

Ford spent more time researching the role of Henry Turner than for any other in his career. Everyone felt a great sense of responsibility to depict Abrams's brain-damage scenario as accurately as possible. Early in rehearsals the writer recalled Ford saying, 'We've got to be extra careful here … this is a very delicate subject. Henry can't be a buffoon.'

Reading every book about brain injuries he could find, Ford also visited a rehabilitation clinic over the course of two months, holding interviews with neurologists, brain surgeons and other specialists. When allowed, he would also sit through therapy sessions. 'It got very emotional at times,' Ford told the *Daily Express* in August 1991, 'watching patients with appalling disabilities who, after a period of depression, realize that there is light at the end of the tunnel.' He found most of the doctors helpful, encouraging and full of anecdotes. The actor's favourite told of a man who was shot in the nose and drove himself to hospital with the bullet lodged at the back of his skull, only to be given a piece of sticking plaster by the doctors and ordered to return home. Ford's most valuable counsel was a Princeton-educated lawyer called Tom Frost, who had suffered approximately the same kind of injuries as Henry. Introduced by Bruce Volpe, the film's technical adviser, Ford studied Frost closely, incorporating many of the lawyer's mannerisms into his portrayal of Henry. For example, he emulated Frost's gait by putting a stone in his trainer. 'This man gave us access to his private life, and he gave me the most faith in the correctness of the choices we made in creating this character. He told us we were right on the mark and that's all I needed to hear.'

In addition, Ford kept three stacks of index cards charting Henry's recovery. He divided each card into three categories – physical capacities, mental skills and speaking skills – numbered on a system of one to ten to keep track of just how handicapped he was supposed to be at any given moment. Because films are generally made out of sequence such a system was invaluable to avoid confusion and to keep himself aligned with Turner's development. Watch the film and Ford's painstaking research never shows, which compares strikingly with such similar films as *Awakenings*, and *Rain Man*. In these Robert de Niro and Dustin Hoffman, playing disabled characters, gave flamboyant star turns. Ford's performance is irresistibly low-key and charming. As Henry he goes further than he has ever gone in revealing depths of vulnerability, but not once does he resort to actorly 'tricks' to make a point or effect. Ford has the modesty and confidence to act as if a film might be about something other than his own performance.

Over and above research, Ford again exploited his own inner personality. Nichols had complete faith in his lead's ability to bring the various aspects of Henry to the surface. 'Both these men are in him,' the director revealed. 'I've seen him make a fuss about a suite at the Savoy, and then I've seen him be wonderful with his kids and with mine.' Ford was quick to agree. If both the arrogant, self-centred Henry and the later, more caring Henry hadn't existed within him he couldn't have played the role with the same kind of conviction. 'Both Henrys are in me, and in all of us.' There's a scene when Henry goes to his daughter's room and makes a so-called apology for yelling at her that ends up as just another lecture. 'That's something I recognize from my own experience with my kids,' Ford explained. 'And something my father did to me.'

Filming got off the ground during the summer and autumn of 1990, principally in districts around Manhattan island. To play opposite Ford, Nichols had chosen Annette Bening, then the rage of the tabloids as the woman who had finally tamed Warren Beatty. Such trivial exposure concealed a blossoming talent, which was sadly given little opportunity for expression in *Regarding Henry*. Still, she enjoyed working with Ford, appreciating his good humour and complete lack of personal vanity on the set, but did find him infuriatingly guarded around strangers. Mikki Allen, Henry's daughter in the film, also commented on Ford's passion for privacy. 'He was really good to me,' she told the *Sunday Express* in July 1991, 'teasing me, keeping me happy. But he kept to himself very much. As soon as work finished, he'd just rush home to be with his own boy and girl. People on set learned to understand: as soon as his hours were over, he was home.'

While Kevin Costner has a gift for exuding quiet self-assurance and Jack Nicholson excels in borderline insanity, one of the things Harrison Ford does best is look puzzled. Some of the most memorable moments in the *Star Wars* and *Indiana Jones* series are when his characters don't quite know what to do next, but always manage something in the heat of the moment. And in his more dramatic roles, like Dr Walker and Rusty Sabich, he was almost perpetually perplexed. In *Regarding Henry* Ford's gift for befuddlement is on hilarious overdrive. Wearing a vacant, childlike look on his face, Ford plays Henry as an eager, but slightly backward infant, a guileless man-child with a beguiling innocence. It is a sweet, funny and often deeply affecting performance – Ford's comic touch has never seemed so delicate or precise – and one which found favour with the critics. 'The finest dramatic performance of Ford's career' – *Newsday*; 'Ford continues to grow beyond his undeniable screen presence and likeability into a performer of impressive emotional range and daring' – *Democrat and Chronicle/Times Union*; 'Ford sets a standard that other potential Oscar nominees are going to have to work hard to meet' – *Minneapolis Star Tribune*. Not all, however, were sympathetic. 'In the worst performance of his career, Harrison Ford isn't awful, just boring' – *Bergen County Record*; 'When Ford's on screen, he blinks, stammers, grimaces and walks funny – it's Indiana Jones in a bad high school play' – *LA Magazine*.

Attending the world première of *Regarding Henry* in New York in June 1991, Ford was in his usual low-key mood. The film did moderately well financially, which was a testament to his pulling power at the box office rather than the bankability of the work itself. Success was also forthcoming overseas, particularly in Japan, which underlined Ford's global popularity. But, critically, the film itself was deservedly trashed. 'Regarding Henry is an unimaginably bad movie, from none other than Mike Nichols, who appears to have lost *his* brain' – *New York*; 'This is a film about amnesia which is just as soon forgotten. It is hard to believe that Ford and Nichols could produce such a mawkish, clumsy bit of cinema as this' – *Financial Times*.

Melted down, Regarding Henry is nothing more than smaltzy disease-of-the-week drama, a sentimental second-chance saga. Henry's conversion from arrogant bastard to warm and wonderful human being is too contrived and overly sentimental. And in trivializing the recovery process, it never achieves any emotional impact. What Nichols seems to be saying is that a man can actually become a better father after a large portion of his brain is destroyed – a prerequisite, it appears, for spending more time with the family. *Regarding Henry* was just one of a crop of Hollywood feel-good movies that were designed to show us the error of our greedy Reaganite/Thatcherite ways. But Henry's affirmation of family values over yuppie consumerism rang particularly hollow. The film might have been more easily swallowed played in reverse, with Henry starting out as the nice guy and ending up corrupted and loathsome.

15

Fugitive Ford

Disappointed with the lacklustre *Regarding Henry* Ford contemplated a return to the action arena and to the kind of role in which he has no peer: the thinking man's hero. He was going to overlook the fact that he was now too long in the tooth for such hi-jinks. 'Well it gets to feeling that way at the end of one of those pictures. But a little rest, relaxation and I'm stupid enough to do it again.' After a run of what he called 'coat and tie jobs', it was perhaps time for a change. 'I reckoned I had to hit somebody in my next movie or lose that as an option.' Ford also needed to connect with a young audience again after a string of dour roles in films like *Frantic* and *Presumed Innocent*.

Conscious of the appeal he has to millions as a man of action, Ford began browsing through the latest scripts for a suitably heroic role in an adventure thriller with ambition – that is to say, not merely an exercise in mindless carnage and gratuitous bloodletting. Ford isn't really much of an action fan and found the recent spate of grossly violent films, the Terminators and Die Hards, morally reprehensible. To him, such movies cater to the basest instincts of the audience. 'I like any kind of film that's successful on its own terms. I've no need to see another virgin deflowered or car chases for the sake of them.' In *Blade Runner*, one of Ford's more brutal pictures, the actor was anxious that his character express an abhorrence towards violence. After every incident of having to kill someone Deckard's revulsion is clear. Projects on which Ford's name was tentatively pencilled in included a Philip Marlowe story, directed by Sydney Pollack, and a comedy called *Good Behaviour*, from the *Working Girl* team of Kevin Wade and Mike Nichols. Most notable of all, Oliver Stone considered casting Ford as Jim Garrison in *JFK*. Ford liked the idea and was keen to work with Stone, but felt apprehensive about making a film about so recent a historical event. Kevin Costner, the usurper to Ford's crown, got the part.

At last Ford found his target: *Night Ride Down*, a fast-paced mystery thriller set against the backdrop of the 1936 Pullman passenger train porter strike. Harold Becker (*Sea of Love*) was slated to direct from a script by Willard Huyck and Gloria Katz, the writers of *Indiana Jones and the Temple of Doom*. Ford would play a Pullman company executive, whose daughter is kidnapped. Scheduled to begin shooting on location in Chicago in autumn 1991, things went horribly wrong. A ballooning budget forced Brandon Tartikoff, the freshly installed chairman of Paramount, to pull the plug on the period drama. Ford had already dropped out by this stage, reportedly due to a disagreement over script revisions. But he was still keen on filling an action role. For a while there was talk of teaming him up with Bruce Willis as Wild Bill Hickok and Buffalo Bill respectively, in a western entitled *Hickok and Cody*. This was to be a fictionalized reworking of the pair's antics *en route* to New York with Buffalo Bill's wild west show in 1873. A great idea that faded and died.

It was precisely Ford's hankering to get tough on celluloid again that led to his controversial replacement of Alec Baldwin in *Patriot Games*. Baldwin was all set to reprise his role as CIA analyst Jack Ryan in the sequel to the money-spinning *The Hunt for Red October* when negotiations hit a stumbling block. Rumours abounded of Baldwin's combative reputation and demands for perks, and his $4 million asking price was considered by the producers to be in excess of his box-office clout. To cap it all, the proposed shooting schedule clashed with an obligation to star in *A Streetcar Named Desire* on Broadway – so Baldwin walked, or was pushed ... Which left Ford free to jump into the breach. David Kirkpatrick, the president of Paramount, sent Ford the script, which he duly read one late August weekend. By Monday morning he was committed. Two weeks after the collapse of *Night Ride Down* the *Patriot Games* deal closed. Harrison Ford was the new Jack Ryan.

The producer, Mace Neufeld, saw the snaring of Ford as a real coup. 'Ford is a star for everybody,' he told *Empire* in October 1992. 'What you see in this movie is Harrison using all of the combination of characters he's played in various films – the cop, Indiana Jones, Han Solo, the lawyer from *Presumed Innocent* – and he kind of rolls them all into one to give a very, very interesting Jack Ryan. When Alec left I was very unhappy. But I guess sometimes adversity turns into good fortune.' The contract Ford signed with Paramount was the most lucrative of his career, a three-picture deal to play Jack Ryan in what the studio hoped would become a fruitful series of films based on Tom Clancy's novels. Ford's price was a cool $9 million per outing. *Clear and Present Danger* looks set to be the follow-up to *Patriot Games*, with *The Sum of All Fears* waiting in the wings.

On release Clancy's champion was hailed as America's answer to James Bond, a hero for the responsible, caring nineties. Here is a family man grounded entirely in reality, who prefers to solve problems by his wits but has the derring-do to fly into action if duty calls. Ford's performance as one would expect, never once echoes Baldwin's, and he claims to have had no qualms about taking over from his younger colleague. Baldwin, on the other hand, felt betrayed and resented Ford's invasion. 'Harrison's not sexy and audiences will not turn out to see him,' he bitched. Clancy complained that, at forty-nine, Ford was too old to play Ryan, who in the novels is a man in his thirties. This was ironic, for in 1987, when Ford was producer Mace Neufeld's first choice to play Ryan in *Red October* Clancy had sung his praises. 'I saw *Witness* last night,' he wrote in a glowing letter to Neufeld. 'You're absolutely right. Harrison Ford is Jack Ryan.' Close to release Clancy dropped further bombshells by publicly slamming the script's deviation from the novel and asking for his name to be taken off the credits, in effect disowning the film. Clancy's loyalty to the celluloid Jack Ryan was secured only after Paramount chiefs waved a very thick chequebook in his direction. Ford's reason for originally turning down *Red October* was plain enough: at that stage Ryan just didn't interest him; if anything he was more drawn to playing the Russian submarine commander, Marko Ramius.

Ford's duties began in the miserable cold of a London November. Jack Ryan has left the CIA to teach naval history at the US Naval Academy, Annapolis. A business holiday to London places him and his family in the middle of an IRA kidnap attempt on a member of the royal family near Buckingham Palace. Originally the Prince and Princess of Wales were the intended targets, but fears of triggering a copycat incident led the makers to change the victim's identity to a distant relative of the queen, the fictional Lord Holmes, played by James Fox. Ryan gallantly foils the attack, killing the younger brother of one of the terrorists, Sean Miller (Sean Bean). When the gunman escapes police custody and begins a terror campaign on Ryan's innocent family *Patriot Games* unfolds as a tale of revenge and retribution.

While *The Hunt for Red October*'s plot was rooted firmly in the days of the cold war, *Patriot Games* presents a new world disorder, in which international terrorism is the key threat. Not the Middle East this time, but a little closer to home. *Patriot Games* has the dubious distinction of being the first major American film to feature Irish militants as the villains. Although the bad guys are a mythical, ultra-violent splinter group of the IRA, the production team drafted in extra security while shooting in London for fear of real-life terrorist reprisals. Ford didn't want to be drawn on the politics of the movie, the Irish protests or the criticisms levelled at its alleged bias – *Variety* called *Patriot Games* 'a right-wing cartoon of the British–Irish political situation'. Ford refused to accept that the film had a right-wing point of view; to him it was about people not politics. The script's depiction of the villains as having a degree of humanity and complexity was one of the reasons that Ford agreed to get involved. *Patriot Games*, though basically a genre picture, defied its genre in his eyes by being more of a character piece. Like many Americans Ford has Irish relatives, and according to an old family story his grandmother took the gold fillings out of her teeth and sent them to the IRA. 'That was a long time ago,' he said. 'That was her history. It's not mine.' Generally Ford took the standard line, deploring terrorism on the one hand whilst recognizing its effectiveness as a trigger to political change on the other. He felt there were some telling comparisons between terrorism and officially sanctioned acts of war. Ford was in Manhattan when it hosted a victory parade for the US troops returning from the gulf conflict. 'I was appalled,' he told *Macleans* magazine in July 1991. 'I'm very sorry that this act of war has been the occasion for the stimulation of pride in this country the likes of which I haven't seen for many years.' For a man so inextricably linked to the macho action genre, it is strangely unnerving that he should hold such strong pacifist views.

Locations in the States were widespread, taking in the Naval Academy in Annapolis, Maryland, Brawley in California, which doubled for a North African guerrilla encampment, and Sea World near San Diego, where the exterior of Ryan's home was erected on a bluff above Mission Bay. The production was also granted unprecedented access to the headquarters of the CIA in Langley, Virginia. The agency, notoriously uncooperative with Hollywood in the past, provided Ford and director Phillip Noyce with a tour and briefing – though both were ordered to sign a pledge of secrecy. They were also allowed to shoot in the foyer and entrance to the HQ – a first for a feature film. Ford's very presence seemed to open doors. According to Noyce, the actor was given the red-carpet treatment, which meant both went deeper into the organization than most outsiders had gone before. Whatever Ford wanted, within reason, he got, including a peek inside the satellite analysis room. 'We were granted some rather extraordinary access,' Ford told reporters. 'We saw things that added to our sense of reality and aided in the replication of that reality.'

In these post-cold war years the CIA see themselves as the guardians of a fragile new world order. Where better to parade their alleged capabilities in the war against international terrorism and drug smuggling, and at the same time justify its expensive existence, than the cinema screen. In *Patriot Games* the CIA's services were bought with the ultimate example of product placement. As a result this slick, if routine, thriller is strengthened considerably by intriguing and accurate scenes of current CIA technology, the most frightening being satellite cameras which can eavesdrop from space on enemy targets.

Although retired from the 'company' Ryan forges an uneasy alliance with the CIA in an effort to track down the renegade Miller. In a futuristic observation theatre at CIA headquarters Ford, as Ryan, stands before a bank of monitors relaying satellite images of a British SAS hit on the Irish terrorists. These are eerie echoes of Desert Storm *à la* CNN. The scene ends on a thirteen-second close-up of Ford, in which we are asked to share in Ryan's ambivalence at the carnage wrought. In order to protect himself from over-familiarity, Ford deliberately stifled his curiosity to see the computer effects footage until the day of the scene. This 'simple reaction shot', in Ford's words, was accomplished in one swift take. Noyce merely let his camera keep on running. 'Harrison just came out with it,' the director told *Premiere* in June 1992. 'Eventually he just turned around and said, "That's it, there's no more." ' Ryan's numb realization of how easy, remote and trivial killing can seem at such a distance moved the critic for the *European* to write, 'At that moment Harrison Ford amply earns his fee. Even in the silliest films he always shows genuine intelligence and a go-with-it, go-for-it commitment that puts flesh and blood on cardboard roles.'

True to Clancy's bullish stance on the intelligence services *Patriot Games* portrays the CIA in a very positive light – a decision many critics insinuated was politically motivated. As the figurehead, so to speak, Ford caught most of the flak. Questions about how he felt playing a member of the dreaded CIA soon began to irritate him. 'I don't think I'm bringing unalloyed glory to the CIA,' he said. Ford was, nevertheless, fascinated by his close encounter with one of the most feared and secretive organizations on earth. He was pleasantly surprised that the headquarters in Langley looked indistinguishable from any other large office building, while inside he took special care in observing the behavioural patterns of all employees. 'Meeting CIA staff was interesting,' Ford explained to *Film Review* in October 1992. 'When you do specific research for a character, what you find is that what makes them interesting and worthy of exploring is not what makes them different, but what we all have in common.' Again it was such small, trifling details as how they worked at their desks, whether they drank coffee out of paper cups or mugs from home, or whether they felt relaxed enough to work in shirtsleeves, which Ford was to find the most useful.

To offset all the state-of-the-art spy technology, *Patriot Games'* denouement is a good old-fashioned punch-up: a terrific speedboat chase which culminates in an underwater hand-to-hand between Ryan and arch foe Miller. The scene contained little in the way of dialogue – 'unless you count glub, glub, glub,' Ford joked – and was filmed over several nights on the backlot of Paramount studios. There, a half-acre site was filled with one million gallons of water (the very water tank in which Cecil B. DeMille parted the Red Sea), and the conditions were horrendous. Picture the scene: it is cold and miserable, the end of a demanding five-month shoot. Fully clothed, a soaking wet Ford, teeth chattering audibly, warms himself by a giant heater waiting for his next cue. Once again he plunges into the freezing water, all around him an array of outsized machinery whips up a tempest of wind, waves and rain. Before each take, the two actors hyperventilate, then take deep breaths from an oxygen tank and go under. The idea is to stay down for as long as possible, but when they run out of air a stuntman is on hand to administer more oxygen.

It was all extremely uncomfortable – 'tortuous' was Ford's own description. 'It went on forever!' Imagine his horror, then, when he was summoned back to the water tank just one month before the release to frantically reshoot the climax. This decision followed negative audience test screenings, and the altered scene pushed the budget up to its final tally of $42 million. Tabloid hysteria didn't help either. Claims that Ford had been grievously injured and had to be rescued from the bottom of the tank were rejected out of hand. He received nothing more calamitous than a tiny scratch on the forehead, thanks to a collision with some rocks. Everyone agreed that the underwater fight footage didn't work. 'We made a mistake,' Ford confessed. There was no power in watching two men struggling in balletic slow-motion; it lacked the necessary visceral effect for what was intended to be a highly emotional resolution. Instead it was replaced by a more savage, crowd-pleasing duel aboard Ryan's wildly out-of-control boat.

Released to good business in the States in June 1992, *Patriot Games* was rather less well received by the critics. 'It's rot, but much better rot than I expected' – *Independent on Sunday*, 'So duff that you wonder why they didn't ask Roger Moore to star, this is no feather in Harrison Ford's cap' – *Time Out*. By far the most vitriolic attack was from *Variety* who, like some other American liberals, slammed the film for its anti-Irish prejudice and with political incorrectness on all fronts. Joseph McBride described it as, 'mindless and morally repugnant', a point of view which so enraged Paramount they withdrew all its advertising from the showbiz trade paper, which resulted in *Variety*'s editor publicly castigating McBride, which in turn resulted in a journalistic uprising. It was a storm in a teacup really. The politics of *Patriot Games* is the politics of the kindergarten, its pontifications on the Irish question are shallow and meaningless in a boneheaded script full of improbabilities. The film completely cops out by establishing the Irish terrorists as a psycho-mad IRA splinter group so as not to offend the romantic sensibilities of Irish Americans. Still *Patriot Games* is an enjoyable, if faintly perplexing film in which there is a serious mismatch between the expertise with which it has been fashioned and the superficiality of its plot and characterization.

Again, as in many of his films, Ford is the linchpin of the enterprise.

His Ryan is older and more subdued than the glib whizz kid as personified by Alec Baldwin and in contrast to 007 is a paradigm of suburban virtue; wholesome, clean-cut and technocratic. Appearing in turn quizzical and harassed – as is his usual bent – Ford as Jack Ryan is allowed to run through his full range of characters: he is at once the reborn, sensitive husband and father in *Regarding Henry*, the man about town executive from *Working Girl* and the irrepressible, indestructible hero we all know and love from the Spielberg and Lucas universe. *Patriot Games* may not be Ford's best work, but his participation in so brazen a piece of formula action film-making is an acknowledgment by the actor that you can't escape destiny. The embodiment of the thoroughly modern matinee idol Ford, in recent years, has been reacting against his past. Having expanded his repertoire to breaking point Ford is now finding himself being drawn back to his origins and is resigned to the fact that in the end people always have a pre-formulated picture of one's first success story. And for Harrison Ford that was *Indiana Jones*. He has no intention of returning to that comic strip world but would like to pursue stories involving more complex heroics, characters in the mould of Rick Deckard and John Book, very human heroes. Ford believes he's found that in Jack Ryan. 'I think that there's much depth to the character of Ryan,' he told *NME* in September 1992. 'And I think that he will be continually interesting in that the dilemmas he finds himself in will be rich stuff for myself.'

The Fugitive, Ford's latest movie, also fits the bill perfectly. As a man attempting to prove he is innocent of murdering his wife, Ford stars in the role originally made famous by the late David Janssen. Under the stewardship of Andrew Davis (*Under Siege*), work began in February 1993 on the $30 million-plus screen version of the hit 1960s television series. Getting into the spirit of the character Ford underwent his usual intense trawl for research, spending several days hanging out with the physicians at the University of Chicago Medical Centre, joining doctors on their rounds and even watching how they scrubbed up for surgery.

Grauman's Chinese Theatre, a 1920s art deco monolith, remains one of the most visually striking picture palaces ever built. Its oriental styling and fortress-like appearance is reminiscent of something Genghis Khan might have felt at home in. *Star Wars* opened to the public at this cinema and in June 1992 it played host to a curious ceremony. Harrison Ford had used the première of *Patriot Games* to, at last, join the ranks of movie immortals by putting his footprints in cement on Hollywood's walk of fame. So much had changed since he first refused the offer back in the early eighties. Then he was content enough to allow his namesake to take all the glory; even now he submitted reluctantly. 'I'll tell you very frankly, I didn't consider it an honour,' Ford carped to reporters afterwards. 'Just an opportunity to sell *Patriot Games*. That's why I was willing to do it.' Childishly defiant to the last Ford wore odd baseball boots for the ceremony.

Since those early heady days of fame we have seen the elevation of Ford to the Hollywood pantheon – from pulp genre hero to one of its legitimate leading men. He has proved to be a mature actor of some distinction, and one who has a tenacious grip on his own destiny. As the eighties drew to a close the mass media proclaimed him the most popular film star of the decade. All manner of industry/magazine surveys bore this out, for his films have raked in more dollars at the box office than any other actor. This testifies to an uncommonly good sense when picking roles, and a choice of scripts that, for the most part, has been exemplary. Since achieving genuine stardom as Indiana Jones Ford has been conspicuous for barely putting a foot wrong. *Presumed Innocent* surprised many by making a greater profit than most of the blockbuster action films released that same summer; and even the commercial flops of his career, *The Mosquito Coast* and *Frantic* for example, have demonstrated the consistent strength of Ford's acting. Even in the beginning Ford seems to have had a clear-sighted estimation of his talents and how they were best employed.

The trick has been to remain level-headed about it all – Ford still prefers to be regarded as a 'working actor' rather than a movie star – helped no doubt by the good grace to accept his success as the fortuitous accident of fate it was rather than because of any inherent superiority over his fellow man. The guileless youth who first entered Hollywood at the time of the Beatles' blitzkrieg on the States and the Tokyo Olympics never predicted, nor was ambitious for, the phenomenal success he would go on to achieve. 'I always thought I was going to do character parts. It never occurred to me for a minute that I'd be a leading man.'

That actors have a public image at all has always greatly annoyed Ford. He finds the celebrity bestowed upon those in his profession distasteful, and resents the fact that he is now and will forever be public property. It did affect him. That type of exposure was bound to make him withdraw even deeper into himself. But he tries hard not to concern himself with it. The business side of his character is aware of the importance of the image he projects to the public, but as an actor he doesn't much care about his heroic persona. As opposed to most modern screen heroes, who are full of bravado and menace, Ford's professional image is that of a recognizably human, vulnerable tough guy, with a quiet strength of character. He is self-confident without being overbearing. And therein lies his appeal and great strength – an ability to capture the foibles of ordinary men, like John Book or Dr

Richard Walker. The everyman actor. Audiences respond emotionally to Harrison Ford. He brings conviction to all his roles, so that whatever he cares about, we care about too. His heroes are Americans of integrity, firm of purpose, honest, decent and true, men with moral values and steely resolve who get the job done. And that's important. Because of his upbringing, Ford is naturally drawn to films that deal with moral issues, and also feels he has a responsibility, towards himself, his children and his audience, to produce work that is positive rather than negative. Producers have learned that Ford cannot be tempted by vast sums of money alone; he is only interested in making high-quality movies which avoid the stale formulae of revenge, rape and death – what Ford calls, 'Tit-flash-die movies. Those films where as soon as the girl takes her clothes off, you know she's gonna die. I like to see the power of film used for the good of mankind rather than merely to excite the baser instincts.'

Ford once made a jibe about the fact that he employed no particular method as an actor. 'I really don't think I know anything about this acting shit in general,' he confessed. 'I'm from the Let's Pretend School of Acting. Let's-get-some-stuff-outta-the-closet and we can pretend that we're whatever. That's where I'm from. I just get dressed up and pretend I'm somebody else.' It goes deeper than that though, for techniques do vary from performer to performer. 'Method' acting, which was originated by Konstantin Stanislavsky and developed at the Actor's Studio in New York during the fifties, is still the most preferred and widely used, particularly in the States. Brando and Dean were its archetypal exponents. While Ford is a defiant non-subscriber – he doesn't live his characters outside office hours or take them home with him – he does bring a brooding, sometimes neurotic intensity to nearly all his roles, most notably Deckard, Fox and Sabich. Thereby, he succeeds in totally immersing himself in a character. In the fifties Lee Strasberg, one of Stanislavsky's most influential American disciples, argued that stars like Gary Cooper, John Wayne and Spencer Tracy, all actors to whom Ford had been likened, were, in effect, method actors, since they 'try to be themselves and do and say what is consonant with their own characters'. With those words Strasberg inadvertently summed up the acting technique Ford has been using since *Star Wars*.

Ford has made no secret of the fact that, when creating a role, he uses his own resources – his history, experiences, emotions and physical body – as tools. Critics who accused him of not really acting in those classic eighties blockbusters might have said precisely the same thing about Wayne, Bogart or Gable. Ford is the opposite of a chameleon in this respect – his surroundings adapt to him. 'I don't hide myself behind my characters. I don't go for accents or vocal characterizations.'

When building a role Ford does rely heavily on physical detail, what he refers to as 'indicators of character'. He gets much mileage out of props and costumes, for instance. The straw cowboy hat of *American Graffiti*; the fedora and whip of Indiana Jones; the crewcuts in *Blade Runner* and *Presumed Innocent* – all were more than mere window dressing, they seem to become a part of him. Ford also appreciates the value of research. Most of his preparatory work leading up to filming is taken up with intense investigation. His primary research method is 'hanging out' – spending enough time in the world he's about to film so that it filters into his unconscious. 'I listen. I watch. I make myself a fly on the wall.' Everything is digested – if a film is based on a novel he will use that as resource. For John Book he spent time with the police force; to bring accuracy to his portrayal of Rusty Sabich's desperation he drew on painful childhood memories ('all children remember being falsely accused'); for Indiana Jones he read archaeological yearbooks. And what of Allie Fox, his most complex role? That was the exception to the rule; no research was needed. 'I was just a maniac,' he said. 'Any actor can do that.' Ford crams in all manner of information and detail then lets it slip out unconsciously during the actual act of performing. It is this process of investigation, of building and inventing the history and attributes of a character and then using his technique to convey all these facets to an audience that Ford most enjoys.

When Ford started out in Hollywood he recognized that the best way to pursue acting was not to imitate someone else's success but develop what was particular about himself. 'I was always a very detailed, very neat carpenter, so I began to apply the same rules to my work as an actor.' Ford was to teach himself how to act precisely the same way he taught himself carpentry. To him they are crafts and his approach to both is almost entirely technical. Ford sees building a character as no different than turning a stack of timber into a bookshelf or a cupboard. It is a question of submitting oneself to the logic of the craft, and if one starts with a firm foundation, every subsequent step becomes part of that logical process. 'As an actor, he's a carpenter. I've watched him "build" a role. He starts research early and makes his "foundation" months before we shoot. He planes his edges. He plans how things are going to fit together. Harrison brings supreme intelligence and a moral centre to his work.' So says Mike Nichols. 'What I learnt from carpentry, above all, was a work ethic,' Ford explained to *The Times* in July 1981. 'I used to be very lazy, but now I find I can't enjoy myself when I'm not working.'

Doing work that he finds satisfying is what changed Harrison Ford from being an unambitious, lazy youth into a man who finds honour in work, contentment in sweat and grind. The collar around Ford's neck is blue; he knows what it is to work hard and admires the same diligence in others. 'I'm basically a workman. I've made myself into a working class person; by virtue of my interests.' It's certainly not by virtue of his breeding. Like the appeal of a rural idyll Ford's working-class ethics are of his own making, and do not stem from his parents, who were comfortably well off. Christopher Ford did, however, help to shape his son's belief that he should always do his best, at whatever he did. 'I was taught the work ethic in its most fundamental form.' What he cannot abide is laziness, people with no appetite for work, who don't understand its rewards and pleasures. 'There's a lack of ambition to work in this country, the loss of our work ethic is probably the greatest threat we face.'

As an actor Ford is happy to sit in a cinema and feel pleased that audiences are deriving enjoyment from his performance. But at the same time he can't help brooding that the whole could have been better – that is central to his perfectionism. Besides, he has never particularly relished seeing himself on the screen. The pure joy is in the work itself: the wrestling with and overcoming of obstacles; the day-to-day process of figuring out how scenes should be played; deciding what to do in rehearsals and then attempting to bring it to life when the camera is rolling. To Ford film-making is a method of communication, and the actor's job is to give life to ideas – he sees himself as little more than a storyteller. As far as technique goes, Ford is mostly informed by instinct, although technically he always decides beforehand what he wants to accomplish. The emotions he shows may be spontaneous, but the bricks have been carefully and painstakingly laid beforehand. By the time the director calls 'action' Ford has arrived at a stage where something takes over and real feelings start to work; the technical side of his ability then ensures that the camera records it. The one great trick is never to be caught acting.

Above all there is the thrill of being part of a team, or 'family', of artists endeavouring to make movie magic. 'I find my mind is engaged on a level that I rarely find anyplace else,' Ford says. 'And that's exciting and very fulfilling. I feel as though it's a process which can be endlessly improved and perfected. And it's different everytime. It is for that reason endlessly interesting.' A touch grumpy about insisting that movies are a cooperative effort, Ford sees being a good team player as one of his greatest strengths as an actor. While fervently against film-making by committee, he likes to think he works best in a collaborative atmosphere, participating in the decision-making and working closely with every one of his directors. 'If I'm told that a director is autocratic by nature, I'm not likely to be interested in working with him.' According to Mike Nichols it is the simple questions he asks about the material that are so penetrating. Ford once told Nichols that the only thing that interests him in a script is: can it be a good film? Does his part advance the action? Many of the changes that came about in *Working Girl* were of Ford's own making. The fact that Trainer is in trouble, the fact that he risks his position by refusing to carry on with the deal without Tess – those were both his contributions. Ford approaches his work in a very practical manner, and he needs a certain number of answers so as to have a clear understanding of the film as a whole. The actor often uses the words 'practical' and 'logical' when discussing himself, because he considers them to be virtues. 'If I think of someone as being impractical, it's because he's being a pain in the arse.'

As well as taking a keen interest in the preparation of the final screenplay Ford also involves himself in post-production right up until they begin striking the prints of the negative. He is virtually a prisoner and feels he cannot walk away until the film is entirely at an end. He watches various cuts of the picture, attends test screenings and, during production, usually goes to dailies, 'because I'm technically very interested in my performance'. Some actors are unnerved by seeing their imperfections writ large on screen, but Ford doesn't mind – for him the rushes are an essential part of the film-making process. It is like referring to a recipe book while the pot is still on the stove; one can still add a pinch of this or that. 'I know how bad it can be,' he told *Films and Filming* in September 1981. 'I just go to see how bad it is. If it's really awful, then I'll make a fool of myself by begging to do it again.' Once the film is completed he watches the final version twice, then never sees it again. It is the work that interests him, remember, not the product. And when the process is over, the case is closed, 'and I go on to another one'.

Wit, geniality, commitment to the craft and utter professionalism has made Ford popular among film crews and earned him the respect of colleagues. 'He works fast, in a fundamentally unegotistical way,' Helen Mirren remembers, 'essentially finding the work more important than himself.' To this day Ford would rather submit to the good of the overall project than thrust himself centre stage. Mike Nichols calls Ford 'the Ferrari of actors'; and Fred Roos sees him as a star in the mould of Bogart, 'tough, cynical, totally capable of taking care of himself'. Spielberg, too, likened Ford to that most gritty star of Hollywood's golden age. When he spoke to the Lucas fan club magazine in the spring of 1989. 'He's more like Humphrey Bogart every day, but better looking. I think when Harrison moves into his late fifties, the way Sean Connery has, he's going to really fall into the Clark Gable/Humphrey Bogart roles even in a more suitable fashion than he's assuming those roles today. I think the older he gets, the better he's going to get and he's never going to lose his popularity. I see Harrison being a real face on the Mount Rushmore of Hollywood.'

Ford finds such praise and sentiment hard to take, embarrassing even. He knows he is very lucky to be where he is today and is modest enough to attribute much of his good fortune to having worked with the right people. He has now reached fifty, having barely survived a lingering mid-life crisis which he claims lasted from when he was twenty-five until he was forty. But he came out the other side a more confident, mature, serious, reflective man, more at peace with himself. The encroachment of old age holds no threat; Ford believes any age is good if you know how to live it. 'I never think about age,' Ford told *Today* newspaper in September 1992. 'I liked being young, even though I had no success. When I was thirty I could walk down any street and not be recognized. That was wealth of a sort. Then being forty held no fears, because I felt some of my best work lay ahead. Now I have no plans to fall apart.'

All outward signs indicate that Ford is currently content with his lot in life. He is eager to pass on his philosophy of the simple, peaceful, close-to-nature life that he has discovered on his ranch. Unlike John Book and Allie Fox, Ford has managed to find his Eden, one that is infinitely more important than earning millions. 'I want my colleagues and fans to say of me: He understands the true value of life, the importance of traditional values. He didn't lose touch with reality like most people who head off to seek fame and fortune in Hollywood.' Being as boring as Harrison Ford needs a special talent, a remorseless dedication to the inconsequential and the saintly.

Happiness is a queer companion. For Ford it was a long time arriving; being happy was something he had to learn. One day he realized, 'Wow, this is it, this is happiness, I guess. I can't think of anything to complain about. I must be happy.' And what would he change given the chance? 'I guess I am judgmental in some ways,' he told *Playboy* in March 1988. 'I know when I'm full of shit. I know when I'm wrong. I know when I'm bad. And I know I could be better in certain things. I'd love to be more fit. I'd love to have more talents in other areas. I'd love to have taken advantage of the education I sort of slept through. I'd love to be more clearheaded. And I'd love to be able to play a musical instrument for my own pleasure.' Apart from that he wouldn't change a thing, except maybe his nose.

The former philosophy student once defined his own philosophy of life by quoting Buddha, who admonished, 'Work out your salvation through diligence.' Ford has always found satisfaction in the work he does and cannot think of a better job than being an actor. 'I love what I do. The only thing I've traded away was my anonymity – but look what I got for it.' A lack of privacy, that is the price Ford has had to pay for the success he's enjoyed these past fifteen years. The simple pleasure of being able to go wherever he wants to, without drawing attention to himself or being hassled, has been taken from him for ever. 'It has had a most powerful and disturbing effect on me. Shattering, in fact.' But the rewards – that ranch in Wyoming, and the financial security to have total freedom of choice in his work – have more than compensated.

Ford remains as enthusiastic as ever about film-making. But mention theatre and he cringes visibly. Ford gets immortalized on the cinema screen. He doesn't tread the boards in the flesh. 'It's too much like a real job' is all the breath he will waste on the subject. Ford makes movies and cannot yet foresee a time when he'll stop. Cinema is a medium from which Ford still feels he can learn much. He wants to carry on taking risks in the sort of parts he plays, and there is the possibility of a return to comedy in the future, preferably something with Woody Allen. 'Otherwise you start churning out bullshit – and that lives on long after you've flushed yourself. It's still up there forty feet high and sixty feet wide screaming, "Bullshit, bullshit, bullshit! This guy was a fraud." '

And what of his talents? Ford is the first to admit that he is by no means a great actor. 'I suppose I'm adequate. I suppose I'm capable'. He is scarcely in the same league as De Niro, Pacino or Hoffman, in part because he is not the most innately interesting or dynamic performer; his acting, at times, leans towards the wooden. There are days when the magic just won't come. 'On those days we do as little as possible. I become a minimalist. Those are the days that kill you by the way. They just take the wind out of your sails.' But he is a diligent actor, whose style and self-assurance increase from film to film. Perfection takes time.

Like the stars of old Hollywood Ford appears to have no offscreen personality. As he intends, his films remain the only available touchstone from which the public can hope to fathom Harrison Ford. Self-effacing to the point of invisibility, he is a screen natural. Steve McQueen and Kevin Costner, other natural loners, are probably the closest to Ford in attitude and style. Interestingly too, Ford built his success on films which the old Hollywood would have no trouble in recognizing. But his true achievement has been to diversify and mature in other roles without sacrificing his appeal or losing a substantial portion of his audience. Today he stands alone for principles that are now more mythical than real. He has an outmoded American doggedness, a strong sense of what's right and what's wrong and defends the notion of being a regular, decent guy, even though the business he serves would prefer him to be a selfish egoist.

There is no one else in Hollywood quite like Harrison Ford. Most icons can't help playing the part to the hilt. Once mythhood sets in, there is no turning back. For those fame is the only reality, and their life is completely in the public domain. Ford is right on that border, desperately trying to remain ordinary, while going through the motions of celebrity simply because he knows it comes with the job. Fame, he knows, is the reason why many people in the public eye crack up, turn to drink or drugs, womanize. But Ford's rigour and practicality, his living with and for his family, and his aversion to the limelight have insulated him from the forces that destroy so many who negotiate the minefield of Hollywood. Harrison Ford's simplicity is of the highly complex variety.

Presenting himself as a man to be counted upon, he is, in fact, a very old-fashioned kind of hero. He is a throwback to yesteryear's ruggedly masculine screen idol: the acceptable face of America.

Filmography

Made-for-Television Films

The Intruders (1970)

Director: William Graham
Producer: James Duff McAdams
Teleplay: Dean Riesner
Running time: 95 minutes

CAST: Don Murray, Edmond O'Brien, John Saxon, Anne Francis, Harry Dean Stanton, Harrison Ford

Dynasty (1976)

Director: Lee Philips
Producer: Buck Houghton
Teleplay: Sidney Carroll
Running time: 120 minutes

CAST: Sarah Miles, Stacy Keach, Harris Yulin, Amy Irving, Harrison Ford

Judgment: The Court-Martial of Lt. William Calley (1976)

Producer and director: Stanley Kramer
Teleplay: Henry Denker
Running time: 120 minutes

CAST: Tony Musante, Richard Basehart, Bo Hopkins, G.D. Spradlin, Harrison Ford

The Possessed (1977)

Director: Jerry Thorpe
Producer: Philip Mandelker
Teleplay: John Sacret Young
Running time: 78 minutes

CAST: James Farentino, Joan Hackett, Harrison Ford

Cinema

Dead Heat on a Merry-go-round (1966)

Director: Bernard Girard
Producer: Carter DeHaven
Screenplay: Bernard Girard
Studio: Columbia Pictures
Running time: 107 minutes

CAST: James Coburn, Camilla Sparv, Aldo Ray, Robert Webber, Harrison Ford

Luv (1967)

Director: Clive Donner
Producer: Martin Manulis
Screenplay: Elliott Baker
Studio: Columbia Pictures
Running time: 95 minutes

CAST: Jack Lemmon, Peter Falk, Elaine May, Eddie Mayehoff, Harrison Ford

A Time for Killing (a.k.a. The Long Ride Home) (1967)

Director: Phil Karlson
Producer: Harry Joe Brown
Screenplay: Halsted Welles
Studio: Columbia Pictures
Running time: 83 minutes

CAST: Glenn Ford, George Hamilton, Inger Stevens, Paul Petersen, Max Baer, Todd Armstrong, Dick Miller, Harry Dean Stanton, Harrison Ford

Journey to Shiloh (1968)

Director: William Hale
Producer: Howard Christie
Screenplay: Gene Coon
Studio: Columbia Pictures
Running time: 101 minutes

CAST: James Caan, Michael Sarrazin, Brenda Scott, Don Stroud, Paul Petersen, Jan-Michael Vincent, Harrison Ford

Getting Straight (1970)

Producer and director: Richard Rush
Screenplay: Robert Kaufman
Studio: Columbia Pictures
Running time: 124 minutes

CAST: Elliott Gould, Candice Bergen, Jeff Corey, Harrison Ford

American Graffiti (1973)

Director: George Lucas
Producer: Francis Ford Coppola
Screenplay: George Lucas, Gloria Katz and Willard Huyck
Studio: Universal Pictures
Running time: 110 minutes

CAST: Richard Dreyfuss, Ron Howard, Paul LeMat, Charles Martin Smith, Cindy Williams, Candy Clark, Harrison Ford, Bo Hopkins

The Conversation (1974)

Director: Francis Ford Coppola
Producers: Francis Ford Coppola and Fred Roos
Screenplay: Francis Ford Coppola
Studio: Paramount Pictures
Running time: 113 minutes

CAST: Gene Hackman, John Cazale, Allen Garfield, Frederic Forrest, Cindy Williams, Teri Garr, Robert Duvall, Harrison Ford

Star Wars (1977)

Director: George Lucas
Producer: Gary Kurtz
Screenplay: George Lucas
Studio: Twentieth Century Fox
Running time: 121 minutes

CAST: Mark Hamill, Harrison Ford, Carrie Fisher, Peter Cushing, Alec Guinness, Anthony Daniels, Kenny Baker, Peter Mayhew, David Prowse

Heroes (1977)

Director: Jeremy Paul Kagan
Producers: David Foster and Lawrence Turman
Screenplay: James Carabatsos
Studio: Universal Pictures
Running time: 113 minutes

CAST: Henry Winkler, Sally Field, Harrison Ford

Force Ten from Navarone (1978)

Director: Guy Hamilton
Producer: Oliver Unger
Screenplay: Carl Foreman and Robin Chapman
Studio: Columbia Pictures
Running time: 118 minutes

CAST: Robert Shaw, Edward Fox, Harrison Ford, Carl Weathers, Franco Nero, Barbara Bach, Richard Kiel, Alan Badel

Hanover Street (1979)

Director: Peter Hyams
Producer: Paul N. Lazarus III
Screenplay: Peter Hyams
Studio: Columbia Pictures
Running time: 109 minutes

CAST: Harrison Ford, Lesley-Anne Down, Christopher Plummer, Alec McCowen, Patsy Kensit, Shane Rimmer, Max Wall

Apocalypse Now (1979)

Producer-and director: Francis Ford Coppola
Screenplay: John Milius and Francis Ford Coppola
Studio: Columbia–EMI–Warner
Running time: 150 minutes

CAST: Marlon Brando, Robert Duvall, Martin Sheen, Frederic Forrest, Albert Hall, Sam Bottoms, Larry Fishburne, Dennis Hopper, G.D. Spradlin, Harrison Ford, Scott Glenn

The Frisco Kid (1979)

Director: Robert Aldrich
Producer: Mace Neufeld
Screenplay: Michael Elias and Frank Shaw
Studio: Warner Brothers
Running time: 122 minutes

CAST: Gene Wilder, Harrison Ford

The Empire Strikes Back (1980)

Director: Irvin Kershner
Producer: Gary Kurtz
Screenplay: Leigh Brackett and Lawrence Kasdan
Studio: Twentieth Century Fox
Running time: 124 minutes

CAST: Mark Hamill, Harrison Ford, Carrie Fisher, Billy Dee Williams

Raiders of the Lost Ark (1981)

Director: Steven Spielberg
Producer: Frank Marshall
Screenplay: Lawrence Kasdan
Studio: Paramount Pictures
Running time: 115 minutes

CAST: Harrison Ford, Karen Allen, Paul Freeman, Ronald Lacey, John Rhys-Davies, Denholm Elliott

Blade Runner (1982)

Director: Ridley Scott
Producer: Michael Deeley
Screenplay: Hampton Fancher and David Peoples
Studio: Warner Brothers
Running time: 118 minutes

CAST: Harrison Ford, Rutger Hauer, Sean Young, Edward James Olmos, M. Emmet Walsh, Daryl Hannah, Joanna Cassidy

The Return of the Jedi (1983)

Director: Richard Marquand
Producer: Howard Kazanjian
Screenplay: Lawrence Kasdan
Studio: Twentieth Century Fox
Running time: 133 minutes

CAST: Mark Hamill, Harrison Ford, Carrie Fisher

Indiana Jones and the Temple of Doom (1984)

Director: Steven Spielberg
Producer: Robert Watts
Screenplay: Willard Huyck and Gloria Katz
Studio: Paramount Pictures
Running time: 118 minutes

CAST: Harrison Ford, Kate Capshaw, Ke Huy Quan

Witness (1985)

Director: Peter Weir
Producer: Edward S. Feldman
Screenplay: Earl W. Wallace and William Kelley
Studio: Paramount Pictures
Running time: 112 minutes

CAST: Harrison Ford, Kelly McGillis, Josef Sommer, Lukas Haas, Alexander Godunov, Danny Glover

The Mosquito Coast (1986)

Director: Peter Weir
Producer: Jerome Hellman
Screenplay: Paul Schrader
Studio: Warner Brothers
Running time: 117 minutes

CAST: Harrison Ford, Helen Mirren, River Phoenix, Conrad Roberts, Martha Plimpton

Frantic (1988)

Director: Roman Polanski
Producer: Thom Mount
Screenplay: Roman Polanski and Gerard Brach
Studio: Warner Brothers
Running time: 120 minutes

CAST: Harrison Ford, Emmanuelle Seigner, Betty Buckley, John Mahoney

Working Girl (1988)

Director: Mike Nichols
Producer: Douglas Wick
Screenplay: Kevin Wade
Studio: Twentieth Century Fox
Running time: 113 minutes

CAST: Harrison Ford, Sigourney Weaver, Melanie Griffith, Alec Baldwin, Joan Cusack, Philip Bosco

Indiana Jones and the Last Crusade (1989)

Director: Steven Spielberg
Producer: Robert Watts
Screenplay: Jeffrey Boam
Studio: Paramount Pictures
Running time: 127 minutes

CAST: Harrison Ford, Sean Connery, Denholm Elliott, Alison Doody, John Rhys-Davies, Julian Glover, River Phoenix, Michael Byrne

Presumed Innocent (1990)

Director: Alan J. Pakula
Producers: Sydney Pollack and Mark Rosenberg
Screenplay: Frank Pierson and Alan J. Pakula
Studio: Warner Brothers
Running time: 127 minutes

CAST: Harrison Ford, Brian Dennehy, Raul Julia, Bonnie Bedelia, Paul Winfield, Greta Scaachi

Regarding Henry (1991)

Director: Mike Nichols
Producers: Scott Rudin and Mike Nichols
Screenplay: Jeffrey Abrams
Studio: Paramount Pictures
Running time: 107 minutes

CAST: Harrison Ford, Annette Bening, Bill Nunn, Mikki Allen

Patriot Games (1992)

Director: Philip Noyce
Producers: Mace Neufeld and Robert Rehme
Screenplay: W. Peter Iliff, Donald Stewart and Steven Zaillian
Studio: Paramount Pictures
Running time: 116 minutes

CAST: Harrison Ford, Anne Archer, Patrick Bergin, Sean Bean, Thora Birch, James Fox, Samuel L. Jackson, James Earl Jones, Richard Harris

The Fugitive (1993)

Director: Andrew Davis
Producers: Arnold Kopelson and Keith Barish
Screenplay: Jeb Stuart and David Twohy
Studio: Warner Brothers

CAST: Harrison Ford, Tommy Lee Jones

Index

Index